Psychology Revivals

Cognition

Originally published in 1962, the problems of cognition dealt with in this book include learning, perception, thinking, memory and linguistic behaviour.

It is not a textbook in the ordinary sense, since it presents a particular approach to the subject through experimental psychology, and also, to some extent, through philosophy, cybernetics and logic. A brief mention is made of ethological and physiological matters.

It argues that cognition is a stepping-stone to integration with allied sciences. A large-scale study of the organism-as-a-whole needs to be supplemented by other biological and logical studies, but preparatory to this, cognitive psychologists must try and discover more rigorous ways of presenting their theories and models, since the mode of communicating an idea can never be wholly separated from that idea.

Furthermore cognition, even at the organism-as-a-whole level, needs to broaden out and link up with social studies and studies in personality and individual difference.

This book, pointed to a new direction that psychology should take; without contributing greatly to existing knowledge in the obvious sense, it suggests new methods and new ways of regarding the existing knowledge at the time.

Cognition

F.H. George

Psychology Press
Taylor & Francis Group
LONDON AND NEW YORK

First published in 1962
by Methuen & Co. Ltd

This edition first published in 2015 by Psychology Press
27 Church Road, Hove BN3 2FA

and by Psychology Press
711 Third Avenue, New York, NY 10017

Psychology Press is an imprint of the Taylor & Francis Group, an informa business

© 1962 F.H. George

All rights reserved. No part of this book may be reprinted or reproduced or utilised in any form or by any electronic, mechanical, or other means, now known or hereafter invented, including photocopying and recording, or in any information storage or retrieval system, without permission in writing from the publishers.

Publisher's Note
The publisher has gone to great lengths to ensure the quality of this reprint but points out that some imperfections in the original copies may be apparent.

Disclaimer
The publisher has made every effort to trace copyright holders and welcomes correspondence from those they have been unable to contact.

A Library of Congress record exists under LCCN: 68007251

ISBN: 978-1-138-91970-9 (hbk)
ISBN: 978-1-315-68760-5 (ebk)
ISBN: 978-1-138-91985-3 (pbk)

COGNITION

by F. H. George

*Department of Psychology
University of Bristol*

METHUEN & CO LTD
36 Essex Street · Strand · London WC2

First published in 1962
© 1962 by F. H. George
Printed in Great Britain by
Butler & Tanner Ltd, Frome & London
Catalogue No. 2/6496/10

CONTENTS

	Foreword	page 7
1	The Nature of Cognition	11
2	Definitions in Cognition	24
3	The Conditioned Response	37
4	Learning and Theories of Learning	56
5	Hull's Theory of Learning	77
6	Tolman's Theory of Learning	103
7	Philosophy, Introspection and Cognition	123
8	Psychological Theory of Perception	141
9	Gestalt Theory	151
10	Empiricism and Transactionalism	160
11	Ethology and Cognition	173
12	A Theory Language for Cognition	186
13	Cybernetics and Cognition	208
14	Cognition and Programming a Computer	232
15	Memory	251
16	Thinking	258
17	Language	272
18	In Summary	286
	References	296
	Index	305

FIGURES

1	The Brain and the Nervous System	*page* 16
2	Maier's Problem-solving Experiment	44
3-5	Partial Reinforcement	65-69
6-8	Tolman Diagrams	107-109
9	The Tolman-Honzik Maze	115
10	Krechevsky Hypotheses	116
11	Normal Conditioning	118
12	Loucks' Conditioning – Stage 1	119
13	Loucks' Conditioning – Stage 2	120
14	Figural After-effect – The Inspection Figure	142
15	Figural After-effect – The Test Figure	143
16	The Plateau Spiral	144
17	The Schröder Staircase	147
18	The Neckar Cube	148
19	Galli-Hocheimer Figures	155
20	A Schumann Figure	155
21	Some Logical Net Elements	218
22	A Classification Net	220
23	A Classification and Storage Net	221
24	Retinal Elements	222
25	A Stochastic Route	245
26	A Modified Route	246

FOREWORD

A book on cognition needs some justification and explanation. As far as justification is concerned this book aims to fill a fairly definite role. It is intended to be something between a textbook and a series of more or less original papers on cognition. The main aim is a survey and reinterpretation of existing knowledge of cognitive processes.

This book is certainly not a textbook in the sense of documenting the vast range of experiments and theories that have occurred in the field of cognition; such a work written by any single mortal would no longer be possible. It is an attempt to present a coherent view of cognition with selected experimental evidence.

To turn now to *explanation*, I should say that this book represents my own attitude to cognitive problems. It emphasizes the things I think are important, and omits those things that either interest me less or seem less important. The methods used in explaining are themselves a matter of great importance.

The field is the so-called "molar" field of psychology. This is the field of observation of the organism as-a-whole. There is no serious attempt to discuss the nervous system, although inevitably a certain amount is said about it. A certain amount is also said about animal work although the book is not primarily concerned with animal behaviour. This is in no way meant to imply that neurological or animal studies are irrelevant to the study of cognitive behaviour; on the contrary I believe they will play a part of ever increasing importance in psychology in the future. I do think, however, that they have a better chance of success, progress and integration if we can learn first to say, succinctly and clearly, what we know about behaviour in general terms, with respect to information derived from psychological experiments.

It is for this last reason that I would like to encourage psychologists to take some interest in philosophy, and the closest possible interest in logic and language. Since herein lies a key to the presentation of evidence, in order to facilitate what seems to me the urgent need for integration between ethologists, physiologists and psychologists.

Certain sections of this book are concerned with Cybernetics and cybernetics is itself partly the result of applying precise and formal methods of analysis to psychological problems. I would like to make clear that Cybernetics is not a major feature of this book, since I have only recently attempted to supply an account of Cybernetics in a separate book called *The Brain as a Computer*. That book is complementary to this in being primarily concerned with Cybernetics and incidentally being concerned with neurology and cognition. This book is concerned with Cognition and only incidentally concerned with Cybernetics in so far as it affects cognitive studies and points of view.

It should be explicitly stated that much of Chapters 13 and 14 on Cybernetics are a re-statement of what the earlier book (1961) treated in greater detail. As a result, readers of the earlier book will tend to find in these chapters a re-statement, in summary form, with some additions and modifications, of views that are already familiar.

In similar fashion the analysis of Hull, Tolman, and the briefer discussion of the work on Skinner and Guthrie can be found in somewhat briefer form, with a somewhat different emphasis in the earlier book.

The bulk of this book is concerned with developing *a theory language for cognition*, and also with explicitly discussing memory, thinking, language and the schools of perception, and in dealing with cognitive material not discussed at all in the book on Cybernetics.

The origins of the book go back to early attempts by me to understand everyday human behaviour, and many of my own early ideas came from reading the theories of Freud and others. To include this development and discuss the problems of abnormal behaviour, although wholly relevant to the present task, would make the whole book too large. However it must be emphasized that the present text should ultimately be understood only in the wider context of normal *and* abnormal behaviour, at the level of nervous activity, chemical and endocrine activity, as well as social studies and a great deal more besides. What we formally call "cognition" is abstracted from all these things and represents a somewhat idealized account of how human beings observe the world around them, how they store their information and how they generalize on it to form concepts and how they think and learn. Thinking, problem solving and learning, involve language and finally may involve physical action – all this is the field of *cognition*.

More specifically I have attempted to lay out clearly some of the evidence relevant to the finding of appropriate models and theories for predicting human behaviour. I would hope the book would be of direct interest to honours students in psychology, as well as postgraduate students in the same subject. But one would like to think that it would be of interest to a wider audience of philosophers, physiologists, biologists and sociologists generally, and I would also like to think that the book was written with sufficient clarity to be of interest to the non-specialist, and that almost mythical character usually referred to as the "intelligent layman".

Chapter 1

THE NATURE OF COGNITION

This book is intended to describe the subject of cognition; but since "cognition" is the name given to the whole of the foundations of normal human behaviour, it will be necessary to limit the breadth of the investigation.

In the first place, it is not intended to discuss animal cognition as such, although so much of the theory of cognition is based upon animal experiments, that examples drawn from work on animals will often be used, and some aspects of ethology will be discussed (Chapter 11). Secondly, we shall not be concerned with clinical or abnormal psychology, except in so far that discoveries in these fields have a suggestive value for those interested in normal cognition. Paranormal cognition, which is the technical name for work on telepathic and other obscure, but possible, forms of communication, is also quite outside the scope of the present book.

It would be nice to be able to add that the philosophy and physiology of cognition are also irrelevant, but they are not. A chapter (Chapter 7) is devoted to cognition and philosophy, and other references will certainly be made to the approach of philosophers and physiologists to our common interest, for their work is in some ways very close to that of the psychologist; but to enlarge on the detail of philosophical and physiological matters alone would involve far more space than the present volume affords.

By cognition, we shall mean the way human beings *perceive* and *learn*, how they reason and think, even how they remember and imagine; and how their "minds" work in the ordinary day-to-day activities of life. This means that we want to know how they learn a poem, or a part in a play; how they remember what they have learnt; how they perceive the relations and layout of a map, a scene, or a painting; how they recall certain events in their pasts, and how they imagine things that may never have occurred, or at least, things that they themselves did not see.

Perception may perhaps be usefully thought of as being connected with our *input* of information. "Perception" refers, of course, to all the special senses, but the eyes have been most extensively studied. Now we know only too well that we may be wrong about just what is happening around us. To use a simple example: we may be led into saying that we saw three men walking down the road, whereas actually there were two men and a woman. Often the difficulty is that we cannot stop our minds (or brains) from making inferences all the time about what the eyes see (even unconscious inferences), and this leads to many errors. Making unwarranted assumptions, taking things for granted, jumping to conclusions, all these affect our perceptual efficiency.

This, so far, seems reasonable enough, but we must recognize that there may be many complications. We shall find that we have to dwell upon our own actions, and take care to be aware of what we are doing: this is the process called "introspection" or, when it involves much that is in the past, "retrospection".

Now most of us discover, rather to our surprise, that we are not very good at introspection. People often find that they are unaware, consciously, of many things that seem to have influenced their actions. They may solve problems of a logical kind, but be quite unable to say what steps they took to reach their solutions. It is not only that they cannot remember things well enough, but that, even while they are actually cogitating on a problem, they find it difficult to say exactly what it is they are doing. It is a well-known and well-validated fact that one may go to bed with an unsolved problem on the mind, and wake to find it solved. This seems to show that the cognitive operations do not stop during sleep, but we must be careful on this point, since many psychologists have defined cognition as that part of perceiving, learning and thinking that *is* conscious.

These problems become more complicated when we consider the findings of Sigmund Freud; in particular, that unconscious motives apparently influence the behaviour of man. Everyone has motives or reasons for learning things, and it is a reasonable guess that these motives are closely connected with the foundations of human survival. At the same time, answers to questions about our motives would need to be somewhat more mundane, in that we are usually asking about what *immediately* influenced our behaviour, and not

The Nature of Cognition

about what is the ultimate driving force. In any case we surely cannot say what our unconscious motives are by introspection.

Our main difficulty here is that cognition could be regarded as referring to the unconscious processes as well as to the conscious; but if this is agreed, then we are going to be using the words "learning", "perceiving", "thinking", and the other cognitive terms, in rather a special and unusual way. This way is sometimes called "behaviouristic".

This last point raises a special problem of science: that of definitions. We must be prepared to say, and in a fairly definite and clear way, what it is that we are talking about, because many of the most important terms of ordinary, everyday language are ambiguous, and may mean many different things according to the context in which they are used; they have all sorts of *shades* of different meaning. This question we shall postpone till the next chapter, since defining terms can be a rather tiresome business – tiresome, but necessary, even if we still cannot make the definitions as precise as we should like.

Apart from the fact that the science of cognition must be in accord with common sense, and follow step by step in a clear, logical argument, the language used must be precise enough to allow experiments to be carried out in order to confirm the truth, or otherwise, of our cognitive theories. These are all points at which philosophy touches cognition.

To illustrate the relation between psychology and the biological sciences, it is convenient to think of a motor-car. If we merely observe its outward characteristics, check its speed and acceleration, and the action of the gears and brakes, then we are what we might facetiously call "car psychologists". But if we open the bonnet and take up the floorboards, investigate the carburettor and ignition system, take the engine to pieces, and so on, then we are, by the same analogy, in the domain of "car physiology". Mainly, this book is about the *psychology* of cognition – human cognition.

Out of these problems, dealt with in many ways over several hundreds of years, has emerged the method of psychological approach called "behaviourism"; this is the method of studying the human being objectively, and not relying on introspective evidence, at least, not directly. We must now trace out some of the main historical developments which brought about the present state of affairs.

Cognition and early Experimental Psychology

Psychology began to emerge as a scientific discipline slightly over a hundred years ago, and it has been evolving more and more as a separate discipline ever since. At the same time there has been an increasing awareness that it is only artificially separated from philosophy and sociology, as well as the biological sciences generally, and even the physical sciences.

This may appear to be something of a paradox, but it is a peculiar fact that, while sciences have become increasingly specialized and compartmentalized, there have been – perhaps for this very reason – movements to unify it; and there have been claims that science really represents a homogeneous mass of well-validated information.

The background of psychology is in philosophy, biology and, as far as method is concerned, physics. It is almost as if scientists had said that the methods of science, having worked so well in dealing with the physical world, could now be applied to the mental world.

Herbart's *Textbook of Psychology* appeared in 1816, heralding the subject in its slender beginnings, but it was not until the work of Fechner, Helmholtz and Wundt, among many others, that the beginnings of the use of experimental methods could be seen.

Kant influenced the development of psychology, and was one of the first people to distinguish cognitive, or reasonable, from conative, or emotional, activities. After Kant, other philosophers – notably Jeremy Bentham and John Stuart Mill – continued the development of psychological theories, though without using experimental methods.

The early work of Fechner, Muller and Weber, as well as Helmholtz and Wundt, was in experimentation on sensation and perception, especially hearing and vision. One well-known outcome of this was the famous Fechner-Weber law, which said that, "in observing the difference of two magnitudes, what we perceive is the ratio of the difference to the magnitudes compared". Even now this law is thought to hold over the bulk of the range of normal sensory stimulation.

While these early beginnings were occurring, physiology had been developing in such a manner as to facilitate its inevitable link-up with behaviour.

The Bell-Magendie law, as it is sometimes called, named after the two physiologists who first propounded it, made the distinction which is now widely accepted between sensory and motor nerves. This anatomical distinction is between nerves running into the nerve pathways of the spinal cord, and carrying incoming messages from the various specialized receptors in the skin, and the outgoing nerves which carry messages to the output organs such as the muscles of the arms and legs. This is closely connected with our distinction between sensory and motor activity; the stimuli are sensory and the responses are motor.

Helmholtz, although perhaps primarily famous as a physicist, was also an eminent physiologist, and was one of the founders of what we tend, now, to call physiological psychology. His work in the latter field is closely connected with colour vision and hearing. Indeed, his theories in both these domains are now regarded as essentially correct, although they have naturally been considerably elaborated since the time of his original work. He is also especially well known for his theory of unconscious inference.

Helmholtz's theory of unconscious inference has been used to explain the constancy effect that occurs in our perception of colours and shapes. We shall discuss this in Chapter 8, but it can be said now that Helmholtz adopted a characteristically empirical attitude in accounting for our ability to recognize coal as black even when seen in a very bright light. Helmholtz suggested that we remembered the real colour of coal ("real" here means its colour in white light) and made allowances for the illuminating conditions which changed its immediate appearance. The use of the memory in interpreting may not, of course, be a process of which we are conscious.

This empiricist interpretation of constancy was opposed by Hering, who suggested that the effect was due to the functioning of our peripheral visual system in the retina. This alternative view is sometimes called "Nativist", and the two views are collectively referred to as the "Nativist-Empiricist Controversy" – a dispute which is still not finally settled.

Another noteworthy milestone in the development of early experimental psychology was the work by Flourens on localization of function in the highest level of the brain: the cerebral cortex. Flourens' work, published in 1824 and 1825, was primarily based upon the removal of different areas of the brain, especially in the cerebral cortex. He found that relatively definite functions were affected by such removal. Perhaps the most significant of all his discoveries was that, with suitably chosen destruction of the nervous system, the subjects appeared to retain sensations in their eyes, and in the special senses generally, but lost the ability to make perceptions, i.e. to co-ordinate and utilize the information that was still being recorded by those special senses.

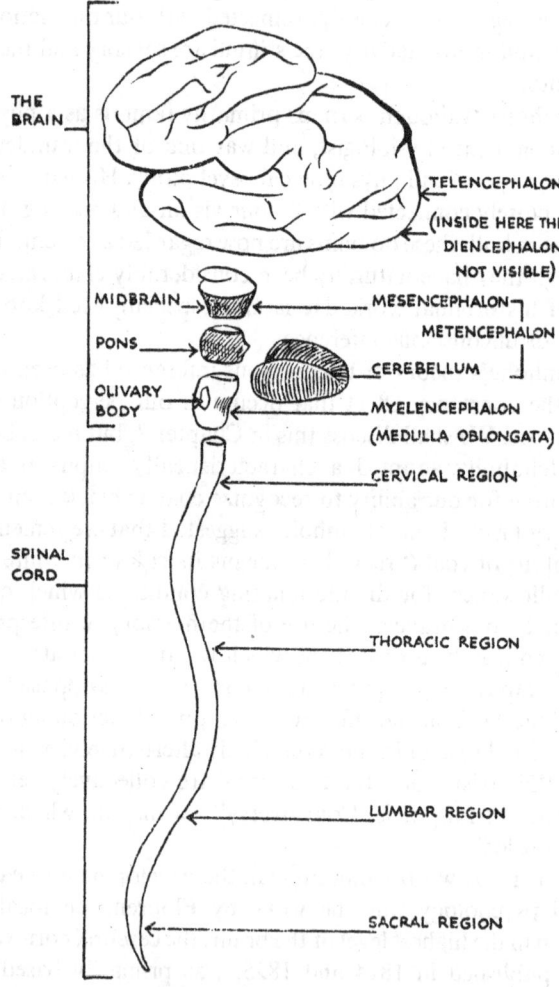

Fig. 1. The Brain and the Nervous System

A diagrammatic representation of the brain and the nervous system, showing the main parts which are separated for convenience of illustration. The Telencephalon includes the cerebral cortex, and the Diencephalon includes the thalamus and hypothalamus.

Even more important than this, Flourens showed that a large part of the brain, called the cerebellum, was concerned with motor co-ordination, a finding which modern neurophysiologists nave been able to confirm (injuries to the human cerebellum certainly interfere with the ability to co-ordinate muscular movements). The same techniques gave hints as to the function of other brain areas, and supported the doctrine of functional localization in the brain, although Flourens himself gave a somewhat different interpretation. The view that the cerebral cortex is localized in its function is still widely accepted, but with some modifications and reservations.

Of the many famous physiologists who have influenced our views on the relation between behaviour and the function of the nervous system, none has had a greater influence than Sir Charles Sherrington, who was able to develop a more complete picture of the nervous system and its function than anyone previously. He found that the cerebral cortex itself seemed to have an inhibiting effect upon some of the lower levels of the central nervous system and, indeed, that the idea of such levels, which was developed by Hughlings Jackson and Flourens, was consistent with the experimental evidence available.

From Sherrington's work we have acquired the concept of inhibition. This is, essentially, an antagonism to excitation which takes place when a particular nerve or set of nerves is stimulated. The stimulated nerves connect with other nerves at the synapses, and these (the second) sets of nerves ramify to make a sort of network throughout the body. The synapses are the controlling centres as far as the distribution of local nervous activity is concerned, and they can be either in an excitatory or an inhibitory state, i.e. the state of the synapse decides whether, when an impulse arrives, it will pass through and fire the next nerve in the chain or not. The complicated co-ordination of this process leads eventually to nerves firing (or not firing) particular muscles, and thus activating bodily movements. This whole process is now thought to be under cerebral cortical control.

By removal of the higher levels of the nervous system – the cerebral cortex at the top, the basal ganglia beneath it, then the thalamus, hypothalamus, pons and medulla (see Figure 1), we can gradually reduce the animal to a spinal animal (i.e. having only the spinal cord intact), from which simple responses can yet be elicited. The seresponses were analysed in great detail by Sherrington and his many followers, and are still being analysed right up to the present day.

We shall have more to say later about Sherrington's theory of nervous activity and its relation to cognition, and we should note that it represents perhaps the greatest single contribution to our present knowledge, although naturally it too is being modified as a result of a steady influx of knowledge.

In the meantime, and rather before Sherrington, we have the development by Fechner of psycho-physics, the first systematic attempt to measure sensation by appeal to strength and conditions of stimulation. This body of methods is closely bound up with the history of experimental psychology.

The psycho-physical methods will be discussed in Chapter 8, but we can say now that their importance lies in the fact that they represent a first attempt to link the objective, or publicly observable, world with the subjective, or private, world of our own feelings. Such a link is clearly necessary to allow the direct application of measurement to our subjective behaviour.

Perhaps even more directly relevant to cognition was the early work on thinking by Kulpe and the Wurzburg school of psychologists. This school was concerned – in rough distinction from the experimental work of Wundt, Fechner and others – with systematic introspection. The operations of judgment, feeling, association and will were all studied. An analysis was made of thinking, and although a great deal was learnt about our higher mental processes, it was often of a negative character, showing the limited usefulness of introspection as a source of information about the internal processes of thought, such as may be involved in finding the solutions to particular problems.

It should be understood that we have selected from the full breadth and depth of psychology, or cognition, but a few of the milestones in the last hundred years of its development, taking those especially which have led to the recent development of "schools" of psychology. These schools are now being replaced by one or two principal integrated theories, the discussion of which will be one of the main themes of this book.

Many of the schools were working on problems which seemed, to those concerned at that time, to differ radically one from another, and so appeared to be less comparable than they do now, from the present historical standpoint. Their differences, indeed, are now seen to have been more imaginary than real.

Psycho-analysis, under Freud, is widely known for its clinical interpretations of abnormal behaviour and its themes of the unconscious influences on our behaviour, the repression of the unconscious infantile wishes, the Oedipus complex, and the like. Freud's school of thought did not embrace all psychologists, and rival theories were built up by Jung and Adler; but this sort of work, embedded in the clinic and derived from the abnormal patient, is only peripheral to the development of cognition as such.

The Development of the Theory of Cognition as a Science

In the last section we mentioned some of the most prominent contributors to the development of experimental psychology, and their most important contributions. Most of them, of course, were responsible for much more than we have mentioned, and there are many other distinguished contributors, of whom the names of Titchener, Francis Galton and William James come immediately to mind as outstanding omissions from our selected group.

The omission of Francis Galton can be usefully remedied now, since he, like Darwin, and Lamarck, gave much to the evolutionary way of thinking which greatly influenced the manner in which cognitive and psychological problems generally came to be regarded.

If we had time to develop the history of psychological ideas it is probable that evolution – the idea of man as developed from more primitive species, in a constant state of modification by a process like natural selection – would be among the first to merit comment. Out of this has sprung the concept of instinctive activities and their direct inheritance from generation to generation, as well as the more simple tropisms, or automatic movements, of one kind or another. Another result has been the gradual development of the belief that man owes something to his genetic background *and* something to the environment in which he lives. To separate the two influences is not easy.

Galton examined the inheritance of genius by statistical survey methods and drew some conclusions, now very well known, about inherited genius. His results showed that genius was something that we tended to acquire by virtue of our parents' abilities. Families of eminent scientists and public men on the one hand, and unfortunate families of mental deficients on the other, both showed that Galton's contention of the importance of heredity in deciding our abilities was supported by statistical evidence. Perhaps more important, though, were his methods, because they represent almost the first example of the use of mental tests; he was, in fact, one of the originators of measurement in psychology. This tradition of measurement has been followed up by many well-known psychologists, notably Cattell, Spearman, Ebbinghouse and, recently, Eysenck.

McDougall's work is relevant to Galton's, because he shows the effect of the influence of theories of biological evolution on his own theory of cognition. His idealist philosophical background also influenced him, and he attempted to explain human behaviour in terms of instinctive behaviour patterns, emphasizing *purpose* as a central feature of human behaviour. He was led to carry out some animal experiments which were designed to show that organisms could inherit acquired characteristics. This was the view proposed by Lamarck, in opposition to the more mechanistic view of evolution proposed by Darwin. McDougall's experiments appeared to support the Lamarckian view, but it is now generally recognized that they were not sufficiently well controlled. It is a point to remember that our knowledge of how to carry out experiments in a way that will ensure reliable results is something that has also increased greatly in the last few years, though it is still by no means a simple matter to draw valid results from an experimental situation; but we shall be discussing this further at a later stage.

McDougall's work in the development of a large-scale theory was in opposition to the work of the behaviourists who, under the leadership of Watson, proposed a somewhat extreme view of cognitive development. They suggested that learning was the literal and immediate association of different processes; that a particular pattern of muscular activity becomes associated with particular circumstances, and that there is a sort of automatic pattern of response which, however, may become complicated as the different patterns interact with each other.

This early behaviourism was a reaction against the introspective technique, which had a rather poor record of results. Kulpe's researches on thinking were dependent on introspection, and had a completely catholic influence and a pre-determined end. Classic philosophical views still haunted the subject, including many forms of dualism (such as body *and* mind) which created more problems than they solved, and so on. Behaviourism, greatly influenced by animal research, cut across all this and suggested the methods which should be used in what was regarded as the proper study for psychologists, the study of behaviour.

Looking back over the early development of experimental psychology, and its roots in philosophy going back to a much earlier

The Nature of Cognition

period, it is easy to see the seeds of the modern behaviourist movement, and the idealist opposition to it. For want of a better name we shall call the anti-behaviourists "idealists", but in this group we shall have to include many scientists with quite diverse attitudes and ideas.

Among the idealists – although rather peripheral to the outlook exemplified by McDougall – there can be found the Gestalt school (the Configurationist school, as they are sometimes called) who had their origins in philosophy; and whereas behaviourism came to fruition via the mechanistic materialism of Diderot and Helvetius in the eighteenth century, Configurationism came through the more immediate background work of the philosopher Husserl, though it was Wertheimer, a pupil of Kulpe, who was most responsible for its development as a psychological school. The names of Köhler and Koffka are now the best known of its followers.

Gestalt theorists have opposed the behaviourists on the grounds that they oversimplified their associationism, and neglected many properties of a more complex character which are particularly obvious in perception: the fact, for example, that we tend to see patterns in a perceptual field as-a-whole. That this view has now been widely accepted is borne out by a modern behaviourist theory – proposed by Tolman – which is called "sign-gestalt theory".

We shall be discussing the disagreements that surrounded the development of behaviourism, and opposing theories, in greater detail in the next chapter. For the present, it will suffice to remember that the old philosophical controversy between materialism and idealism, in all its various manifestations, was inherited by psychologists, and still underlies many current disputes on the theories of cognition.

In the field of cognition it is perhaps over concepts such as insight that the warmest disputes have arisen, but whether it can still be regarded as a bone of contention between the behaviourists and the idealists is somewhat doubtful.

There are, however, still various doubts hovering over modern theories of cognition, of which, perhaps, the most important concerns the status of consciousness. In the past, this might be described as creating a dead-end line of research, and the early behaviourists dispensed with it altogether. Certainly, progress seemed to be possible without the use of the concept, but even so, more recent, and more liberal-minded, behaviourists have admitted that this is a problem which we cannot forever avoid.

This book will be principally concerned with tracing the evolution of a liberal behaviourism, while including a statement of other sorts of views not inconsistent with behaviourism: for example, the views of cyberneticians, of ethologists, of physiological psychologists and of philosophers.

We shall be devoting some chapters to a more detailed analysis of some of the behaviouristic systems that are in existence. In particular, we shall describe Hull's and Tolman's theories of learning and, more briefly, the views of Thorndike, Guthrie and Skinner, among learning theorists. The empiricists, especially the transactionalists among the more behaviouristic perception theorists, and the Gestalt theorists (borderline idealist in view) are also to be discussed.

The central controversies of learning and perception have to some extent strayed over into thinking and the rest of the cognitive processes, but not in quite such a clearcut fashion. These will be considered as subjects in themselves, rather than being directly associated with schools of psychology.

The cyberneticians, whom we mentioned above, represent in some ways the most extreme behaviouristic school, but this is only one aspect of a rather complicated system. They are interested primarily in *effective* definitions, so that the theories evolved are virtually blueprints from which machines, or even organisms, could be constructed. Indeed, from the standpoint of cybernetics there is no hard and fast distinction between machines and organisms, in that both are capable of being analysed, synthesized and described in exactly the same terms.

Many readers will be familiar with Grey Walter's "tortoises", and with other such cleverly constructed electronic systems which simulate simple organic behaviour. The computer can be made to simulate more complex cognitive behaviour and, from these beginnings, theories can be constructed that are in many ways similar to the behaviouristic theories of Hull and Tolman, who are the two principal remaining learning theorists, the others having now been amalgamated with one or other of these two for all practical purposes. Hull and Tolman have, in fact, moved a long way towards agreement in recent years.

It should be borne in mind throughout the book that all cognitive psychologists do not have clearcut theoretical attitudes, and do not necessarily subscribe to the principal points of view outlined here. Many experimental psychologists, especially in England, are inclined

The Nature of Cognition

to believe that theory on a large scale is premature, but even for these, the *problems* of cognition remain.

This book, then, will aim to outline the most important contemporary attitudes to cognition, which is a central problem in human behaviour. It cannot deal with so vast a subject in great detail, but it will outline the main features, and these will be supported by references which will be sufficient for those who are curious to follow them up in much greater detail.

The next stage

From the foregoing brief resumé of the history and background of the subject, we have developed certain lines of thought. In a sense, the rest of the book is spent examining these in greater detail. In order to see where we are going it is essential that a few important points are understood. In the first place we are aiming to make cognition rigorously scientific, and to do this we shall be guided by the need for some strictness in methods and in our ultimate scientific aims. This being so, it follows that we must be careful to give fairly precise definitions to our terms, and make a precise expression of our purposes. As these definitions become more explicit we shall find ourselves resorting more and more to carefully reasoned arguments, which might in turn become mathematical in form. Some indication of this sort of tendency in cognitive theories is already apparent in Hull's theory (Chapter 5) and in cybernetics (Chapters 13 and 14).

We must, in short, now prepare ourselves to leave the vague usage of everyday language, at least as far as our special key terms are concerned, and start defining these terms more carefully. This, among other things, will be a function of the next chapter.

Chapter 2

DEFINITIONS IN COGNITION

The word "cognition" means, according to a recent dictionary of psychology (Drever (1952)):

> a general term covering all the various modes of knowing: perceiving, imagining, remembering, conceiving, judging and reasoning. The *cognitive* function, as an ultimate mode or aspect of the conscious life, is contrasted with the affective or conative – feeling and willing . . .

In this definition there are apparent difficulties for us since, as we have mentioned in Chapter 1, we may well apply the word "cognition" to processes of which we are not directly aware. Indeed, in pursuing a behaviouristic approach to these problems, we shall not be thinking primarily in introspective terms at all, and therefore should amend the definition, for our purposes, to the extent of omitting the clause, "as an ultimate mode or aspect of the conscious life". If, of course, we were trying to decide on rigorously appropriate terminology, we should have to consider this matter with great care; but we are now only trying to indicate the meaning of terms with a fair degree of precision, a precision which still falls short of what cognitive theory will ultimately demand.

The word *recognition* is better known than the word "cognition", although "to be cognizant of" is still a fairly standard phrase in our everyday language. The word "cognition" is therefore primarily concerned with knowing and knowledge, and deals with those aspects of thought that have been largely separated from the emotional aspects of knowledge. The distinction between cognition and conation (also, affection) is due primarily to Kant. This fractionation of the psychological states of human beings is certainly somewhat artificial, and we should bear in mind that the organism should properly be thought of as working as-a-whole, and that in separating emotions from more intellectual attitudes, some violence is certainly being done to the facts. In modern terms, this is seen when we realize

Definitions in Cognition

that learning is never to be thought of as independent of motivation.

Since cognition is so much concerned with knowing, it will be no surprise to find that philosophers have had much to say that is relevant.

The study of epistemology, which is the foundation-stone of philosophical studies, deals with the questions: how does anyone *know* what he *knows*? and what is the nature of knowledge? Epistemology is in fact just another name for theory of knowledge. Philosophers have, for centuries, asked these sorts of questions, with the emphasis less on the process by which knowing takes place, than on the extent to which people know, and the extent to which they can rely on their cognitive experience.

If this book were philosophical it would dwell primarily on the use of language, on logic, and on the sort of arguments that are used to try to justify whatever it is that people think they understand and know. This has also raised questions about what they perceive; whether they can talk of a real world of hard matter outside themselves, or whether they should confine themselves to talking of appearances. The philosophical question is as to how, logically, to distinguish reality from appearance, when by the very nature of things one can only be directly aware of appearances.

These are chiefly philosophical matters, and are not our direct concern here; at the same time we believe that an awareness of the philosophical problems, especially over the use of language, is a great help to any experimental psychologist who is approaching such problems from a scientific point of view. This very problem of appearance and reality becomes of the first importance in our assessment of the Transactionalists in Chapter 10. The distinction implied here between a logical and a scientific approach is one over which there is still much debate; however, we are interested in the experimental psychologist, and how he approaches these matters of cognition, and what he thinks of cognition. But this much must be said about the debate: it has sometimes been thought that perception could be regarded from a purely logical point of view, as opposed to the empirical or scientific view, which is what the scientist is concerned with. The logical point of view deals with the language used, and the propriety of that language, as well as the logical consistency of the argument, whereas the scientist is interested in constructing a model of the process in much the same way as we build maps of our countryside, with the idea of making predictions about what happens, in fact, when certain things are done. This difference between logic and science is clearly valid up to a point, but beyond that point, you *cannot analyse the language used without also considering the things that are described by the language.*

The experimental psychologist is strictly a scientist in his method of observation. He uses experiment, gathers together the experimentally derived observations, and then makes generalizations (hypotheses) about these observed facts, and proceeds to deduce consequences from them. Scientific method is actually more complicated than this makes it appear, but the business of observing and formulating general hypotheses are among its most important features. It is therefore now necessary to decide upon the scope of cognition.

We should perhaps say once more that, as far as this book is concerned, we shall think of cognition as the fundamental problem of psychology: the problem of how people (organisms) learn, how they perceive, how they think, how they imagine, and so on. Since these aspects of human skill are not independent of memory and motivation, these subjects must also necessarily be discussed. They have been developed partly independently in the past, and therefore theories of learning and theories of perception exist which do not always fit easily together, and these make up the bulk of the well-established part of modern experimental psychology.

Another preliminary to be settled before we can get to grips with our subject is that of method and subject-matter. Experimental psychology is a vague name for a subject which includes many different approaches to human and animal behaviour. We must here distinguish at least two of them. The first is the so-called "molar" approach, which is concerned with the organism-as-a-whole, and carries out experiments on organisms that are intact, guessing at the internal changes that accompany the externally observable changes, so that theories are constructed which rely on what are called *theoretical terms*.

To understand this, imagine you are confronted with a big box, and find that if you touch it at one point it moves in a certain manner; touch it at another point and it moves in a different manner; and then, if you touch the first point again, it behaves differently from the way it did the first time. Since you are not allowed to open the box to discover the causes of its behaviour, and there is nothing to guide you as to whether the inside mechanism which causes the box to move is made up of springs, or weights, or chemicals or anything else, you proceed to invent a sort of hypothetical mechanism, and a terminology for it which is logically consistent, and that is all. You may say, for example, "I assume that it has a set of 'rings' inside it, and then some 'rods'," and so on; but these terms ("rings" and "rods") are not necessarily intended to be the kinds of rings and rods we normally think of: they are theoretical terms. We are, in fact, defining terms to suit our own purpose, and we can subsequently impute *any* meanings to them that we find convenient, provided that they are logically consistent with each other. It may seem a little odd, but this is exactly how the terms "ego", "id", and "super ego" are used in psychoanalysis, and even the term "mind" is used in this way in ordinary discourse.

The second method – the "molecular" approach – entails opening the box and investigating its contents. You will now rename the parts, which you may find are of the nature of "nerve fibres", "nerve cells", "nuclei", and so on – terms used in "physiology". It is generally considered that neuro-physiology is the primary ingredient of the "molecular" approach. The word "molar" (in spite of its dental sound) merely indicates that relatively large-sized slices are to be taken as basic data and investigated; "molecular" indicates very small slices to be treated in the same way. The distinction, however, is quite arbitrary, and any number of different levels of distinction may be defined. They are, in any case, complementary studies. We shall be dealing with both, but will be concerned primarily with the former – the molar or larger scale organism-as-a-whole methods.

The Scientific Problem of Cognition

The scientist – here, the experimental psychologist (but including the physiologist, the zoologist, the logician, the cybernetician and others) – is trying to find out how organisms are able to modify their behaviour so as to survive in the world around them. It is generally accepted that the ultimate aim is to make these discoveries for the benefit of man, but we have necessarily used animals as experimental tools in trying to fill in the larger gaps in our knowledge.

The ability to survive by our ability to adapt to changing circumstances is, roughly, what we mean by "learning", although there are many automatic types of adaptation that are not learnt, but are innate. The movement of flowers and insects towards the light, for example, is the result of an innate mechanism inside them. There is, in fact, a large range of instinctive behaviour patterns which have been investigated, and which we must discuss.

It is obvious that the way information is acquired is through our special senses, and it follows from this that our methods of collecting that information are vital to what is stored, and must involve the study of perception. The distinction between seeing (or hearing, touching, etc.) and perceiving is of the first importance, because we often learn, from subsequent inference, that things we think we have seen differ from the actuality. To repeat a previous example: we thought we saw three men when actually there were two men and a woman.

We shall require, then, in cases of learning and perceiving, to carry out our scientific investigations on at least two levels: the psychological, or direct observational, level of the behaviour of the organism, and the physiological and biochemical, or internal, level; the two levels that we have called above "molar" and "molecular". If these two sets of investigations can be brought into a consistent picture with each other, then we shall have taken a great step towards a predictive theory, which is precisely what science is aiming at. We might add *understanding* to prediction, but prediction is a minimum requirement.

"Cognition", it must be remembered, means more than just learning and perceiving; it also means thinking, reasoning and remembering, and these are more difficult fields in which to experiment. Our aim, though, as with all science, is to construct a model from which can be derived a theory, and this must be such as will allow us to make predictions for the future.

The model will sometimes be a physical model, for example, the model aircraft in a wind-tunnel, but it may also be mathematical or verbal. The term *model* will signify something which is relatively simple and logically clear, such as a simple map, or a geometrical drawing, or blueprints or block diagrams in engineering, or it may be some *symbolic* equivalent of these more pictorial models. The idea is that around the skeleton of the model (usually a logical model) can be built a scientific theory with the full equipment of empirical predictions. The theory-model relation is complicated, and relative in the same way as the molar-molecular distinction. The best examples are in the field of mathematical physics; there, a statement in the theory would be about the physical world, and a statement in the model would be about mathematics. A simple analogy is that of man with a desk computer. The man uses the numbers and their relations in the computer as a model, and temporarily designates them to stand for particular units such as pounds, shillings and pence – or pounds and ounces – when they are part of some theory.

In the ideal situation we would also *understand* what the model implies, although it is clear that it may be possible to use the model to predict without such an understanding. For example, a patient may be given a certain drug whenever he exhibits certain symptoms, which may prevent the recurrence of those symptoms, even though no one knows why the drug should have this effect. Again, the operation called frontal leuchotomy, which alleviates certain states of tension in affected people, does so by virtue of effects that can only be guessed at. Scientific explanation may take two forms: it may make an intuitive appeal as being reasonable (i.e. understood), or it may simply work in practice for no ostensible reason, or it may, ideally, both appeal *and* work.

With these rough methodological ideas in mind, a further enquiry must be made as to the various aims and approaches with respect to cognition. Physiologists working on the cognitive systems have tried to give a sort of explanatory model of the internal working of the organism and, in order to work more on the lines of what is called a "comparative approach", some of them have enlisted the co-operation of zoologists in considering the changes that occur in the nerves, or the biochemical changes of the body, when perceiving, learning and other cognitive events occur. We are, in fact, more concerned in this book about learning than any other single cognitive problem; let us, therefore, consider an example of an animal experiment which directly bears on the problem, and shows the biologist at work on the *molecular* approach to cognition.

Yerkes (1912), in America, carried out a series of experiments to study the behaviour of earthworms in a T-maze. The T-maze is so called, as one might expect, because it is shaped like a capital T, with a main runway, and two branches at right angles to left and right at one end.

At the end of one of the branches Yerkes put some dry leaves, and the end of the other branch was arranged to give an electric shock to the worm when it made contact. It was found that, when the worm arrived at the end of the long arm of the maze, it would at first turn haphazardly to right or left, but that eventually it *learned* to turn away from the arm with the shock at its end. This was true regardless of which arm contained the leaves and which the shock, provided, of course, that they were not changed over too frequently; but it took Yerkes' earthworms many hundreds of trials to learn the trick efficiently. So far, it will be noticed, this is all strictly *molar*.

From the *molecular*, or biological, point of view there is an interesting sidelight on Yerkes' experiment. It was found that if, after learning to run the maze successfully (i.e. avoiding the shock and reaching the leaves), the small nerve ganglia, or primitive brain in the head end of the worm were removed, the learning was still remembered. But worms generate new brains, and when the new brains grew it was found that the learning was lost, and the worms had to be trained all over again. This exemplifies, at the simplest level, and in a very general way, the relation between the molar and the molecular approaches to cognition.

It has been mentioned that zoologists take a *comparative* view of these problems of animal learning, and this means that they would be inclined to test different species of worm with the same apparatus, and to check on the various rates of learning, trying, in an evolutionary manner, to relate the ability and its development to the worm's history and environment.

The experimental psychologist, then, is interested in the character of learning, how it takes place, and how it is modified by changing the conditions of the environment. Those who are also physiologically inclined will then go on to ask how the internal environment of the organism changes with learning.

At this point we should consider the semantic difficulties with which we are faced over the words used to describe these cognitive factors. It is not easy to define "learning" in such a way that the definition is narrow enough to exclude effects of adaptation due to fatigue, or instincts, and yet broad enough to include every type of adaptation that occurs through experience and is still capable of being unlearned again. This condition, that associations should be capable of being destroyed as well as created, is a vital feature of learning.

The dictionary says that "learning" is a modification of a response, following upon and resulting from experience of results. It must be distinguished from remembering, etc. The philosophically or semantically inclined reader may readily find fault with this, as indeed he might with any other definition we might propose; we must therefore endeavour to arrive at an approximate idea of what is involved, and realize that we want to exclude instinctive, or automatic, behaviour

Definitions in Cognition

patterns acquired by genetic means, and other obvious artefacts, and yet include the process of systematically adapting to an environment. This is the problem of learning, and one of the central problems of cognition – certainly the one which has been most often examined. Let us consider some examples.

If a horse is put into a field near to a railway line, it will probably run to the furthest end of the field when a train goes by for the first time. However – assuming that the trains pass fairly frequently – in time, it will gradually show less and less response, perhaps eventually to the extent of completely ignoring the passing trains. This sort of simple learning is sometimes called "habituation". It is the setting up of simple habits.

More complex than habituation, although not obviously different in essence, is the manner in which the game of chess is learnt. Rules are remembered, then tactics are learned, and gradually the tactics are adapted to playing experience. What seemed a good opening under certain circumstances is no longer good if the opponent replies with a particular move, so a modification is made in the original opening. In the meantime it may be discovered that a counter measure exists to the opponent's defeat of the earlier opening, and the original gambit may then be used again.

This continual change or adaptation to new situations, where unlearning is as important as learning, is characteristic of learning in the fullest sense; what is required of the organism is obviously very much more complex than in habituation. Learning will grade over from the simplest to the most complex but, as an early maze-running experiment by Watson suggests, it is necessary to distinguish the process of learning from the habitually used act that was the result of previous learning. Many things which have been difficult to learn eventually become mere habits, and require no thought whatsoever.

Perhaps a sufficiently workable definition of *learning* is that given by Hilgard (1949):

> Learning is the process by which an activity originates or is changed through training procedures (whether in the laboratory or in the natural environment) as distinguished from changes by factors not attributable to training.

We shall return to the subject of learning later; in the meantime let us give some consideration to our second cognitive act: the perceptual act.

Perception has a history different from that of learning – though in many ways analogous – in that it lends itself more readily to introspective treatment. When human beings are involved, it is difficult to get accurate information from introspection about the way they learn, imagine, and solve problems. Learning experiments, therefore, call for the use of animals which have to be treated behaviouristically, whereas it seems natural to ask a human being how he sees something, how he hears certain sounds, and whether he subsequently believes that his perceptions were mistaken, or not. Although a good deal of more recent work on perception has been behaviouristic, the bulk is introspective, and remains to be integrated with the parallel research on learning theory.

Perception, we may say, has been treated less behaviouristically – less as an objective science – than learning, but it has also been the subject of a whole mass of experiments, some of which will be discussed. In many respects, the prototypes of perceptual experiments were those done by Köhler (1925), with his ape called "Sultan", on the island of Tenerife. He was able to show that the problem of reaching a banana outside the range of a single stick could be solved by the ape by putting two separate sticks together. This appears to have been possible only if the two sticks occurred together in his visual field, although once learned, the trick could be repeated under less rigorous conditions. This particular experiment emphasizes the relation between perceiving and learning (or problem solving), and also serves as a reminder of the close relation that exists between them. At the very least, they overlap.

Another basic problem of perception is well illustrated by an anecdote of Gardner Murphy, an American psychologist, who records a visit to his laboratory one evening. He was worried at the time about the destruction of many of his laboratory rats, and believed that a wild rat was finding its way into the laboratory and causing the deaths. On this evening, when he walked into the laboratory he *saw* the wild rat on the floor in a corner. He immediately prepared to take action and then, looking again, realized that what he had seen was, in fact, a ball of screwed-up paper.

Everyone has had this experience of mistaken identification, and it brings out the difference between actually seeing and perceiving. An interpretation is implied when the word "perceive" is used, and it may or may not be that such an interpretation is correct. One would say, "I thought I saw . . .", when and if it was discovered that the interpretation was incorrect. Clearly, then, what is perceived is dependent upon what it is expected to see; what psychologists sometimes call the "set" of the person. It will be observed that the words "see" and "perceive" are here being given a specific or technical meaning, with the object of distinguishing between awareness of visual appearances, and a knowledge of what is actually there – a problem of primary philosophical interest, but also relevant to psychology, as we shall see later.

Perception depends on the structure and function of the special senses, so it may be expected that physiological details will be of the utmost relevance. This means that a study of the special senses must be regarded as proper to a study of cognition.

Let it be said, quite generally, that the problem of cognition will be solved when, if ever, a sufficient model is available, from which one can construct a verbal theory which tells the user what will happen in the future, given certain present conditions. "If I do that to Charlie, then he will do such-and-such, because Charlie is this sort of a person." Perhaps we should always say, "he will *probably* do such-and-such", since however detailed the physiological and psychological theories used, one will never be in a position to be *certain* of the outcome, for it seems highly unlikely that it will ever be practically possible to say with sufficient precision what sort of person Charlie is. Nevertheless, the aim is to supply the general rules which apply to all human beings, with some measures of the individual differences between them. The sense of what has been said above seems virtually to identify cognition with normal psychology, yet that part of normal behaviour of the different types of people and of their individual differences, as well as their emotional responses, is outside the field of cognition. It cannot, of course, on that account be altogether ignored by cognitive theorists.

Much has already been done towards building a cognitive theory and we shall be quoting, later, some of the laws of learning and perception which have evolved from work in the past, while admitting that their status as "laws" is still open to debate. Furthermore, it is not claimed that they are by any means a sufficient set of laws.

Introspection, Behaviour and Body-mind

Now to return to a discussion which was started in Chapter 1, in which a distinction was made between McDougall's psychological theories and Watson's behaviourism, both in turn being distinguished from Gestalt theory. These various distinctions must now be somewhat sharpened.

Watson and Thorndike, and the work of Pavlov on the conditioned response, were the historical forbears of behaviourism, but the early forms of behaviourism show some differences from the present theories constructed under the same name. Watson's attitude can be illustrated by a simple prediction and an experiment (Carr and Watson, 1908). The prediction was that, if a rat were taught to run through a maze with a right-hand turn say three feet from the starting box, and then the right turn was moved further along to say four feet from the start, then the rat would behave automatically, and simply bump its nose on the slide of the maze.

This was doubted by some of Watson's opponents, who denied the underlying assumption that the learning – or at least the performance, once learned – is so unintelligent. But Watson was quite right, and when the experiment was tried the rat duly bumped its nose. Nevertheless, the implications of the experiment really proved very little, for human beings perform a great many complex and skilled acts in quite automatic fashion, and we should often appear stupid and unthinking if we had much of our environment changed suddenly. However, this is certainly no argument against the need for "insight", in favour of which McDougall and the Gestalt school have argued.

It will have been noticed that, in the previous paragraph, a distinction was made between learning and performance. This is an important feature in discussions in modern learning theory, and vital to an understanding of the evolution of Hull's theory (Chapter 5). Briefly it is necessary to infer what is learned from performance; but equally it must be possible to learn things that are never performed. Human beings may learn how to play a game on the basis of a verbal description, but they may never play it.

There is another set of experiments, carried out by Ruger (1910), which illustrates a very important point, and one especially liable to be misunderstood. Ruger worked with wire puzzles which posed the problem of disengaging one piece of wire from another by simple manipulation, that is, without recourse to such tools as pliers, hammers, etc. It was discovered that if the time taken were plotted against the stages of success in solving the problem, then there were various points, or stages, from which a person would more quickly arrive at the solution. In short, the graph of performance against time was not a simple straight line, but showed sudden changes which were suggestive of *insight*. The answer to this is that unless the puzzles are equated for difficulty at each stage (and this is virtually impossible) then nothing is proved at all. Even if we accepted Ruger's argument, we should still need to explain how insight operated, and what its nature was, for it is now well understood that to name something is not to explain it.

Some experiments by Thorndike (1898) are worth quoting at this stage. He kept cats in a cage, from which they could escape by appropriate manipulation of some escape device, such as by pulling a loop of string connected to a latch opening the cage door. Outside the cage, and visible to the cats, was food to motivate the hungry cat to escape.

Thorndike found that the problem of escape was solved slowly at first, but with practice, at increasing speed. He described the initial stages as trial-and-error procedures, and the successes, as they occurred, were stamped in by virtue of the rewards of food. Such simple associative explanation is similar to that of the work on the so-called conditional reflex by Pavlov (1927), which we shall discuss at some length in the next chapter. What is important now is to remember the existence of trial-and-error learning. Thorpe's (1950, 1956) definition of this is as follows:

> Trial-and-error learning is the development of an association, as the result of reinforcement during appetitive behaviour, between a stimulus, or situation, and an independent motor action as an item in that behaviour, when both stimulus and motor action precede the reinforcement, and the motor action is not the inevitable inherited response to the reinforcement.

This is rather heavy going, but defining some of the terms will help to elucidate it. By "appetitive behaviour", Thorpe means the flexible or variable phase that occurs at the start of an instinctive behaviour pattern. "Reinforcement" is a key word in learning theory, and means the result of rewarding any piece of behaviour and the consequent strengthening of that behaviour. The last phrase of the definition about "inherited response", is merely intended to exclude the possibility of an instinctive (rather than learned) pattern of behaviour.

Although awkwardly worded, Thorpe's definition covers precisely the sort of behaviour shown by a Thorndike cat during the early stages of its learning, but it is not so certain whether its later learning was always, or ever, trial-and-error. The familiarity of a situation surely eliminates the need for trial-and-error to a great extent, and might even involve the use of insight.

Thorpe does, in fact, make a distinction between *insight* and *insight learning* which must now be stated. Insight involves the organization of perception and the apprehension of relations, whereas insight learning is defined as follows:

> Insight learning is the sudden production of a new adaptive response not arrived at by trial behaviour, or, the solution of a problem by the sudden adaptive reorganization of experience.

It could be that insight learning is on a higher level of learning than trial-and-error, but it is essentially continuous with it. This is a problem we are very anxious to solve, but we have, as yet, a long way to go to reach a solution.

A discussion on conditioning theory now follows as a natural sequence, and this will occupy us in Chapter 3.

Chapter 3

THE CONDITIONED RESPONSE

The main discovery that led to the growth of behaviourism, and with it the possibility of making behaviour theory scientific, was made by the great Russian physiologist Ivan Pavlov. He, with his many associates, and especially another reflexologist Bechterev, had spent some time working on reflexes of one kind and another, when a new and exciting discovery was made. At that time Pavlov was studying digestion in dogs whose parotid glands in the face had been externalized so that when the dog salivated it was possible to collect the saliva and analyse it; salivation being induced, of course, by presenting food to the dog.

The great discovery occurred when the workers began to realize that merely bringing the dog into the laboratory situation, or even into the presence of any of the other associated signs – such as the persons who carried out the experiment – was enough to elicit salivation.

This led Pavlov to carry out a large-scale investigation of what became known as the "conditioned response". It was found that if the dogs were kept in a soundproof room, and a bell, gong, metronome or other sound was made to occur at the same time as feeding took place, then subsequently the presence of the sound alone would evoke the same response as that made to the arrival of food. The food was called the "unconditioned stimulus" (US), and was assumed to be innately related to some unconditioned response (UR). The sound – the bell or other sound used – was called the conditioned stimulus (CS), and the salivation response to the bell was called the conditioned response (CR).

It was subsequently shown that a whole range of animals could be conditioned in this manner, and that it was also possible to set up what was called "second order conditioning" in which the bell (the CS) was associated with a flash of light (a second CS), and the food

(US) was not present at all throughout this secondary association. It was also realized that the length of time during which the conditioned and the unconditioned stimuli occurred together was important in deciding the strength of the conditioning. Other factors had to be considered, such as the state of hunger of the dog which, of course, varied as between one test and another. It was found, too, that the conditioned response had to be *reinforced* by the unconditioned response from time to time. This intermittent reinforcement was called "partial reinforcement".

It will be of interest here to consider a formal definition of conditioning which was proposed by Konorski (1948).

> The conditioned response is such that if two stimuli S_1 and S_2 are applied in overlapping sequence, the stimulus S_1 being antecedent, then with repetition of such a combination, a plastic change in the nervous system is formed, consisting in the stimulus S_1 acquiring the ability to elicit the response of the same kind as the stimulus S_2.

Thorpe's (1956) definition is rather easier to follow. It says:

> Conditioning is the process of acquisition by an animal of the capacity to respond to a given stimulus with the reflex reaction proper to another stimulus (the reinforcement) when the two stimuli are applied concurrently for a number of times.

It was thought by Thorpe that such a conditioning process never constituted the whole of learning in animals fairly high up in the evolutionary scale. However this may be, we must return to the analysis of the variables that the situation and the definitions imply.

It was next realized that the amount of delay that occurs between the conditioned response and the reinforcement is of importance. This means that, during the process of conditioning, the strength of the response can be to some extent determined by delaying the arrival of food (reinforcement) for a period after sounding the bell, and measuring the time lapse between the sound and the commencement of salivation.

The strength of the conditioning is also determined by the strength of the stimulus, and of course it is also determined by its relevance. Irrelevant motivation has become a subject for special experiments, but in any case it is easy to see that a hungry dog will be less motivated by sexual stimuli than a dog that has recently been fed, and that a thirsty dog will not be so attracted by food as a hungry dog. This means generally that at any instant the needs of the organism will be a factor in determining the strength of the conditioned response.

The Conditioned Response

Many other facts were discovered about how this simple, if rather artificial, association process was set up. This sort of conditioning, it should be added, was only possible under carefully controlled experimental conditions. The animal was kept in a harness in a soundproof room, for any noise source that was not a planned part of the experiment would make conditioning difficult to achieve, if not altogether impossible.

Light was thrown on many other questions as it was gradually shown to be possible to condition every species, from the simplest unicellular ones, such as the amoeba, to man.

In the first place it was observed that an animal will give a conditioned response (CR) to a particular tone of bell (CS), and that the response to a similar, though different, tone is roughly proportional to the difference in tone. This means that there is a sort of *gradient of generalization*, and that the organism behaves towards one sound as if it were like another one, and to other sounds as if they were quite different. This also means that, if an animal were conditioned to respond one way to one sound and another way to another sound, it would be necessary for the animal to *discriminate* the two sounds in order to show the distinct responses.

The act of conditioned discrimination breaks down if the two stimuli are too much alike. If in these circumstances the animals are required to perform one of two mutually exclusive responses correctly, they fail to do so, and become restive and show symptoms which led to the name "experimental neurosis". This state has been set up in the rat as well as in many other animals.

Perhaps the simplest example of this sort of situation is where an animal, such as a rat, is placed on what is called a Lashley Jumping Stand (which presents two cards of different patterns) and forced to jump towards the cards. If the rat chooses the correct card he is rewarded by food which was placed behind the card, and if the wrong card, he bumps himself and falls into the net beneath.

If in this type of experiment the discrimination between the two cards is made too difficult, the rat becomes unable to make any sort of response, and goes into a state of a wholly abnormal kind; either a sort of fit in which no more interest is taken in the problem, or a state of rigidity where the rat will lie quite still and apparently take no interest in anything whatsoever. Both these states are characteristic of what has been called experimental neurosis.

The above experiment also raises the problem of perception in a behaviouristic way; certainly it shows a behaviouristic approach to perception, since the conditioning in the Lashley Jumping Stand depends directly on the abilities of the rat to perceive its environment.

Another, and simpler, fact was discovered, which was that when a conditioned response was extinguished by lack of reinforcement it would show spontaneous recovery under certain circumstances and, after a time, without any further renewing of the conditioning association it would react again as if the conditioning were still effective.

There are many other such effects which we have no space to discuss, and their variety makes the conditioned response complicated in the extreme; but the main point at issue is whether or not Watson and Thorndike and the early behaviourists were correct in believing that such conditioned responses were the basis of all human behaviour, and whether it is only necessary to consider their interaction in sufficient complication to account for all behavioural situations.

The next step, taken more recently, was to say that the classical (or type I) conditioning, as it is sometimes called, is not the whole of conditioning, and that there is also a further, and more interesting, group of experiments which are essentially the same and whose explanation is couched in terms known as instrumental (or type II) conditioning. We shall now outline this extension of the original theory, and illustrate the different types of conditioning that are then available for use in explanation in the behavioural sciences.

First the new categories must be considered. Instrumental conditioning is so called because, unlike the classical examples of Pavlov, the animal has to perform some specific action to achieve the rewarding circumstance; he is not a mere passive receiver of rewards. In this respect instrumental conditioning seems to be a much closer analogue of behaviour. There are four different training schedules which make up this instrumental conditioning, and they are called: (1) Reward training. (2) Escape training. (3) Avoidance training. (4) Secondary reward training.

Reward training is very similar to the classical example of Pavlov's harnessed dog. The difference is that the dog has to perform some more positive action, as a result of the conditioned stimulus, before the reward is forthcoming. A rat running a maze, for example, is rewarded by food at the end of the maze if, and only if, he runs it. Perhaps a better example is that of the guinea pig which was conditioned to turn its head at the sound of a buzzer, the movement being rewarded with a carrot. If he did not turn his head he did not receive the carrot.

The buzzer is the conditioned stimulus (because the guinea pig has learnt to associate the sound with the carrot), and it is also the unconditioned stimulus, the movement towards the sound being an unconditioned response. The same stimulus can elicit a new response by continued association and training, since the trick actually has to be learnt in the first place. This piece of learning is really indistinguishable from problem solving.

Escape training is also fairly simple. Consider a rat in a rotating cage, part of the floor of which is electrified. As the rat runs the cage rotates, and he eventually arrives at the electrified part and receives a shock. He responds to this by running much faster in order to get away from the uncomfortable part of the floor, and by this experience he soon learns how to escape from the shock. Of course he may originally make some inadequate response, or simply stop dead, but as soon as he has discovered that the increased speed has been successful, the trick is learnt.

Thorndike's cats (1898) – discussed in the previous chapter – show an example of reward training from the point of view of achieving the food outside the cage, but of escape training when considered as wanting to escape from the cage. This dual fact has brought about experiments designed to play down the role of motivation, on the grounds that the cat will not always eat the food when he has got outside the cage; but this does not really minimize the importance of motivation, rather, it points out the importance of identifying the relevant motive.

Our rat-in-cage example also illustrates avoidance training. When a sound is used as a conditioned stimulus, occurring just before the rat reaches the electrified part of the floor, the rat can learn to respond to it, and avoid the onset of the shock by running very fast, or by jumping over the electrified part. In this way he avoids, rather than escapes from, the unpleasant situation.

Lastly, secondary reward training. This may be exemplified by the experiment with apes who were made to work for poker chips which they could exchange for food later on, Wolfe (1936). The chips, originally of no value to the apes, became, by continued association, objects to be worked for because they could be stored and subsequently exchanged for food.

This last experiment brings to mind one further variation on the theme of the classical conditioned reflex, which we have intentionally left with a bare mention until now.

If a dog is conditioned to respond with salivation to a gong, a whistle can now be associated with the gong so that the dog will eventually learn to salivate to the whistle alone, even though the whistle and the food have never occurred together. This is called second order conditioning, and it should be noted that even higher order conditioning has sometimes been obtained. There is a close analogy between secondary reward and second order conditioning; indeed all symbolic usage, including language, might conceivably be subsumed under this heading.

At the end of this chapter and later in the book Morris' (1946) sign theory and its implications for philosophy will be mentioned briefly, since it provides a further link with the broader explanations concerned with all human knowledge. In the meantime we shall consider to what extent psychologists themselves have utilized the concept of the conditioned reflex, and how many fields could conceivably be explained in such terms.

The conditioning process is obviously very complicated, indeed probably very much more complicated than any psychologists have yet come to realize. It has been pointed out that in the apparently simple classical conditioning situation, really complex neurophysiological changes occur, and it may well be that it is also complicated at other levels of explanation.

Instrumental conditioning and the attendant problems of reinforcement with motivation, and the nature of inhibition, extinction, strength of conditioning, gradients of reinforcement and discrimination are all constituent parts of learning theory. All such matters are bound up in the work of Hull, Tolman and various others whose theories will be examined in Chapters 4, 5, and 6.

Cognition is much more than learning, and we must ask whether conditioning helps us to understand cognition better when we are thinking of the fields of perception, problem solving, thinking, and even when we cease thinking of the general rules of behaviour, but dwell on matters of individual difference.

These are all questions that will be discussed later in more detail, where the approach will not be confined to a strictly conditioning approach. We should also notice as we go along that the distinction between conditioning and any other association principle is often a matter of terminology alone; it is what we might call a semantic problem. We shall also bear in mind that this must be discussed further at a later stage.

Problem solving could certainly be brought within the compass of conditioning terminology. Indeed, in the case of instrumental conditioning, the distinction between learning, or, for example, the phase of learning that involves setting up the association by which avoidance can be achieved, is indistinguishable from a problem-solving situation. This point, which we have already remarked upon, can hardly be overstressed. At the same time we should presumably avoid saying that all problem solving is learning, since although one *could* always be said to be learning the solution, that fact is that this would be somewhat misleading, and there are many particular problems, perhaps especially of the symbolic type such as in mathematics, in which what is involved is at least more specific than learning in general, as we tend to think of it.

Books on experimental psychology often have chapters on reasoning, thinking, and problem solving, and the detail that goes into these chapters includes a number of particular experiments on animals, some of which have also appeared under the name "latent learning" – which we shall meet later – and some that are the phase of avoidance training in which the actual association is set up. These works also often contain chapters on formal logic which seldom give the impression of a close coherence with the animal experiments, nor even with the human experiments that are often found under problem solving. Of these last, Ruger's wire puzzles have already been mentioned. Let us consider another example.

Maier conducted a series of experiments in which rats had to run a maze such as in Figure 2. The problem can be stated as follows: The rat has been trained to run from R to X when hungry, and also from U to X when hungry, and in each case is rewarded at X. When thirsty, the rat runs from R to U or R to H, and has water at either place. Having been made familiar with these partial steps, he is placed at R with a barrier at B. This leaves a "choice" and, in training, its tendencies at the choice point were balanced in the thirsty state. When hungry rather than thirsty, it is confronted with the "choice" which, although it had never actually occurred previously as a choice, had paths both of which were familiar. If enough rats are used in the above experiment, we can decide whether there is a tendency to satisfy the conditions that would exist if reasoning were being used. Naturally this leaves a doubt as to whether reasoning was actually used, and we must try to be sure to eliminate other possible means of success. This does not tell us, of course, how reasoning works, and we may even be a little doubtful about the use of the word "reasoning" at all. At any rate, theories built upon conditioning must attempt to explain these results. As we shall see later, this is a matter still much in dispute.

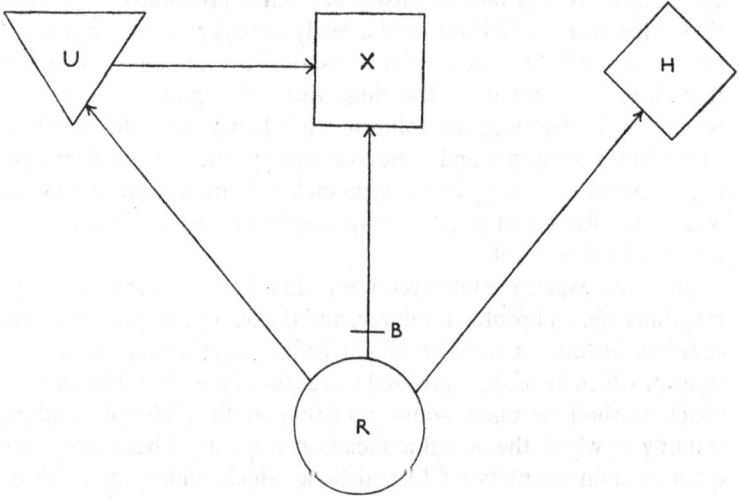

FIG. 2. MAIER'S PROBLEM-SOLVING EXPERIMENT
This figure shows the routes followed by the training schedules of the rats.
The text explains the details.

Human problems abound, and perhaps the most obvious ready-made examples are those of the working scientists, who are all the time trying to solve the problems presented by reality. Although it is possible to use conditioning terminology in stating the problem, and in describing the behaviour of the animals or humans, this is probably not enough, since we must also be sure that steps can actually be built up in terms of the simple conditioning process, and this is by no means certain. Köhler's apes, for example, seemed to solve their problems as a result of satisfying certain perceptual conditions, and this has led to the use of such terms as "perceptual learning", but it is not really clear on this account that any new principle is involved, since all learning will obviously involve perception. It seems that this is rather a matter of degree, and depends on the degree of immediacy of perception in the process of finding solutions. Some human beings, for example, will solve problems by looking at all the ingredients of the problem, but others may not need the pictorial aid, although the difference between the immediate perception and the earlier perceptions, now at the conceptual stage, is not necessarily great.

Because of the work done on experimental neurosis it is possible to approach the subject of personality and clinical behaviour in conditioning terms, but it should be apparent by now that this could always be achieved by a suitable choice of terminology. It has, in fact, often been felt that if conditioning were to be sufficient to explain all behaviour, it must entail something more than a mere change of terminology. This is a problem we must not lose sight of; no definite conclusions can suitably be drawn as yet.

Physiology and Conditioning

Pavlov himself drew up a sort of neurophysiological model of what he thought went on in the brain while conditioning was taking place. We shall briefly describe this model because it has very considerable historical importance. It should, however, be borne in mind that many of the inferences drawn by Pavlov have been much modified in more recent work, as will appear later in this chapter.

Fundamental notions used by Pavlov were *inhibition* and *excitation*, and these were to be thought of as cerebral cortical processes. Sensory stimulation leads to a state of excitation at a particular point of the cortex, and from there it spreads over the entire surface of the cortex, gradually diminishing in intensity as it becomes more remote from the point of origin. This phase of irradiation was followed by a phase of diminution and concentration back at the point of origin. It follows from this that, if the cortex does indeed contain highly localized areas, or points, dealing with the organization of each and every function performed, then we have to chart the points, and regard the cortex as a mosaic that has various patterns continually interacting on its surface. The same sort of activity is assumed to take place for inhibition and indeed, after either process there is a phase of the opposite. An analogy is in the behaviour of an elastic band which has been displaced from an equilibrium position; it does not go straight back to its stable position but overshoots, and gradually settles down after a series of oscillations.

These terms "inhibition" and "excitation" refer to assumed processes of the brain, but are close to the observed phenomena of excitation in nerve fibres, and the inhibition of excitation which occurs probably at the synaptic connections between nerve cells. The model is then supplemented by a series of theoretical terms which try to make for consistency between the theory and the observations. The concept of *induction* now comes into the picture. As we have mentioned, when the cortical process subsides at any point it may be succeeded by the opposite process, and this is called "induction". "Negative induction" intensifies inhibition under the influence of preceding excitation; "positive induction" intensifies excitation, following inhibition.

The conditioned reflex is assumed to be set up in the following way: excitation is set up by a neural stimulus at some point A, excitation irradiates from A, and will be concentrated at some other point of the cortex B, which is the focal point of the unconditioned stimulus. This process provides, metaphorically, a sort of channel from A to B, set up in such a way that "drainage" takes place from "weak" to "strong" points.

Generalization follows from the fact that excitation at B will be aroused by A, or by excitation at some near centres, A', A'', A''', etc., all very similar to (or near to) A. Inhibition arises if B is extinguished by presentation of stimulus without reinforcement, and the process is called *internal inhibition*. Other manifestations of inhibition have terminology as follows.

External inhibition involves the contemporaneous eliciting of an unconditioned response or reaction with the inhibitory conditioned stimulus.

Inhibitory after-effect is a simple generalization of inhibition.

Disinhibition is inhibition which can be temporarily removed under the influence of foreign stimuli.

Inhibition of delay involves a conditioned response, followed after a longish interval by an unconditioned response.

The use of the word "generalization" in the theory implies the use of "differentiation", and of "conditioned inhibition", which is a particular case of differentiation.

Resulting from some concentrated experimental work by another Russian experimental psychologist, Krasnagorsky (see Pavlov, 1911) there exist some experimental generalizations which we may call the "Krasnagorsky generalizations":

1. The more the CS resembles the stimulus originally inhibited (extinguished or differentiated) the more lasting is the inhibitory after effect.

The Conditioned Response

2. The more the CS resembles the inhibitory stimulus, the stronger is the inhibitory after effect, granted equal time intervals.

3. Secondary inhibition of all CS applied after inhibitory stimuli, increases gradually and achieves its maximum after a dozen or so seconds, and then diminishes.

4. The more times the inhibitory stimulus is repeated, the stronger and more lasting is the inhibitory after effect.

5. Secondary inhibition of active CS impinging upon the same part of the cortex as the inhibitory stimuli, is stronger and more prolonged than the inhibition of stimuli impinging upon other parts of the cortex.

Coupled with all that has gone before, there also exist some assumptions about the nature of the cortex itself. The cerebral cortex, as we have mentioned above, is in fact viewed as a mosaic of points in states of relative inhibition or excitation. This introduces one or two further notions. One of these is "capability", a term used to imply that different cells have different capabilities or excitabilities. Applications of more than top excitation brings out protecting inhibition. The second assumption, phase of equalization, occurs when both strong and weak conditioned stimuli evoke an identical conditioned response. With these remarks we must conclude our summary of the Pavlovian model. Let us now consider briefly some criticisms of it.

In the first place it should be said that, in a general way, the picture of the cortex as a mosaic is idealized, and removed from experimental data. Pavlovian excitation and inhibition are essentially inferential, and much of the model is *remotely* metaphorical, e.g. the use of words such as "drainage".

More specifically irradiation is non-demonstrable in the simple form suggested by Pavlov. Certain techniques in modern neurophysiology have demonstrated great variability in spread of excitation in the cortex. Some areas show virtually no spread, while spreading effects in other areas are by no means as simple, or symmetrical, as is suggested by Pavlov.

For Pavlov, the term "inhibition" is at least different from the same term in classical neurophysiological theory. Indeed it is clear that Pavlovian "inhibition" refers to a quasi-permanent state of the cortex, and it is therefore not a probable model of events in the cortex.

In neurophysiology there is action-by-contact, in the sense that neurons fire neurons in a more or less precise manner. Neither of the Pavlovian irradiations of excitation or inhibition behave quite in this manner, although they could perhaps be made to conform to this extra condition, particularly by using the hypotheses of closed chains of activity within the cortex.

From Konorski's (1948) viewpoint, the most important error of a fundamental kind is the assumption, deep-rooted in Pavlov, that excitation and inhibition are not only essentially cortical processes, but that both the excitatory state evoked by application of an active conditioned stimulus, and the inhibition evoked by application of the inhibitory conditioned stimulus, is localized in the cortical centre. This leads to the complete omission of the reflex arc, and more dubiously, to concentration on unspecified states of excitation and inhibition which irradiate or concentrate, summate or restrict, and above all are not committed to particular neuron chains.

Another point made by Konorski is that different states can be introduced at a cortical centre merely on the grounds of whether or not a stimulus is reinforced.

A further difficulty, also noted by Konorski, is that of making sense of the notion of "indifference states" existing between centres of excitation and inhibition.

To summarize briefly the further developments of Konorski's arguments against the internal inconsistencies of the Pavlovian model: in the first place there is the vagueness in the distinction between "excitation" and "positive excitability", as also between "inhibition" and "negative excitability". The notions of positive and negative excitability refer to states (more or less permanent) of cells, as opposed to the processes of excitation and inhibition, but these terms have been used in a confusing manner, such as in the establishment of differentiation which may be followed by an increased conditioned response, thanks to the permanent influence of positive induction from the inhibitory point; for the theory also states that positive induction can be brought about only by inhibition. Another example of confusion is the statement that the administration of bromides increases the strength of the conditioned response and of the positive induction evoked by the concentration of inhibition. When we are also told that a wave of excitation caused by an extraneous stimulus may summate with the excitation of a conditioned stimulus, the confusion is increased because we know that a wave of excitation may "wash away" the inhibitory excitability of a given point, and leave a temporary state of positive excitability.

Another proposition of the theory is that with very strong or very weak stimuli irradiation is immediate, but that with medium strength stimuli it is delayed until the stimulus has ceased. This assumption has not been verified, and indeed it has no place in the explanations of the molecular foundations of cognition. Furthermore, the Pavlovian notion of top inhibition leads to two quite separate, and opposed, mechanisms in explanation of external inhibition: either concentration of excitation, *or* irradiation of excitation and top capability. At best the theory here is confused.

There are many other details of internal inconsistency in the Pavlovian theory; the problem of sleep as explained by internal inhibition is also open to criticism. It should be noticed that other writers have pointed out the inadequacy of the Pavlovian model, and enough has been said here to show that it is not adequate for various reasons. It also appears to be inconsistent with many of the findings of neurology. In fact it may be said that, generally, it appears to be internally inconsistent and confused, and theoretical terms have been used in a manner which reduces their explanatory value to a low level.

To sum up, it must be said that whereas the Pavlovian model had been of considerable use in the past, it is no longer sufficient as an explanatory model for a molecular theory of cognition, and this, at least in outline, is what we are seeking.

Konorski's Molecular Model

It will be useful next to consider another model that appears to be a step in the direction of our objective, the model that is due to Konorski, and represents an attempt to integrate the Pavlovian model with our knowledge of classical neurophysiology. Konorski's first point is that plasticity in behaviour is central to all neurological and cognitive theory, and he suggests that it is a property of the intact organism-as-a-whole. He gives some interesting examples of the properties of plasticity, notably:

The application of a certain combination of stimuli tends to give rise to a definite plastic change, and the repetition of the combination leads to cumulation (i.e. an increase in this change) where this change, like the law of effect, has certain limiting properties; e.g. if the combination of stimuli which is the cause of the plastic change ceases to be applied, the change suffers regression.

These statements represent generalizations from observations of behaviour in the organism-as-a-whole, and it is not easy to demonstrate the neurological correlates. The best known theory of neural growth is probably due to Ariens Kappers (Kappers, Huber and Crosbie, 1936). Kappers proposed that new neural connections were established by growth of the neural processes. After stimulation they grew in such a way that, if two cells were simultaneously excited, the resulting ionization is assumed to lead to the growth of axons toward the cathode and dendrites toward the anode, so that new synaptic connections are set up. This idea has been used by Hebb (1949) recently. The Kappers-type neural growth had been held to be morphologically impossible, but Hebb re-stated Kappers' position and, though it has not in fact been observed over any large distance, it remains a possibility over small distances of a centimetre or so which, in Hebb's treatment, is all that would be necessary. However, this point must be left here.

Konorski's generalization of Pavlov's model starts from the assumption that the simplest and best known type of plasticity is the conditioned response, which involves the setting up of new functional relationships between concurrently excited groups of nerve cells. Konorski calls the centre of the conditioned stimulus the "conditioned centre", and the centre of the reinforcing unconditioned stimulus is called the "unconditioned centre". These centres may or may not be cortical, but they will normally involve the cortex. Unlike the assumption in Pavlov's theory, the connection between these centres is now assumed to be extremely complex, involving a number of intermediary stations. Konorski substitutes for the top capability of cortical cells, the notion of *occlusion* and a *state of saturation* of conditioned connections. This form of modification has been extensively carried out throughout Pavlov's model with the dual aim of increasing internal consistency, and bringing the data of Pavlov into line with our classical neurophysiological knowledge.

Now there is one important extension of the Pavlovian system that needs to be considered before we can say anything general about the Konorskian revision. With respect to plasticity, the classical conditioned reflex is not considered to be the only mechanism. The classical reflexes, or conditioned reflexes of the first type, must be supplemented by conditioned reflexes of the second type, the type which has been referred to as "instrumental conditioning". The details of type II conditioning, as it is also called, are well known to psychologists, and need not be repeated here except to note that the various types have been categorized as: (1) Reward training, (2) Escape training, (3) Avoidance training, and (4) Secon-

The Conditioned Response

dary reward training. They involve the principles of substitution, effect, expectancy, etc. (see pp. 60-1). Konorski takes a type II experiment and infers from it that unconditioned stimuli can be divided into two categories: those which, by reinforcing the animal's movement cause it to perform a movement spontaneously and those which cause an antagonistic movement. He calls these "positive unconditioned stimuli" and "negative unconditioned stimuli", respectively. For example, in the guinea pig and carrot experiment the buzzer is initially a positive unconditioned stimulus; but if the buzzer had been used as a sign of an oncoming electric shock it would have been a negative unconditioned stimulus.

In comparing classical with instrumental conditioning, Konorski notices certain differences. Firstly, the response of type I is the same for unconditioned and conditioned reflexes, whereas in type II it is, in general, quite different and, in special cases, even antagonistic. Furthermore, there is an identical pattern for type I, but for type II there are different patterns, according to whether the reinforcing stimulus is a positive or a negative unconditioned stimulus. Response to type II seems wholly somatic, as opposed to either somatic or automatic for type I. By "somatic" we mean, broadly speaking, "under voluntary control", though that is also a vague phrase. The words "voluntary" and "automatic" clearly demand a further detailed analysis, since it is their uncritical use which encourages one of many unsatisfactory dualisms in science.

A final word about these changes is now necessary. In the first place let it be said, quite generally, that there is at least a doubt as to whether the terminology of the conditioned response is usefully taken over to describe the whole of nervous activity and cognitive activity. It seems that the classical conditioned response is a special case of general associative processes involving the central nervous system; whether or not, then, we regard type II conditioning as a type of conditioned response is a matter of terminology, though this must not be taken to diminish its great importance.

Selecting some aspects of the change in notation that has been made by Konorski, it seems that the phenomenon of generalization of excitatory conditioned reflex seems better accounted for by the notion of partial cortical overlap, since there is considerable independent neurological evidence for such an overlap.

The concept of occlusion, which acts as a limiting mechanism in the top value of conditioned reflexes, seems more satisfactory than the notion of top capability of cortical cells, if only in so far as an integration is thereby attained with the classical theory.

This last remark is, of course, generally true of the Konorski revision. It is to be recommended on the grounds of integration in scientific theory, and the achievement of the use of the same theoretical terms and formulations as classical theory. This is indeed an important and valuable step. Much, also, of the internal inconsistency of Pavlov has been remedied, e.g. the confusion over inhibition, negative excitability, etc. Here we should also mention the formation of the inhibitory conditioned response, which is now explained by Konorski in terms of the contemporaneous excitation of the conditioned centre, with fall of excitation in the unconditioned centre. Also, the increase of the excitatory conditioned response concurrently with the inhibitory response seems more adequately explained by summation of the excitatory conditioned response and the excitato-inhibitory response with facilitation predominating.

If it is assumed that the conditioned response and unconditioned response are special cases of neural association which are, respectively, reinforced and unreinforced, then the question arises as to whether inhibition and excitation are "unitary" processes or not. The answer obviously depends on the meaning of the word "unitary". The argument is that only one neural process occurs in the nervous tissue, and the difference between excitatory and inhibitory processes refers to the state of the synapses on receipt of the neural excitation. This assumption resembles Sherrington's central excitatory state (c.e.s.) and central inhibitory state (c.i.s.), in which a state of excitation would be assumed to take place at a synapse or not, according to the excitable state of the synapse as the impulse reaches it. One somewhat crude hypothesis, by way of illustration, may suffice: if excitability is increasing when the impulse arrives then, up to some limit, the incoming stimulus may have an excitatory effect; if however the excitability is decreasing, the stimulus may be inhibitory in its effect.

In addition to these observations on the new Konorski system, it is important to know whether it implies a sufficient degree of flexibility, even granted that it accepts a certain level of approximation. To restate simply the foundation of Konorski's procedure: He has taken the experimental findings of conditioning, and reformulated the theory in terms of the classical neurological concepts; or, more literally, he has disposed of the theoretical terms used by

Pavlov, and rebuilt conditioning theory into the classical neurophysiological theory. The first question that it is necessary to ask is, Is this process successful? and secondly, what does it entail? The answer to the first question is that as far as it goes it is successful, because the changes necessary to effect Konorski's ends are verbal, i.e. it is possible to take any separate body of facts and integrate it into some known body of facts by explanations involving the same theoretical terms. It should be clear that this is *not* an adverse criticism. The second question, however, raises some doubt. Is the body of experimental knowledge called conditioned responses, with which Pavlov and Konorski deal, central to the problem of cognition? It does seem, in the final analysis, that conditioning terminology – at least, the fundamental notion of the conditioned response – is not by itself adequate as a foundation for cognition, especially when extended to higher organisms.

Before continuing a general review of the relation of conditioning to learning, it will be as well to mention Konorski's definition of learning:

> By learning we shall denote a process leading to the lasting changes in the manner in which an organism reacts to a stimulus, which are due to the application of this stimulus in definite combinations with other stimuli (the application of a stimulus alone is also considered as a definite combination), and which are not caused by any destructive effects which the applied stimulus might produce.

These changes are referred to as plastic changes, and stimulus is defined as:

> Any compound of agents acting on the receptive parts of the nervous system (i.e. on receptors, afferent pathways, or directly on nervous centres) and evoking their excitation.

Konorski also emphasizes the words "lasting character", for it is, of course, true that the question as to what length of time is required for modifiability, to make the effect genuine, is a matter of convention and necessarily arbitrary. The most interesting aspect of the definition of "stimulus" is the evocation of excitation. The more useful model must regard the nervous system as being in a continuous state of change and excitation, and it follows that the complete absence of all external stimuli, even for a considerable period, would not lead to quiescence.

The more important question, however, is that of the generality of conditioning, and Konorski makes it clear that he does recognize other types of learning; indeed a definition of "insightful" behaviour is given, and the notion of latent learning is accepted. This is, of course, where the most difficult part of the problem *starts*.

We have devoted a good deal of attention to the work of Pavlov on conditioning; the reason for this is partly its great historical importance, but much more because the basic idea of conditioning is one that is still central to experimental psychology in general, and cognition in particular, and it also involves both molar and molecular levels of explanation.

This point is brought out more clearly in the work that has been done explicitly in the field where philosophy and psychology overlap. The work of Charles Morris in America is of the utmost importance in this respect. He has used the theories of Hull and Tolman – whose work is directly related to the conditioned response and behaviouristic interpretations of the conditioned response – as a point of departure for an analysis of sign behaviour.

The analysis of signs is the first step towards the analysis of language. The use of signs is also obviously bound up with instrumental conditioning, and this leads on quite naturally to the use of signs in language, sometimes called lansigns (a contraction for language signs); these are first the sentences and later the words that make up a language.

Another important aspect of language and conditioning is seen through the technique of cybernetics. This is a method of giving something more than "ordinary" theories – it is, in fact, giving *effective* theories, or blueprints – for the operations performed by organisms, in particular in using signs and language. The whole matter of cybernetics will receive separate treatment in Chapters 13 and 14; it must suffice for the moment to say that cybernetics is closely related to the analysis of semiotic (with which Charles Morris is much concerned) which entails a behaviouristic analysis of the concepts of language, meaning, etc. (see Chapter 17), hitherto the exclusive province of philosophy; indeed it is viewed by philosophers with mixed feelings, since they claim to be interested in logical rather than causal explanations, and so deny the relevance of science to philosophy. This particular view is one that has become a focus of debate because, for the behavioural scientist, the question is not whether, but to what extent, language and logic are themselves a part of behaviour, and therefore the whole of philosophy is open to behavioural and scientific analysis, just as science is open to logical and philosophical analysis. In spite of opposition by philosophers generally, this view is one that is increasingly gaining ground, and the reason for the change – we might call it progress – is the development of the behavioural sciences. This in turn has depended tremendously on the utilization of the concept of the conditioned response.

Chapter 4

LEARNING AND THEORIES OF LEARNING

In this chapter, as was intimated previously, we shall be saying something more about conditioning; indeed our study of the learning theorists is largely a study of the theories that have been built up around the conditioning experiments.

Before we come to discuss these particular theories of learning, it would be well to consider some of the so-called laws of learning which can be regarded as being, at least to some extent, independent of the various theories.

Every learning theorist – or perhaps one should say, almost every learning theorist – is prepared to accept some version of the law of *effect*, much as it was originally formulated by Thorndike.

This law states that if a response leads to an event (or state) that is satisfying to the organism then, if the circumstances leading to the event are repeated, the same response is likely to occur again. If we substitute the word "dissatisfying" for "satisfying", then we shall have to say that the response is *not* likely to be repeated. It is in this way that responses that lead to pleasure and avoid pain are built into the repertoire of the surviving animal. Clearly this suggests a great deal of complication in the associations that the organism must store, but nevertheless it seems a fair general statement, and one that is almost certain to have application at some level, whether to learning or performance.

The law of *recency* says that the most recently formed associations are most likely to be recalled, everything else being equal. The qualifying phrase obviously applies, among other things, to large differences in the importance of events for the organism, or, more briefly, to differences in their *value*. It is, for example, obviously unlikely that I shall remember the death last year of some remote acquaintance more readily than my own father's death ten years

Learning and Theories of Learning

before. The need for some qualification to any law of recency is fairly clear.

The law of *exercise*, and the law of *frequency*, state that repetitions strengthen connections between stimuli and responses (associations), and the frequency is one factor that contributes to the strength of the associations.

It is in this sort of form that learning laws have been developed, and the problem remains to fit them together into a broad, predictive system or theory that ultimately includes most of cognition.

Some of these laws have also been developed in more mathematical form, and it is easy to see that their quantitative aspect lends itself to such treatment. Experiments in methods of constructing theories are always taking place and, in keeping with the development of physics, attempts are being made, and will continue to be made, to fit suitable mathematical models to the established facts of learning. Our chapters on cybernetics (Chapters 13 and 14) will be especially concerned with precisely this sort of thing.

In the meantime it seems that the bulk of learning theory has been built up around conditioning experiments and other experiments that could be interpreted in conditioning terminology, and is anyway dependent upon associative processes capable of a behaviouristic interpretation. The four types of instrumental conditioning mentioned in the last chapter have lent themselves to different sorts of explanatory principles which we must now consider.

First there is the classical conditioning to explain. Pavlov thought of this primarily in molar terms, as opposed to the molecular explanations briefly outlined in the previous chapter. The idea is that the conditioned stimulus *is a substitute for* the unconditioned response, and that there is a degree of substitution which depends upon the variable factors which we have already mentioned. Principally should be mentioned the time interval between the conditioned stimulus and the unconditioned response (the sound of the buzzer and the salivation), the intensity of the conditioned and unconditioned stimulus, and the number of repetitions of the stimuli. This principle is widely known as the principle of "substitution".

Now it certainly may be the case that one stimulus is in some sense substituted for another, but we should also notice that there is a great deal of evidence that the conditioned response and the unconditioned response are not identical with each other, and that, in fact, many experiments have been carried out which show the different nature of the responses.

An American psychologist, Zener (1937), photographed the full act of conditioning a dog and pointed out that, while a casual glance might make the two responses seem the same, a more detailed observation shows that the dog's posture is different in the two cases. There are various other minor differences, perhaps the most important being the fact that the unconditioned response carries with it an appearance of satisfaction and completeness that is missing in the conditioned response, which still shows signs of anticipation. The conditioned response is perhaps more generalized, and is accompanied by a general sense of readiness and alertness.

It is now widely agreed that a distinction exists between the conditioned and the unconditioned response, and this is something we should bear in mind in considering a substitution principle, for the evidence seems clear that, if substitution takes place, at least it is not because the animal takes the conditioned stimulus and the unconditioned stimulus to be identical. This in itself suggests the operation of something more like a *sign* or indicator, and leads to another viewpoint which has already been mentioned briefly in connection with the work of Charles Morris (1946).

An alternative rendering of the substitution principle has been made by Guthrie (1935) and we shall briefly examine the manner in which Guthrie differs from Pavlov before we consider his principle further.

At first sight, Guthrie's view of substitution seems rather surprising. He says that substitution is the basis of learning, and that when it occurs it occurs completely; there is no question of partial substitution or degree of substitution. He has two simple laws which he suggests as being appropriate to learning.

1. A combination of stimuli which has accompanied a movement will, on its recurrence, tend to be followed by that movement.

2. A stimulus pattern gains its full associative strength on the occasion of its first pairing with a response.

Guthrie's first law is somewhat like the law of effect, but the use of the word "movement" makes it clear that he is thinking of a rather more specific application. He used a problem box, rather like that of Thorndike, and found that the dogs did not always eat the food outside the box when they escaped. Such results have had the effect of putting Guthrie against motivation as a vital, central ingredient in learning, as it tends to be for almost everyone else.

But it is in Guthrie's second law that the main difference between his substitution principle and that of Pavlov's is shown. His statement to the effect that substitution is immediate and complete seems clearly to be incorrect, for we *do* get from experiments degrees or gradations of response when the subsequent stimulus is similar to, but not the same, as the original conditioned stimulus – a bell, or whatever it is, with a tone, say, an octave lower than the bell previously used.

Guthrie seems to answer this objection by saying that his units of substitution are much smaller than those of Pavlov, and that in any molar situation there are many conditioned and unconditioned stimuli and responses, and the full conditioning process depends upon the appropriate pairing and ordering of all of them. This argument for "maintaining stimuli", as he called them, he uses to explain the improvement in performance with practice. The upshot of all this seems to be that Pavlov and Guthrie are really not talking about quite the same thing. The same principle is used, but on different levels of description using different theoretical terms.

Substitution, in Guthrie's sense, is difficult to test since it does not always seem possible to verify the presence of the actual factors being associated. Furthermore, his theory might be criticized on the grounds that he has generalized too freely from experiments done on too narrow a sector of learning.

Seward (1942) and others have performed experiments that might be said to cast some doubt on Guthrie's theory. In particular Seward has shown that rats learn to press a bar more efficiently when they are explicitly rewarded. This also lends emphasis to the importance of motivation to Tolman, who does not treat it with quite the immediacy of Hull.

It should also be mentioned that a partial formalization of Guthrie's theory has been undertaken by Voeks (1950), but this particular formalization will not be discussed here.

If we confine our estimate of the principle of substitution to its use in Pavlov's theory, we must ask how such a principle can account for the different types of instrumental conditioning. For this purpose we can consider reward training and escape training together.

Reward and escape training will be explained, in terms of the substitution principle, by arguing that reward (the word "reward" will be used here to mean both reward and escape unless otherwise stated) will terminate a conditioned stimulus and that the last response made is the one that remains conditioned. This applies more obviously to Guthrie than to Pavlov, but could be taken to apply to both.

Avoidance training (the term will include secondary reward training, in the same way as with reward and escape) is then accounted for by saying that the conditioned stimulus evokes anticipatory responses which have been learned by substitution. So here we see the need for a new sort of response, that of anticipation, and this is certainly a possible explanation.

The next explanatory principle is the law of effect, and we shall see how it works in explaining instrumental conditioning. The principle of effect has been used primarily to account for reward training, but it can be extended to other types. Of course there is an element of effect principle in substitution itself, but not quite in the original form. To make the theory of effect account directly for the classical conditioning situation requires that we add the concept of heterogeneous reinforcement to that of *drive*, and then it is a straight case of *drive* reduction. By *heterogeneous* reinforcement we mean reinforcement through a response that does not resemble the conditioned response. If it does resemble the conditioned response we say that the reinforcement is *homogeneous*. The word "drive" in this context is used to represent the basic motivational factors in the organism – the factors of hunger, thirst, sex, parental drives, and so on. As these drives are set up they are said to represent needs for which the organism demands some satisfaction. Hull has called this *need-reduction*, and it is taken to be the core of his principle of reinforcement.

We can apply the effect principle directly to reward training, but this leaves us with the large problem of explaining avoidance training by the same principle. An explanation once given was that heterogeneous reinforcement supported derived reinforcement, and this was thought to be enough.

In the case of Hull's theory – as we shall see in the next chapter – he postulated from the start a principle that allowed for what he called "fractional anticipatory goal responses". These fractional responses could be integrated to build up the expectancies that seemed to be necessary to account for avoidance and secondary reward. The actual difference between this form of explanation and that proposed by Tolman – which depended directly on the assumption of some state called "expectancy" – is one of the main points of discussion in the comparison of Hull's and Tolman's theories, and we shall be devoting some time to this in Chapter 6.

Taking the principle of expectancy next, we should start by accounting for classical conditioning by saying that learning occurs if, and only if, that learning is part of a behaviour route to a goal. To account for reward training we shall say that the reward confirms an expectancy. What appears to be a "spread of effect", according to the law of effect, is really a gradient of uncertainty regarding probabilities and their expected sequence. From this, avoidance training appears as a direct application of the principle of expectancy.

Before a discussion of other particular theories is pursued, it will be as well to examine more closely these apparently simple explanatory statements.

In the first place it should be asked whether these attempted explanations of *substitution*, *effect* and *expectancy* are really mutually exclusive. We should certainly pause to consider the significant fact that those who have favoured substitution and effect have tended to experiment on more primitive organisms than those selected by people who prefer the expectancy type of principle. Tolman is perhaps an exception in this case.

We should note next the definition of substitution given by Hilgard and Marquis:

> An activity initiated by a stimulus, occurring at the same time as another activity which results in a response, will tend on subsequent occurrences to evoke that response.

Here the word "that" might be generalized slightly to include "similar" responses, or responses associated with the original response. This takes up Pavlov's version of substitution, and makes it closer still to Hull's use of effect; or, to put it in another way, substitution and effect could be brought into line with each other by regarding homogeneous reinforcement as a special case of heterogeneous reinforcement.

In considering the expectancy theory we shall not press the point that the more primitive forms of conditioning could not be regarded in this light, for learning has to be a part of a route to a goal. This is after all mostly a matter of the point of view, and it would be rash to assert that it is impossible to reconcile the principle of expectancy with such a one as effect. It is rather, perhaps, that one group is placing emphasis upon the receptive and passive nature of behaviour, and the other is emphasizing the active participating aspect. These matters come to a head in later chapters.

By way of summary of what has been said so far, the following table is given (Hilgard and Marquis, 1940).

TYPE OF EXPERIMENT	ABSTRACTED PROCESS	SUBSTITUTION	EFFECT	EXPECTANCY
Classical Conditioning	Homogenous Reinforcement	Substitution principle can be directly applied.	Conditioning depends upon drive and heterogeneous reinforcement.	Learning occurs only if response is part of a purposive route to a goal.
Instrumental Reward and Escape	Heterogeneous Reinforcement	Reward (or Escape) terminates conditioned stimulus, and the last response made is the one conditioned.	Effect principle can be directly applied.	Reward (or Escape) confirm expectancy; what appears to be a spread of effect is a gradient of uncertainty regarding the probability that certain expected events will occur.
Instrumental Avoidance and Secondary Reward	Derived Reinforcement	Conditioned stimulus evokes anticipatory responses which are *learned* by substitution.	Heterogeneous reinforcement is necessary to produce and support derived reinforcement.	Expectancy principal can be directly applied.

Thorndike's Behaviourism

The learning theories of Thorndike (1898, 1911, 1949) and Skinner (1933, 1938) are among the most important contributions to the subject. Thorndike's views and his scientific generalizations surrounded the law of effect, but he built up a much broader theory than this law, on its own, would suggest. He talked a great deal about bonds, or connections, being made, and he undoubtedly thought in terms of a simple, conceptual nervous system in which connections were made and broken in something of the same way as we saw depicted in Pavlov's neurophysiological theory in the previous chapter.

Thorndike's cat experiments led him to believe in the central importance of trial-and-error learning. His experiments also laid emphasis upon the nature of motivation and the problem of rewards and punishments. The law of effect gave significance to a law of practice by insisting that learning had direction, and showed a purposive quality. It is interesting to remember, here, that in Thorndike's early days the idea of purposive behaviour was anathema to behaviourists.

Underlying the law of effect, Thorndike also developed a theory of readiness, which he called a "law", and which shows in particular Thorndike's leaning towards a physiological or molecular form of explanation. His law of readiness states:

1. When a conduction unit is ready to conduct, conduction by it is satisfying, nothing being done to alter its action.

2. For a conduction unit ready to conduct not to conduct is annoying, and provokes whatever response nature provides in connection with that particular lack.

3. When a conduction unit unready for conduction is forced to conduct, conduction by it is annoying.

We should regard "conduction units" as typical theoretical terms. Behind Thorndike's terminology was a desire to avoid such problems as are presented by ideas and consciousness, rather than to encourage thought of neuroanatomical and neurophysiological details. The attempt is always to supply an explanation of the need for action, and the direction taken by a particular action.

The law of exercise was the means by which Thorndike hoped to explain the strengthening of conditioning with practice, and its weakening with its lack of practice – the laws of *use* and *disuse* respectively.

Thorndike developed his theory in far more detail than we have space to discuss here, but suffice it to say, by way of summary of some of his other contributions, that he tried to account for characteristics like *set*, the selection of appropriate responses from a set of possible responses, responses by analogy, and by what he called "associative shifting", whereby a response might become associated with a wholly new stimulus. Thorndike's own example is one of teaching a cat to stand up, when ordered, by using a piece of fish to tempt him. The piece of fish acts as a conditioned stimulus, of course, and we can now recognize the situation as classical conditioning of degree one, or more, and involving no new principle.

Thorndike occupies an important historical position in experimental psychology. He derived many principles that are now widely accepted, if in slightly modified form. He was behaviouristic by inclination, but not wholly committed to the older narrow behaviourism, and this made him a liberalizing influence in the development of learning theory. It is now generally thought, however, that he applied his methods in a variety of ways that paid too little attention to the obvious complication and sophistication of human thought, and that his theorizing was not sufficiently rigorous to satisfy modern requirements. We must, I think, now regard his work in the same way as that of the Gestalt psychologists; both he and they have contributed a great deal that has now been integrated into modern theorizing.

For a more up-to-date appraisal of Thorndike's work, placing emphasis on the concept of Spread-of-effect, reference should be made to Hilgard (1958) as well as Thorndike (1949).

Since we are not concerned in this book with the sort of completeness aimed at in a textbook, and because we believe that this particular discussion is already incorporated in other discussions such as that comparing Tolman and Hull (Chapter 6) this matter will not be pursued here. What can be said is that it is fairly widely accepted – or so it seems to the writer – that the simple Thorndike concept of spread of effect can only be understood in the background of more complicated principles. In other words, it seems clear that stimulus-response connections is only one way in which learning takes place. Stimulus-stimulus connections also occur, and indeed possibly response-response connections may occur as well. Furthermore, for the human being the whole problem of association is complicated by the nature of motivation, and the subsequent evaluation of events. Much the same is probably also true of the lower organisms.

A further set of representative experiments in learning must be examined next.

Partial Reinforcement

Before we can complete even a preliminary assessment of molar theories of learning, it is essential to consider some of the other principle variables and theoretical terms in the molar psychological field. We shall start with "partial reinforcement", and for reference purposes we shall first give a working definition of this term.

Partial reinforcement is reinforcement which is given on only a certain percentage of trials (or following responses). Thus the limiting cases are total reinforcement – 100 per cent., and no reinforcement – 0 per cent.

In partial reinforcement, our interest will be centred on a short summary of the experimental evidence, and a brief study of the suggested theories.

Platonov, a Russian psychologist, is one of the first to be credited with partial reinforcement experiments. In his experiment a con-

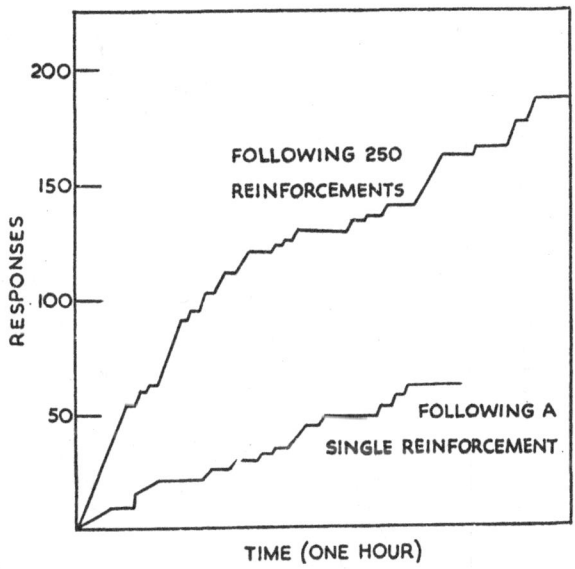

FIG. 3. PARTIAL REINFORCEMENT

The graph shows in one case the extinction of lever-pressing following a single reinforcement and in the other case following 250 reinforcements.

ditioned response was maintained by application of the unconditioned stimulus on the first trial only of each day.

Since the work of Platonov, many experiments have been performed on partial reinforcement, the most important of which would appear to be those carried out by Skinner (1933, 1938). It will not be possible in one short chapter to investigate each slight variation in design; Skinner's work, therefore, will be taken to be typical. It is important to notice that Skinner's principal concern is in the operations performed, rather than in theoretical terms, such as "reflex reserve", which are invoked to explain them.

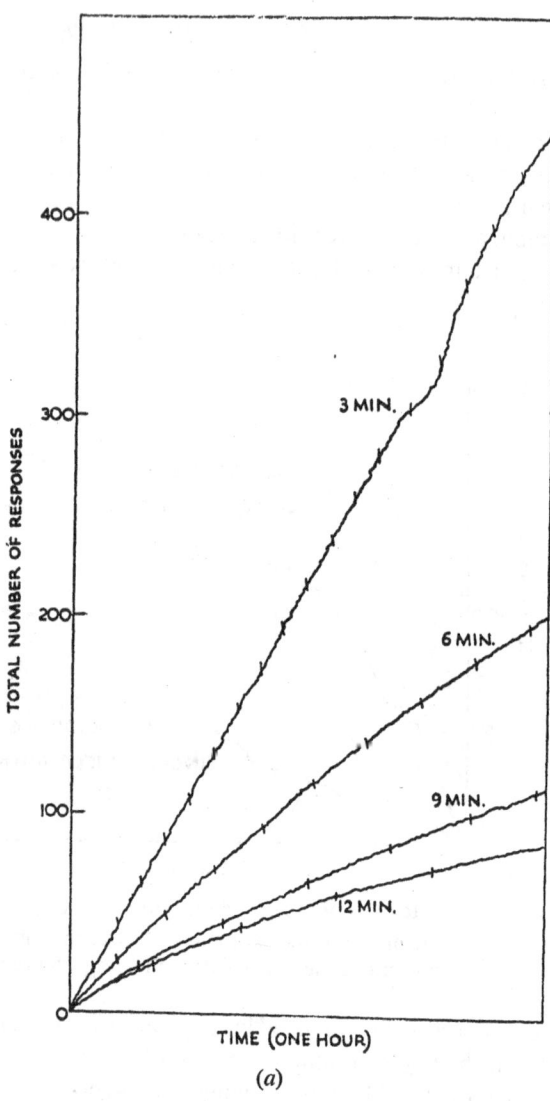

FIG. 4. PARTIAL REINFORCEMENT
Responses within a single session of fixed-interval reinforcements are illustrated by the graph (a). The graph (b) shows the same thing for repeated sessions.

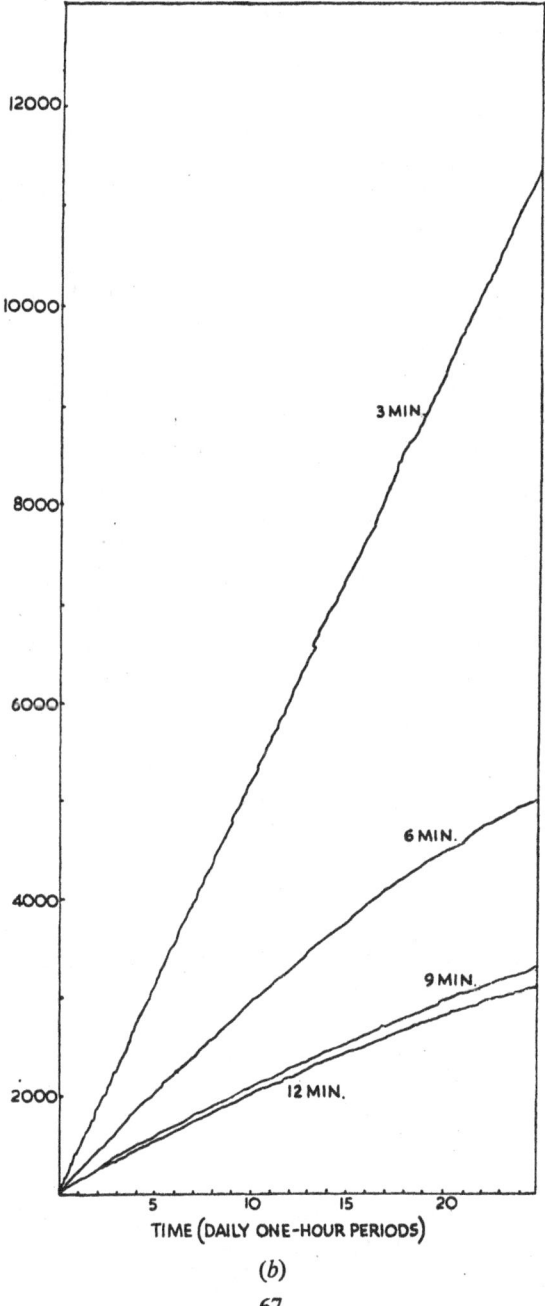

(b)

Skinner's work divides conveniently into sections. His first experiments compared lever-pressing performance in rats following a single reinforcement with performance following 250 reinforcements (Figure 3). He found that the relationship was by no means a linear one. The actual performance demanded of the rats was that of lever-pressing, and the reinforcement was the pellet of food received from the apparatus.

Using the same apparatus, Skinner has shown two different sorts of partial reinforcement. The first he called "periodic reinforcement", and it involved the use of reinforcers at standard intervals of time. This implies a constant amount of reinforcement per unit of time, and leads to a constant reponse performance; in fact over a considerable range Skinner found the roughly constant response rate of 18 to 20 responses (Figure 4). From this is derived the notion of "extinction ratio", which we shall define as the uniform number of responses per reinforcement. This is taken to be a measure of learning under varying conditions of drive. Incidentally, we should note here that the greater maintenance of response-rate which is observed in partial reinforcement is accounted for by Skinner simply by employing the theoretical term "reflex reserve".

Skinner's next type of partial reinforcement is called "reinforcement-at-a-fixed-ratio" (Figure 5); in this the pellet of food is delivered after a standard number of responses, instead of after a standard interval of time. The result is a very high response-ratio, the extinction ratio changing from 20 : 1 (as in Skinner's first situation) to 200 : 1 in this one. Some graphs will illustrate these results.

Some further explanation of work on partial reinforcement will be undertaken in the following chapters; in the meantime it will be convenient to give some general description of the design of partial reinforcement experiments.

In these experiments "frequency" and "pattern" will be seen to be two of the more important variables, i.e. continuity of reward and regularity of reward are variables which require particular attention, and this has been illustrated by Skinner. However, two kinds of experimental situations need to be distinguished: (1) those where the responding is independent of the experimenter and of the environment; this covers both types of Skinner's conditioning, and is sometimes called "free responding", and (2) experiments in which trials are involved and there is control of opportunity to respond, e.g. mazes,

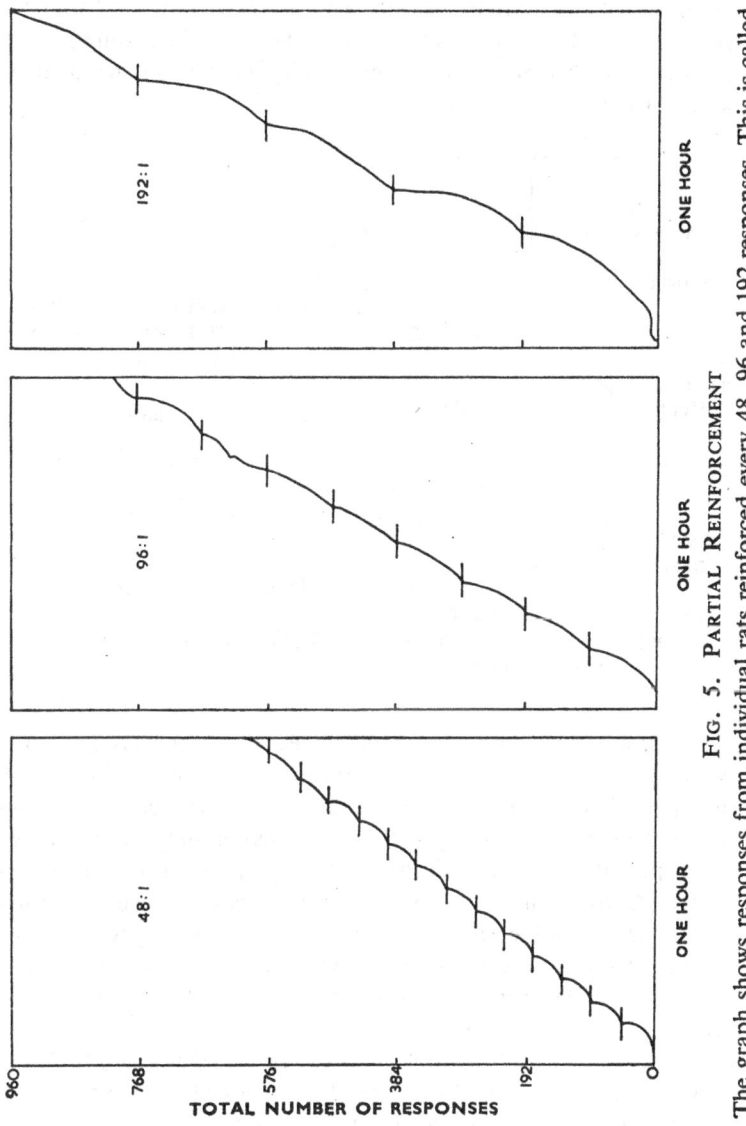

Fig. 5. Partial Reinforcement

The graph shows responses from individual rats reinforced every 48, 96 and 192 responses. This is called 'reinforcement-at-a-fixed-ratio'.

multiple response situations, etc. This is referred to as "trial responding". (1) and (2) differ with respect to their timing. The following table (Jenkins and (Stanley, 1950) summarizes the different kinds of partial reinforcement.

VARIATIONS OF REINFORCEMENT	SITUATION			
	Free-responding	TRIALS		
		Simple response	Alternative response	Multiple responses
TIME				
Regular	Periodic reinforcement	Time variation not ordinarily used		
Irregular	Aperiodic reinforcement			
NUMBER OF RESPONSES				
Regular	Fixed ratio reinforcement	Fixed ratio reinforcement		
Irregular	Random ratio reinforcement	Random ratio reinforcement		

One important point to notice in all these experiments is that initial training has always been on reinforcement, and only subsequently has partial reinforcement been introduced. In another experiment in this field (Keller, 1940), a group of rats was continuously reinforced for a period, and then split into two groups, one group being subjected first to continuous, and then periodic, reinforcement; the other group was given the same reinforcement, but in the opposite order. Using resistance to extinction as a measure, the second group was found to be far superior for the first five minutes of extinction only.

There are many other problems altogether too numerous to detail, but perhaps one or two more should be mentioned, such as inter-trial interval, massed and spaced training, and the complex relationship between number of trials and number of reinforcements. For example, a partially reinforced group of rats can be compared with a continuously reinforced group, with respect either to number of trials or number of reinforcements, but not both. Another problem is the variability of response strength, at the end of learning, in resistance to extinction as between continuously reinforced and partially reinforced groups. We have tried to extract here only the major aspects of the problems.

One point of great importance should be noted. Trotter (1957) has pointed out the arbitrary nature of what is regarded as a response in the Skinner experiments. Many rats touched and fondled the lever without pressing it far enough to allow a pellet to be ejected, and none of these responses was included in the count. This goes some way to vitiate the experimental results; but there is much other evidence which suggests that the results are probably valid.

For a brief explanation of partial reinforcement, it may be said that the problems can be stated under the five headings of (1) acquisition, (2) performance, (3) maintenance, (4) retention, and (5) extinction. As far as acquisition is concerned, the general findings are that there is little apparent difference between the continuous and the partially reinforced groups, although the former appear to have a slight advantage. Much the same state of affairs holds in (2), (3) and (4), and it is only in extinction that a serious reversal is apparent. Here the partially reinforced group was significantly ahead of the continuously reinforced group.

We shall see in due course how these results are explained by molar psychologists, but in the first place there are certain minor difficulties that require comment. Skinner's experiments on reinforcement at a fixed ratio (see Figure 3) shows oddities in its graph that appear to call for explanation on three scores, (1) the very high rate of responding, (2) the delay after reinforcement, and (3) the acceleration between reinforcements. Skinner explains these by saying that each lever-pressing in the early part of a run acts as a secondary reinforcement. (2) is explained by the "negative factor" associated with reinforcements, and the weakening of what Skinner called the *reflex reserve*, and (3) is a function of (1) and (2). This sort of explanation by appeal to theoretical terms, and functional relationships between them, is typical of molar theory, and is often difficult to test. These matters will be considered further in the next two chapters.

The general problem of partial reinforcement will be discussed further in the chapters on Hull and Tolman for, in so far as a problem is involved, it is their rival explanations which are most interesting and important.

Latent Learning

Latent learning is to be considered next, and there is a difficulty here that does not wholly apply to partial reinforcement, in that there is a doubt as to whether latent learning actually takes place or not – at least in terms of the definitions framed by some workers. Many psychologists have been suspicious of the evidence.

Thistlethwaite (1951) has classified latent learning into four groups:

(1) Type 1. The Blodgett (1929) variety in which the rats are given a series of unrewarded or mildly rewarded trials in a maze, and then a relevant goal object is introduced before further trials take place.

(2) Type 11. The organisms are allowed to explore the maze prior to a trial in which a relevant goal object is used (Haney type, 1931).

(3) Type III. Organisms (e.g. rats) which are satiated with food and water are given trials in a maze the pathways of which contain the goal objects with which the animals are satiated (Spence-Lippett type, 1940).

(4) Type IV. Organisms (rats) which are either hungry or thirsty are placed in a maze with relevant and/or irrelevant goal objects. The rats are then satiated for formerly desired goal objects, and deprived of the previously undesired goal object (Kendler type, 1947).

Further, the term "latent learning" has the twofold historical usage:

(1) learning not manifest in performance scores, and
(2) learning that occurs under conditions of irrelevant incentive.

More recently (Hilgard, 1958) we find latent learning experiments classified into five different types. The fifth type added is a variant of type II, above, and a variant on Maier's (1929) reasoning experiment. It is concerned with the exploration of pathways leading to distinctive goal-boxes, when pre-feeding has taken place in one of the goal-boxes.

Now returning to the question of the existence of latent learning, it has been asserted that type 1 and type 11 (Blodgett and Haney types) do not reveal latent learning, and can be explained in terms of the Hullian theory of reinforcement (see next chapter). It will be noticed that there are two quite separate points involved here. One is that, since there is an improvement in performance in the unrewarded period, then any subsequent distinction in performance is invalid, and therefore the statistical significance of the results are in question. However, it appears that there is some confusion over the definition of "latent learning", resulting apparently from the lumping together of the two separate points, one maintaining that latent learning is not revealed, the second point is that the phenomena revealed can be explained in terms of the Hullian theory of reinforcement. Let us be clear that no one is averring that latent learning is not explicable in Hullian terms, though it is claimed by some that it is not shown in particular circumstances.

The Haney design is the one in which a group of hungry rats were permitted to explore a 14-unit T-maze for four days for 18 hours per day, while a comparable control group spent the same periods of time in a rectangular maze. The experimental group, therefore, could acquire knowledge of the T-maze which was denied to the control group. Neither group was rewarded with food in its maze in this initial stage of the experiment. Then both groups were run, while hungry, in the T-maze for 18 days, and rewarded in one trial per day. The result showed no statistical difference in the performances of the two groups, which indicates that learning can take place without reward, or at least without *obvious* reward. The main point to notice here is that *performance* is taken to imply learning, and it is therefore presumed possible to identify them in a negative sense. Many experiments have been carried out which have claimed to include all the stated conditions of latent learning, but they have failed to show that it took place.

Involved in all this is a point of logic which has been mentioned before. It has been said of both the Blodgett and the Tolman-Honzik experiments that they led to the conclusion that maze performance did not necessarily mirror maze learning, and Kendler makes the point already referred to, namely that in comparing the food and no-food groups, performance is taken as a measure of *learning*, whereas the same level of *performance* does not necessarily imply the same level of learning. However, although this is a serious criticism, it is possible that, if the motivation and reward-value of the incentive are equivalent, then (but only then) can *performance* be taken to be the same as learning. This reply is implied in Tolman's theory (see Chapter 6).

The important point here is as to whether or not motivation can be sufficiently controlled, and the burden of proof for this lies with the experimenters. Advocates of latent learning have defended themselves initially by reference to experimental evidence which, they claim, should end controversy; but this is obviously over-optimistic in practice, since the results of experiments are never so precise as to allow of only one interpretation.

The status of motivation and reinforcement is a matter of convention in the problem of latent learning. Reinforcement may be defined in such a way that it is *always* necessary to every performance; or it may be independently defined, and so may or may not be necessary to the performance. The particular *convention* adopted commits us to one of several very different interpretations of reinforcement. Of these the first is typical of Hull's learning theory, while the second is typical of Tolman. The position is that, if the hypothesis that reinforcement is necessary to *all* learning is granted, then it is necessary by definition (and by operational methods if possible) to show that such a definition is logically consistent. This would indeed appear to be an embarrassment to the theory of Hull, but we shall see later how he dealt with it. There always remains, of course, the possibility that suitable sources of reinforcement may be found. Indeed, in the Blodgett type experiment, curiosity and escape are obvious candidates for the job.

Let us see what partial reinforcement and latent learning mean in common-sense terms. Partial reinforcement is exemplified by the success achieved by occasional sporting successes as opposed to regular success. Latent learning is exemplified by the fact that we may be taught how to solve certain problems, or how to deal with certain situations, without immediately demonstrating that learning. Although we usually demonstrate human skill as soon as we have acquired it, by way of practice, we clearly do not always need to do so.

We shall now move away from the established aspects of learning and learning theories, and consider some more isolated problems with which these theories were not primarily concerned.

Transfer of Training

Transfer of training is a way of describing, or a measure of the empirical fact that similar tasks have a degree of "carry over".

It is easy enough to see how transfer could occur. In fact it could be through either of the two well-known principles:

1. By virtue of some large task involving whole sequences of events, where two sequences had many common pairs, and

2. by virtue of stimulus generalization, which means that two sequences of events are treated as the same, or as being two sub-cases of some more general relation.

The first explanation is self-evident, but the second needs some elaboration. We should note, though, that this appears to be a case in which two rival explanations – as they appear to be – could and would both be appropriate to the same theory; furthermore, they smack of the sort of distinction that might be made at the "habit level" in the first case, and the more "cognitive level", or reflective level of activity, in the second.

In everyday life we see transfer of training in many activities. We learn to drive one car and can then easily drive another car, or certainly more easily than if we had not driven any car before.

On the other hand, when two cars are very similar in all but one respect, then this one respect might be the cause of confusion.

Stimulus Generalization

Continuing the discussion of our second explanation of the way transfer of training takes place, we must look further at the concept of stimulus generalization. This must, in fact, be a characteristic of any system which classifies events, for the term implies that sometimes differences may be either overlooked or not observed. The only way in which such generalization could be revealed or discarded is in circumstances where the outcome of the generalization was unexpected or undesirable, and this would be revealed in its effect on the motivation of the organism. Need reduction would then fail to take place, and the necessary condition for registering approval would not occur.

Of course what has been said does not tell us what any particular person will generalize upon at any particular time. This will be partly a matter of individual differences, both hereditary and environmental, and in so far as it is a general matter, it will depend on *set* and *value* for the organism.

Set, here, being merely the fact that the probabilities associated with the perceptions made will interact with knowledge of the context in which the perceptions are made. This is simply saying that the probability with respect to the perceptual process is never independent of its place in the temporal sequence of events. It is the probability over the larger interval that will lead the organism to expect some particular outcome to its response, and this will depend especially on the use of language. Value will arise in so far as different stimulus-response activities will be associated with different degrees of need-reduction. This matter is obviously complicated, and for the moment we shall discuss it no further.

We must also bear in mind that organisms have the capacity to draw logical inferences. To illustrate the principle in the simplest case, we say that sometimes two pairs of events may be seen, or perceived, to be interdependent. Consider the following scheme of events involving A, B, C and D:

$$A \rightarrow B$$

and

$$C \rightarrow D$$

Let us suppose the symbol→means "is followed by". Now suppose that $A \rightarrow B$ is *always* followed by $C \rightarrow D$; this means that the relations $B \rightarrow C$ is a *necessary* relation; it still remains a matter for public verification to say that $A \rightarrow B$ and $C \rightarrow D$ are necessary relations. $A \rightarrow B \rightarrow C \rightarrow D$, as we should now write it, is a slice of behaviour that involves one necessary relation with or without the other two relations being necessary, and this means that the probability for $B \rightarrow C$ must be 1, or certainty. This necessity, and indeed the probability for the other purely contingent relations, may be said to be dependent upon, or independent of, some response on the part of the organism.

The above interpretation is simply that of a typical Markoff process, as statisticians call it (George, 1961). The consequential conditional probabilities are stored with the letters representing the stimuli and the responses. This whole problem will be discussed further in Chapters 13 and 14.

This chapter has made a general survey of learning and learning theories. In the next chapter we shall consider Hull's theory of learning in greater detail.

Chapter 5

HULL'S THEORY OF LEARNING

Hull's theory is primarily a theory of learning; it has something to say about the other cognitive functions, but very little about perception.

Hull has taken the early work on the conditioned reflex seriously and literally, and he has tried to construct from it a systematic theory of learning – this, for him, is the fundamental aspect of behaviour – in the same mould as Newton's theory of the physical world. In this attempt to construct a thoroughgoing scientific theory it is natural that Hull should spend a certain amount of time on methodological matters. There are, however, many people today who feel that the empirical generalizations that Hull builds into his theory are bound to need so much revision as to change the original form almost beyond recognition; and other extensions which may be needed and carried out in a variety of different ways are likely to have a similar effect. Nevertheless, many people believe that his work is the precursor of systematic and scientific psychology; it is certainly, in any case, of great methodological interest.

Since our interest here is primarily in the cognitive content of his theory, we shall spend but a brief moment on his methodological principles.

Hull's method of theory construction is sometimes called "hypothetico-deductive". It assumes the need for the axiomatic or postulational method which has proved so successful both in mathematics and in the physical sciences. His postulates are hypothetical physical generalizations that refer to organismic behaviour, and from these hypotheses he derives, by rules of deductive inference, the theorems that are the description of behaviour – this at any rate is the aim. In fact the greater part of Hull's work was concerned with trying to find a suitable set of postulates on which to construct his theoretical edifice.

His technique was to start from the observables – the stimulus and response in human behaviour – and then make inferences about what occurred in between, in order to connect these observables with his theoretical terms.

Theoretical terms have already been discussed, and we must now deal further with them. Theoretical terms are words that refer to some hypothetical process, and of course they differ from each other in their degree of "concreteness". Whereas Tolman has referred to his theoretical terms as "intervening variables", Hull has called his "logical constructs". Tolman is concerned with descriptive variables that can be manipulated, but do not refer to any definite process of a neurophysiological kind. Hull's terms are to be understood as specifically needing subsequent redefinition in such a neurophysiological manner. They are theoretical terms in a chain which has appropriate logical connections, and they make up the theory of the organism. The theory is to be tested and refined, and gradually brought into line with all the known facts of behaviour.

Motivation is a central feature of Hull's learning theory, but perception, on the other hand, plays a very small part. Indeed, perception is a process separated from learning, and one that Hull takes for granted. He sees the organism as perceiving its world through the stimulation of its neurological structures. In Hull's (1943) own words:

> Sequences in the outer world evoke parallel reaction in sensitive organisms ... The organism has thus acquired an intimate functional copy of the world sequence, which is a kind of knowledge.

This hardly gets to grips with the problems posed by the interpretation of the incoming sensory stimuli, in deciding whether it is stimulus-response, stimulus-stimulus or both types of connection that are utilized in learning. Hull's system was avowedly a miniature system based primarily on rat psychology, and it is this fact that makes it tend to neglect these apparently "higher order" problems.

It must also be said that the problems of thinking and understanding are not really adequately pursued beyond the most general statements at a fairly primitive level of behaviour. He has, however, discussed the possibility that the organism's own responses are the "surrogates of ideas", since they furnish stimuli, particularly anticipatory stimuli, for which Hull uses the name "fractional anticipatory goal responses", by which he appears to mean stimulus-response activities that are not overt, and are run off without necessarily

Hull's Theory of Learning

involving overt change in the organism's state. This is, perhaps, a realistic suggestion, but it certainly needs to be followed up in some detail, and this has not yet been done, even by the Neo-Hullians.

It is not altogether a criticism of Hull to say that he has not covered the full range of significant behaviour activities. There are certainly more important criticisms arising from within the field that he aimed to cover, but before we can illustrate them we must develop to some extent his theory of learning.

The Theory of Learning

Miller and Dollard (1941), who have been interpreters of Hull's theory, have stated that the four principal factors underlying learning are: drive, cue, response and reward. Cue, here, is really a stimulus which elicits responses. It is really a part of a perceptual theory implying that it is an interpreted stimulus, deciding the type and detailed nature of the response elicited.

Drives are strong stimuli that bring about the need for action. Drives may be primary, such as sex, hunger and thirst, all ultimately necessary for survival. They may also be secondary, such as the desire for money, for social approval, etc. This notion of secondary drive, and the accompanying idea of a secondary motivator, are seen to be manifested in symbolic activities; the example of the poker chips (Chapter 3) well illustrate this.

The above statement has reintroduced the word "reward"; what is meant here is the use of the law or principle of effect. Responses are made to cues in the presence of drives and as a result of drives; learning takes place if the responses are rewarded. If unrewarded, the tendency to repeat the response will be seriously weakened.

The picture is a fairly simple one, and has already been discussed in Chapter 3, where the principle of effect was discussed as an explanatory principle. If you are thirsty you drink, and if the drink satisfies your thirst you are, for the time being, no longer in need of a drink. When you are thirsty again you will tend to repeat the same procedure as before. If the drink was not satisfying ("need reducing", as Hull calls it) then you will try something else.

This system has the one possible defect (also alluded to in Chapter 3) that it may not sufficiently account for anticipatory behaviour. This we shall examine later, with other possible defects, but now we must discuss the form in which Hull himself presented his theory. It would be inappropriate to set out a complete list of his various postulate systems, the theorems he derives, and the mathematical rendering of the theory, but we shall give a sample that will help the pertinacious reader to grasp what it is about.

One further difficulty arises in discussing Hull's theory: it is not quite a single theory. He naturally modified it as he went along, and there were ultimately three versions of his postulate system. We shall discuss two of these, and compare them briefly because the modification from one to the other shows an interesting development in Hull's ideas.

In one of his earlier systems Hull's (1943) central postulates were stated in the following form:

POSTULATE 1. *Afferent neural impulses and the perseverative stimulus trace.*
Stimuli impinging upon a receptor give rise to afferent neural impulses which rise quickly to a maximum intensity and then diminish gradually. After the termination of the stimulus, the activity of the afferent nervous impulse continues in the central nervous tissue for some seconds.

POSTULATE 2. *Afferent neural interaction.*
Afferent neural impulses interact with other concurrent afferent neural impulses in a manner to change each into something partially different. The manner of change varies with every impulse or combination of impulses.

POSTULATE 3. *Innate responses to need.*
Organisms at birth possess a hierarchy of need-terminating responses which are aroused under conditions of stimulation and drive. The responses activated by a given need are not a random selection of the organism's responses, but are those more likely to terminate the need.

POSTULATE 4. *Reinforcement and habit strength.*
Habit strength increases when receptor and effector activities occur in close temporal contiguity, provided their approximately contiguous occurrence is associated with primary or secondary reinforcement.

And the final sample:

Hull's Theory of Learning

POSTULATE 5. *Generalization.*
The effective habit strength aroused by a stimulus other than the one originally entering into conditioning depends upon the remoteness of the second stimulus from the first on a continuum in units of discrimination thresholds (i.e. just noticeable differences).

There are some sixteen further postulates, progressively decreasing in importance, and dealing broadly with drive, inhibition, and the conditions for the elicitation of response.

Postulate 1 formally states the need for the process of stimulation to be spread over time, and thus permit the integration and interaction of impulses that Postulate 2 caters for. Postulate 2 is noneffective in its vagueness, and clearly would need to be supplemented by some further statements to have any practical predictive value.

Postulate 3 caters for a built-in set of responses.

Postulate 4 is a restatement of the law of effect.

Postulate 5 is the basis of learning in that it allows for novel situations to occur. Postulates 4 and 5 taken together are fundamental to Hull's, and most other writers', concept of learning. Postulate 5 is the basis of the well-known gradient of generalization.

Hull's system does in fact throw up two very important variables which the postulates are supposed to define sufficiently. They are called "habit strength", written $_sH_r$, and "reaction potential", which is written $_sE_r$. The concept of $_sH_r$ is already embodied in the first five postulates, and especially and explicitly in Postulate 4.

There are various further derived principles, such as that of the *goal gradient principle* and the *habit family hierarchy*, which can be derived from the postulates, and which state further conditions attendant upon learning. The goal gradient principle was applied especially to maze-running, and stated that responses nearer to the goal box were more strongly conditioned than those that occurred further away. The habit family hierarchy is a general principle that is intended to account for variety in behaviour, such as maze-running behaviour. This allows for adaptation and anticipation in the range of the organism's behaviour.

The units of measurement suggested by Hull for use with the system are physical ones, and obtained by the operations of counting, timing, or otherwise measuring the observables of stimulus and response and whatever else is directly observable. From these he makes inferences to find the measurements for the theoretical terms.

Perhaps the most important single principle which is found directly in the primary postulates is that of secondary reinforcement. The idea is that any reinforcer, when operating, will contaminate other stimuli occurring at the same time, so that the stimuli acquire the property of being reinforcers themselves. This is a central concept, and one we shall return to more than once.

Among the many criticisms of Hull's theory, as it stood in the form of which the five postulates quoted are a sample, the experiments on latent learning raised particular difficulties. It will be remembered that latent learning is dependent upon the fact that changes can occur in the organism which need not necessarily be immediately manifested in performance.

Hull's followers sometimes defended his theory by trying to show that latent learning probably did not really occur, or that, even if it did, Hull could easily account for it. Be this as it may, Hull himself changed his theory in some respects, and in such a way as to meet these criticisms. A brief outline of the modifications follows.

The Evolution of the Theory

To compare the old Hull theory with the newer one it is perhaps easier at first to look at his mathematical rendering. Originally, Hull defined $_sE_r$, which we might roughly equate with the performance of the organism, as

$$_sE_r = f_1(_sH_r) \cdot f_3(D) \tag{1}$$

and $_sH_r$ as

$$_sH_r = f_2(V, K, J, N) \tag{2}$$

where N is the number of rewarded responses to some stimulus, V is the intensity of the stimulus, and K and J are motivational variables. K is called incentive motivation; J is the delay in reinforcement. In the first equation D is the drive. By substituting 2. in 1. we get

$$_sE_r = f_1(f_2(V, K, J, N) \cdot f_3(D)) \tag{3}$$

and before we show the new set of equations we will just indicate how one typical variable, say J, is defined.

$$J = e^{-j}t \tag{4}$$

where the implication is that delay of reinforcement is an exponential mathematical function such that its effect dies away with time. Most of the other variables are thought of as such die-away variables.

Hull's Theory of Learning

Now in the new system Hull defines $_sE_r$ in the following terms:
$$_sE_r = f_1(D, V, K, J, {_sH_r}) \tag{5}$$
and $_sH_r$ as
$$_sH_r = f_2(N) \tag{6}$$
then by substituting 6. in 5. we get
$$_sE_r = f_1(D, V, K, J, f_2(N)) \tag{7}$$

The changes are not, of course, restricted to those suggested by the functional rearrangement alone. Indeed we have omitted to discuss the particular functions f_1, f_2 and f_3, which Hull adopts, and these vary a little from the first case to the second.

What Hull in fact achieved by his changes was to make motivation enter directly into performance, rather than indirectly through learning. It could be shown then that, for the functions Hull chose, sudden changes in performance were allowed that were previously not possible. The separation between learning and performance was thus made clearer in a manner that we had primarily associated with Tolman and the expectancy theorists.

That Hull's theory still lacked cogency on other grounds has been pointed out by many people working in the field. Particularly, the idea of learning being a function of the number of rewarded responses alone is unsatisfactory, and there seems to be a need for motivation to be explicitly represented in the equation of learning.

The final form of Hull's theory which differs little from the second version has postulates 1, 3 and 4 taken over much as before, and has postulates concerned with the exact nature of the variables D, V, J and K and reaction potential and inhibition. Finally it has an important pair of postulates 3 and 10 that must be quoted. First though let us quote the new postulates 5, 6, 7 and 8 dealing with D, V, J and K.

POSTULATE 5. *Primary drive (D).*

A. A primary drive (at least that resulting from food deprivation) consists of two components: (1) the drive proper, which increases with the number of hours of food deprivation, and (2) an inanation component which reduces drive as starvation continues.

B. Each drive condition generates a characteristic drive stimulus (S_D) which is an increasing function of the drive condition.

C. Some drive conditions may motivate into action habits set up on the basis of different drive conditions.

POSTULATE 6. *Stimulus-intensity dynamism (V).*
The greater the intensity of the stimulus, the greater the reaction potential for any given level of habit strength. The magnitude of the stimulus-intensity dynamism (V), as a component of reaction potential, is an increasing logarithmic function of the stimulus intensity.

POSTULATE 7. *Incentive motivation (K).*
The greater the magnitude of the incentive used in reinforcement, the greater the reaction potential for any given level of habit strength. The incentive reinforcement (K), as a component of reaction potential, is a negatively accelerated increasing function of the weight of food or quantity of other incentive.

POSTULATE 8 (Corollary 3). *Delay in reinforcement (J).*
A. For a response in a chain, the greater the delay in reinforcement, the weaker the reaction potential leading to that response.
B. For a single response, the greater the delay in reinforcement, the weaker the reaction potential, according to a gradient that falls off rapidly at first and then more slowly, approaching the asymptote at about 5 seconds.

We now quote the two important postulates 3 and 10 of the final Hull system.

POSTULATE 3. *Primary reinforcement.*
When a response (R) is closely associated with a stimulus trace (s) and this stimulus-response conjunction is associated with a rapid decrease in drive-produced stimuli (S_D) there will result an increment in the tendency for that stimulus trace (s) to evoke the response (R).

The rapid decrease in the goal stimulus (S_G) is also reinforcing.
Corollary 1. *Secondary drive.*
When a neutral stimulus trace (s) has been closely associated with the evocation and rapid decrease of drive-produced stimuli (S_D), the hitherto neutral stimulus trace (s) acquires a tendency to bring about these drive stimuli (S_D), so that the previously neutral stimulus trace (s) becomes the occasion for a secondary drive $(s \rightarrow S_D)$.
Corollary 2. *Secondary reinforcement.*
When a neutral stimulus trace (s) has been closely associated

Hull's Theory of Learning

with a rapid diminution in drive produced stimuli (S_D), the hitherto neutral stimulus trace (s) acquires a tendency to bring about the reduction of S_D, so that the previously neutral stimulus trace (s) acquires "the power of acting as a reinforcing agent".

POSTULATE 10. *Stimulus generalization.*
A. Generalized habit strength ($_{s_2}\bar{H}_R$) associated with a stimulus trace (s_2) differing in quality from the stimulus trace (s_1) involved in the habit ($_sH_R$) depends upon the remoteness of s_2 from s_1 on a qualitative continuum in units of discrimination thresholds (j.n.d.'s).

Provided D, K and V remain constant, the generalized reaction potential ($_{s_2}E_R$) will vary directly with $_{s_2}H_R$.

B. The generalized habit strength ($_{s_1}\bar{H}_R$) associated with a stimulus trace (s_2) differing in intensity from the one (s_1) involved in the prior learned habit ($_{s_1}H_R$) likewise depends on the remoteness of s_2 from s_1. Because the difference is one of intensity, log units may be used instead of j.n.d's in determining the stimulus separation. The amount of generalization, furthermore, is a function of V_1, the stimulus-intensity dynamism of s_1 during conditioning.

Provided D and K remain constant, the generalized reaction potential ($s_2 E_R$) will vary directly with $_{s_2}\bar{H}_R$ and V_2, the stimulus-intensity dynamism of s_2 during testing.

C. Generalized conditioned inhibition ($_{s_2}I_R$) follows the same principles of generalization from $_{s_1}I_R$ along qualitative and quantitative stimulus continua as generalized habit strength and generalized reaction potential.

All these changes in Hull's system have undoubtedly improved it in the sense of bringing it increasingly into line with the experimental facts, and also into line with Tolman's theory. There is however much to be dissatisfied with in the fact that the theory in spite of its apparent precision is in fact vague and not effective in the technical sense of an *effective procedure* in logic.

But in any case Hull's work, although precise in many ways, and having great methodological interest, suffers from many other blemishes of inconsistency, not only internal to his various versions but also, sometimes, between the verbal and the mathematical renderings of the postulates. A most detailed analysis of Hull's theory has been undertaken by Sigmund Koch (1954) and published in a book analysing the principal theories of learning. This analysis, while giving credit to Hull's important historical contribution, also points out many of the errors in his system, some of which take the form of a great vagueness, which destroy the predictability of the theory. Unfortunately Koch's analysis is not beyond question, and he has been much criticized for being so literal in his analysis of Hull. Much more unsatisfactory, however, are the underlying assumptions about theory construction in science, of which Koch himself seems quite unsure. He often judges by a yardstick which is itself as much open to question as Hull's own theory.

Hull has naturally leaned strongly towards formalization, by which we mean the construction of precise theories, even to the extent of reducing a mathematical theory to its own logical foundations. Perhaps this requires a little further explanation.

In constructing a theory we are inclined to start from simple beginnings, such as statements from everyday life, e.g. "Charlie seems to see better than Joe", or "Harry thinks quicker than Bill". This leads to the formulation of less informal statements about people and their behaviour, and this in turn to generalizations that are based on different types of people and postulated circumstances. Even now we shall still be relying on ordinary language, although at this stage we shall probably have given special meaning to certain terms which have a broader meaning in ordinary language. We might even be able to use mathematics to describe certain parts of our theories. All this suggests steps towards greater precision, but even when the theory has become mathematical there is still much to be done to show that it is logically consistent and watertight. It is also difficult sometimes to be completely clear about the meanings of theories, and it will be worthwhile restating them in the language of logic. This process is called "formalization", and is a lengthy and difficult one which sometimes reveals flaws in the edifice of the theory itself. To those who feel that this is really going too far, the answer is that a computer, for example, can only handle a system that is in a sense formalized, and there are many reasons for believing that computers will be needed to derive the logical consequences of particular behaviour theories in the future. Whether or not it may be valuable to formalize Hull's theory as yet is a different question but, apart from any other consideration, the knowledge gained for methodological purposes alone seems to justify the step. However this may be, two sorts of formalizations have been carried through for Hull's theory, and we shall look at both of them.

Hull's Theory of Learning

Formalization of Hull's Theory

Fitch and Barry (1950) have formalized Hull's theory, or the central core of it, for the purpose of seeing more clearly what it states. It is interesting to note, in passing, that Koch (1954) in his analysis makes no reference to this particular work. This formalization was undertaken for the earlier version of Hull's theory, and we shall state the formalization in full.

They start their formalization with precise definitions, insofar as that is possible, for thirteen of the crucial terms that occur in the postulates.

D1. Stimulus Event

Each stimulus event is a specific event of very short duration, taking place in the body of the subject, and having a causal effect on the central nervous system of the subject. Events of longer duration can be viewed as sequences of these very short stimulus events.

D2. Response Event

Each response event is a specific event of very short duration, taking place in the body of the subject and resulting from the operation of the central nervous system. Responses of long duration are regarded as sequences of these short response events.

D3. Time of Occurrence

The "time of occurrence" of a stimulus event or a response event is the time at which such an event occurs. Since these events are of very short duration, this time of occurrence could be taken as the time at which the event begins, or equally as the time at which it ends, or some intermediate time, because these times would all differ by very little. The time of occurrence of a stimulus event is expressed as $T(s)$. Similarly the time of occurrence of a response event r is expressed as $T(r)$.

D4. Initial Time

The "initial time" is a hypothetical time at which the nervous system of the subject can be supposed to have started functioning. We will let T_0 designate the initial time.

D5. Tendency

By "tendency" is here meant a quantity corresponding to each stimulus-response pair (s, r), and measuring the likelihood of the occurrence of a response of the same kind as r, given the occurrence of a stimulus of the same kind as s. Tendency is a function of time. We write $_sH_r(t)$ to stand for the tendency corresponding to the stimulus-response (s, r) at time t.

D6. Increment of Tendency

By "increment of tendency" is here meant the part of the total tendency $_sH_r(t)$ due to the occurrence of a stimulus event s' and a response event r'. Increment of tendency is a function of time, because it depends on the "effective drive reduction" $J(t_1, t_2)$, which is itself a function of time. (See all below and axiom $A2$.) Negative increments of tendency may perhaps be regarded as positive increments of inhibition. We write $\delta_s H_r(t, s', r')$ to stand for the increment of $_sH_r(t)$ due to the occurrence of stimulus event s' and response event r'.

D7. Stimulus Similarity

This is a quantity corresponding to each pair of stimulus events and measuring the similarity between them as they affect the subject. We write $S(s, s')$ to stand for the amount of similarity between stimulus events s and s'. Stimulus similarity is important in connection with stimulus generalization. In computing the increment $\delta_s H_r(t, s', r')$ it is necessary to take account of $S(s, s')$.

D8. Response Similarity

This is a quantity corresponding to each pair of response events and measuring the similarity between them as actions of the subject. We write $S(r, r')$ to stand for the amount of similarity between response events r and r'. Response similarity is important in connection with response generalization. The increment $\delta_s H_r(t, s', r')$ depends on $S(r, r')$ as well as on $S(s, s')$.

D9. Function for Amount of Drive

This is a mathematical function of a time variable t and serves to express the amount of drive at any given time t. It is written as $D(t)$. The axioms will not assume that there is a special drive stimulus, but such an assumption would be consistent with the axioms.

D10. Goal-gradient Function

This is a mathematical function of time, taking values between 0 and 1 and expressing the decrease in effectiveness of drive reduction relatively to the increase in the time interval between the conditioning response r' and the occurrence of the reduction in drive. This function

Hull's Theory of Learning

therefore embodies the notion of "goal gradient". It is written as $G(t)$, where t is the time interval referred to above. As t increases, $G(t)$ decreases.

D11. Function for Effective Drive Reduction

This is a mathematical function of two time variables t_1 and t_2. It represents the total decrease in drive taking place during the time interval from t_1 to t_2, but as corrected in accordance with the goal-gradient hypothesis, so that those decreases or increases in drive which take place near the later time t_2 are less heavily weighted than those near the earlier time t_1. The weighting is brought about by an appropriate use of the goal-gradient function $G(t)$. This is done in axiom $A3$. The function for effective drive reduction is written as $J(t_1, t_2)$. If the conditioning response r' occurs at time t_1, then the increment $\delta_s H_r(t_2, s', r')$ at time t_2 depends on $J(t_1, t_2)$, as well as on $S(s, s')$, on $S(r, r')$ and on the time interval between the occurrences of s' and r'.

D12. Function for Dependence of Increment of Tendency

This is a mathematical function denoted by the letter F and expressing the dependence of the increment $\delta_s H_r(t_2, s', r')$ on effective drive reduction $J(t_1, t_2)$, on stimulus similarity $S(s, s')$, on response similarity $S(r, r')$, and on the time interval from s' to r', namely on $T(r') - T(s')$, where $t_1 = T(r')$.

D13. The Constant of Proportionality between increment of Tendency and effective drop in Drive

This constant will be called K. It is used in axiom $A4.2$.

With these definitions we have gained a measure of precision which to a large extent counteracts objections frequently raised that words like "stimulus" and "response" are hopelessly vague, and used for both gross and minute occurrences. We should perhaps use the phrase "stimulus pattern", or "event", for a complex of such simple stimuli, though this may still leave a doubt as to the identification of what is actually stimulating the organism.

Now to the postulates; it should be noticed that greater precision is achieved as compared with the more informal postulates stated by Hull himself.

Axiom A1

If s is a stimulus event and r is a response event, then

$$_sH_r(t_2) = {_sH_r}(T_0) + \Sigma \delta_s H_r(t_2, s', r'),$$

where the summation is over all stimulus events s' and all response events r' such that T_0 $(T(s'))$ T_2, and T_0 $T(r')$ t_2.

This axiom asserts that at any time t_2 the tendency $_sH_r$ (t_2) of a stimulus event s to evoke a response event r is equal to the initial tendency $_sH_r$ (T_0) plus the sum of all increments of tendency δ_sH_r (t_2, s', r') at time t_2 due to the occurrence of stimulus events s' and response events r' in the interval of time between T_0 and t_2.

Axiom A2

δ_sH_r $(t_2, s', r') = F(x, y, z, w)$, where $x = J(t_1, t_2)$, $t_1 = T(r')$, $y = S(s, s')$, $z = S(r, r')$ and $w = T(r') - T(s')$.

(For explanation, see D6 and D12)

Axiom A3

$$J(t_1, t_2) = \int_{t_1}^{t_2} G(t - t_1).(- D'(t)).dt.$$

The essential meaning of the above axiom will first be presented without use of calculus. We start by considering a special case in which the drive is assumed to be constant at all times except in a very small interval (t_3, t_4), where it drops from amount p to amount q. In other words we will assume that $D(t) = p$ for $t \leqslant t_3$, and that $D(t) = q$ for $t_4 \leqslant t$, where $t_1 < t_3 < t_4 < t_2$ and where (t_3, t_4) is a very small time interval during which the drive drops by an amount $p - q$. In computing an increment of tendency $\delta_sH_r(t_2, s', r')$ at time t_2 due to a conditioning stimulus s' and a conditioning response r', the effective drop-in-the-drive $J(t_1, t_2)$ will be assumed to be equal to $G(t_3 - t_1).(p - q)$, where t_1 is the time of occurrence of r'. (See axioms A5.1–A5.6 for the properties of G.) If we let R be the average rate of drive reduction during the small interval of time from t_3 to t_4, then $p - q = R.(t_4 - t_3)$ and we obtain,

(1) $\qquad J(t_1, t_2) = G(t_3 - t_1).R.(t_4 - t_3)$.

Instead of the special case where the drive is constant everywhere except over one very small interval, we next consider the more general case where the drive varies (or remains constant) over each of a series of very small intervals a_1 to a_2, a_2 to a_3, a_3 to a_4, and so on, ending with a_n, and covering the whole interval from t_1 to t_2. Thus a_1 is the same as t_1, and a_n is the same as t_2. As before, we assume that t_1 is the time of the conditioning response r'. Let each of the very small intervals be equal in magnitude to a fixed time interval δt. Let the average rate of drive reduction from time a_1 to

Hull's Theory of Learning

time a_2 be R_1, and from time a_2 to time a_3 let it be R_2, and from time a_3 to time a_4 let it be R_3, and so on. If the drive increases in one of the intervals instead of decreasing, then of course the average rate of drive reduction for that interval would be negative instead of positive. If no change occurs, the average rate of drive reduction is zero. The total effective drive reduction $J(t_1, t_2)$ is assumed to be given approximately by the following equation, and this equation is assumed to be more and more exact as δt is chosen smaller and smaller. Notice that the equation is simply a generalization of (1) above.

(2) $$J(t_1, t_2) = \Sigma(G(a_1 - t_1) \cdot R_i \cdot \delta t),$$

where the summation is from $i = 1$ to $i = n - 1$. If the drive varies continuously and if we consider the limit approached by the right side of (2) as δt approaches zero and as n approaches infinity, the limit is seen to be the integral constituting the right side of axiom $A3$. Observe that R_i of (2) corresponds to $(-D'(t))$ of $A3$. This is because $D'(t)$ is the time derivative (time rate of increase) of the drive at time t, so that $(-D'(t))$ is the rate of drive reduction at time t. It is clear that (2) can be regarded as a rough approximation to the principle embodied in more precise form in the equation of axiom $A3$.

Axiom A4.1
$$F(0, y, z, w) = 0$$

This axiom may be regarded as asserting that if there is no effective drop in the drive there is no corresponding increment of tendency. (See $D6$, $D12$, $A2$).

Axiom A4.2
$$\frac{\partial F}{\partial x}(x, y, z, w) = K > 0$$

The increment of tendency is proportional to the effective drop in the drive (other things equal), where K is the positive constant of proportionality.

Axiom A4.3
$$\frac{\partial F}{\partial y}(x, y, z, w) > 0$$

The greater the similarity of the conditioned stimulus to the conditioning stimulus, the greater the absolute value of the increment of tendency (other things equal). The symbol $\delta/\delta y$ indicates the mathematical operation of forming the partial derivative with respect to y.

Axiom A4.4

$$\frac{\partial F}{\partial z}(x, y, z, w) > 0$$

The greater the similarity of the conditioned response to the conditioning response, the greater the absolute value of the increment of tendency (other things equal).

Axiom A4.5

$$\text{If } w \geqslant 0, \text{ then } \frac{\partial}{\partial w} F(x, y, z, w) < 0$$

If the conditioning response does not precede the conditioning stimulus, then the greater the time interval between them the less the absolute value of the increment of tendency. Perhaps some analogous assumption could be made for the case where the conditioning response precedes the conditioning stimulus, but the axioms are non-commital on this point.

Axiom A5.1

$$0 \leqslant G(t) \leqslant 1$$

The goal-gradient function takes values between 0 and 1 inclusive.

Axiom A5.2

$$G(0) = 1$$

The goal-gradient function G is equal to unity when its argument t is equal to zero, so that for a drive reduction simultaneous with the conditioning response r', the corresponding effective drive reduction is equal to the actual drive reduction. Briefly, G equals unity at the conditioning response.

Axiom A5.3

$$\text{If} \quad t < 0, \quad \text{then} \quad G'(t) > 0$$

The function G is increasing previous to the conditioning response. $G'(t)$ is the derivative of $G(t)$ with respect to t.

Axiom A5.4

$$\text{If} \quad t > 0, \quad \text{then} \quad G'(t) < 0$$

The function G is decreasing after the conditioning response.

Axiom A5.5

There is some time u_1 and some time u_2 such that if $t_1 < u$ or $u_2 < t$, then $G''(t) > 0$, while if $u < t_1 < u_2$, then $G''(t) < 0$.

There are times u_1 and u_2 such that G is positively accelerated outside the interval (u_1, u_2), and negatively accelerated within that interval.

Axiom A5.6

If $\quad t > 0, \quad$ then $\quad -G'(t) > 2G'(-t)$.

The function G rises to its maximum more than twice as fast as it declines from its maximum.

This last axiom $A5.6$ Fitch (1954) later suggested should be revised or omitted.

It will be realized that the value of formalization is that it removes vagueness from a theory, and makes the underlying ideas explicit, although it does not necessarily provide a metric by which measurement may be carried out. Furthermore, the process of formalization is one of degree, and the present definitions and axioms could be further refined and put into the symbolism of mathematical logic. Of course the precision does not add to the psychological content of the statements; it merely makes them explicit, easier to test, and therefore easier to confirm or deny. As we have already mentioned, their value may turn out to be very great indeed when, and if, we choose to programme a computer with the details of a theory to test its predictive content. In all these respects Hull's theory is admirably placed, and is far ahead of all rival theories of learning.

Criticisms of Hull are much more in terms of the psychological content, and perhaps also of the premature nature of the attempts to introduce precision as far as actual measurement is concerned. A more basic criticism will be deferred to the end of the next chapter, where a comparison is made between the respective theories of Hull and Tolman.

Many people working together produced a second, and better known, formalization in a book called *The Mathematico-Deductive Theory of Rote Learning* (1940). This book has caused some amusement as well as criticism in psychological circles, for it concentrates the enormous powers of mathematics and logic on experimental evidence that is derived from simple learning experiments. The result is certainly rather striking, and a little frightening, and should serve as a warning that if we have to formalize any behaviour system to this extent in practice, it will keep a large number of people very busy for most of a lifetime; yet this may well be necessary before we achieve a predictive theory of behaviour at the level of precision we seem to need. However, it is not our concern here to worry over whether this is a serious example; all that is important for us is its methodological interest. We might though mention again that the greatest advantage of this sort of system is that it can easily be put on to a computer, and this may be an important criterion for future cognitive theories.

Hull's Theory and Experimental Data

Our next step is to relate Hull's theory more closely to the experimental evidence from which it is derived. Ideally, a theory is derived from experimental evidence by appropriate inductive generalizations which are subsequently tested, and the theory modified accordingly. In psychology, the great complexity of the necessary theory has made it difficult to construct a sufficiently cogent set of generalizations; many feel that the search is still for generalizations, and therefore that concentrated effort should be given to exploratory experiments. This may be partly true, but the time is rapidly coming nearer – if indeed it is not already here – when we shall look to experiment primarily as a tool for testing the hypotheses that seem plausible.

Hull's theory starts by assuming the truth of Pavlov's earlier generalizations and of his general experimental findings. The various examples of instrumental conditioning we have considered may be regarded as fuel for the Hull system, with the possible exception of latent learning experiments at a later phase, although these, too, might now be regarded as being eligible, at any rate in the last version of Hull's theory.

A number of Hull's experiments were concerned with rote learning, not only because of his interest in the subject itself, but also because it seemed to suggest a set of experiments which could be used for confirming his theory. In particular, he investigated three phases of rote learning: (1) Serial learning, especially of nonsense syllables; (2) Forgetting and the act of reminiscence and (3) The response thresholds and the general pattern of memory in these experiments.

In one experiment by Hovland (1939), 32 subjects were tested with the object of discovering whether reminiscences varied according to whether the material was originally learned all at once, in what is called a "massed" manner, or whether, for the same amount of learning time, the learning was distributed over varying periods of time.

The materials used were nonsense syllables such as *HAJ, ZOX*, etc. These were presented both singly and in pairs. It was presumed that the pairs would be easier to recall because of a definite association set up between them. The timing used was: for massed practice, six seconds between trials; for spaced practice, two minutes between trials. The words were first presented on a revolving drum such that only one word could be seen at a time, the drum revolving at a uniform speed. At the second trial, as each word was presented the subjects were asked what the next word would be. Gaps between trials were filled with the presentation of colours which the subjects were asked to name. Hovland found that distributed practice resulted in a significant reduction of the trials required to learn serial material as compared with the number required to learn the paired associates.

The explanation given is in terms of the interference between the words, with the maximum interval delays and the minimum interference results. Other such experiments have confirmed the notion that distributed learning facilitates reminiscence in the same way as in Hovland's experiment. These results are claimed to confirm Hull's theory, and they led to a consideration of memory in the rote learning theory.

Hull (1934) himself was able also to confirm to some extent his goal-gradient theory. Rats kept hungry were made to run a straight maze for a food reward, and it was found that their speed increased in successive sections of the maze.

Many other experiments have been carried out, but whether or not they may be interpreted as confirming Hull's theory is a matter on which opinions differ. Some of these equivocal experiments will be discussed in the next chapter, but in the meantime we must ask some more fundamental questions about Hull's theory of learning.

In the first place, are individual differences really accounted for? This question should not be taken to imply serious criticism, for it is difficult to see how they could have been introduced. Some later attempts were in fact made to show how individual differences occurred, but in any case it is an explicit assumption of the behaviouristic approach to learning theory that it aims to deal first with general principles before attempting to apply them to particular cases, and that behaviour shall be approached in the manner that physicists adopt in their own subject.

In considering practice, we want to know what is the effect of repetition of a task. On the face of it, it would seem that practice should improve performance, and we should enquire as to whether Hull's theory confirms this. The answer is that repetition alone does not do so; on the contrary it produces an inhibition to that performance, for practice is only effective in that it goes with reinforcement. In other words, reinforcement of tendencies is what improves performance, and not mere repetition. Of course motivation through drives and need-reduction is the core of Hull's whole theory.

Transfer of training, which is systematically observed in learning, is accounted for by Hull by stimulus equivalence or response equivalence. By stimulus equivalence Hull means, by generalization; and by response equivalence he means to imply that there is an ordered set of possible responses – which he calls the "habit family hierarchy" – all of which have led to the goal before, and will be utilized in the order they occur in the hierarchy, one being discarded and the next used in the event of failure.

Next we should consider partial reinforcement experiments. Why is it, as Skinner found, that, at least within certain limits, reinforcement at a low frequency elicited more responses than reinforcement at a high frequency? Hull's theory seems to suggest that the higher the rate of reinforcement the higher the tendency to respond. To deal with this situation Hull has suggested that it is the secondary reward, becoming associated with the trials in between reinforcement, that keeps the rate of responding high. Miller and Dollard have argued for Hull's theory on much the same basis, claiming that unrewarded behaviour followed by reward would certainly lead to greater resistance to extinction; their argument is fundamentally the same as Hull's, although couched in terms of the gradient of generalization.

The fact is that while Hull's theory could account for partial reinforcement, it does not seem wholly convincing in its dependence on secondary reinforcement. The concept of expectancy looks much more likely material as an explanation here, and it is not easy to see why it should not be invoked, since organisms are clearly able to store and utilize information. At the same time, if we think of secondary reinforcement as being stored responses to cues connected with the goal, then their role is almost exactly similar to that which is embodied in the concept of an expectancy. We shall look carefully to see how Tolman regards an expectancy as being brought about.

Partial Reinforcement

It is clear that a direct application of Hull's theory could not readily account for partial reinforcement. The fact that a *reward* strengthens a response, and the omission of a *reward* weakens it, would be insufficient to account for partial reinforcement, since it would fail to account for the greater resistance to extinction following partial training. Hull and his followers have formulated an explanation in terms of secondary reinforcement, although it has been pointed out that an alternative definition of response would suffice, and the meaning of the term could be widened to meet the difficulty, and further, that our treatment of the basic units of molar behaviour is at fault. All this may be true, but it does not lead to an adequate explanation. Miller and Dollard have suggested that greater resistance to extinction may be expected to occur when unrewarded behaviour is ultimately followed by a reward, and their argument is essentially based on a gradient of generalization.

Mowrer and Jones (1943) have accepted the fact that a response more than 30 seconds in time removed from a reward is not reinforced, and yet they accepted an explanation in terms of a "temporal gradient of reward", even though intervals of far greater duration than 30 seconds have been found to result in adequate responses.

The following comment has been made by Jenkins and Stanley (1950) on the above view:

> It would seem that some mechanism of the response-unit variety is operating. Otherwise, behaviour could not be maintained when reinforcements occur only once in nine minutes, or every 192 responses. A temporal gradient, restricted solely to strengthening behaviour occurring not more than 30 seconds before the reward is, at best, an incomplete account. A temporal gradient may well be one of the factors interacting with several others, but clearly it cannot explain many of the findings that Mowrer and Jones fail to mention.

Another view compares the acquisition and extinction of a running response under the escape and avoidance procedures, and points out that extinction practically always involves a change in the cue patterns present in training, while escape training does not permit the conditioning of the consequences of failure to respond. This alternative theory correctly predicts greater response strength for escape procedure in training, but greater resistance to extinction following avoidance conditioning. This would seem to mirror accurately the sort of unavoidable circularity that is so often criticized in behaviour theory; it is apparently not always realized that our theory job is to mirror the events of behaviour, i.e. it *must* restate the actual events in verbal terms. Generally, of course, it will do more than this. Here we are reminded again of the fact that description and explanation are not essentially different.

The modern Hullian interpretation of partial reinforcement would appear to depend wholly upon secondary reinforcement. Spence has made the assumption that the gradient of reinforcement is a special case of the stimulus generalization gradient. He goes on to place emphasis on the vital nature of secondary reinforcement. Now secondary motivation in Hull's postulate system is said to arise when neutral stimuli are repeatedly and consistently associated with the evocation of a drive which undergoes an abrupt diminution. Secondary reinforcement occurs when a neutral receptor impulse occurs repeatedly and consistently, in close conjunction with a reinforcing state. The *secondary reinforcing* is the fractional antedating goal response (r_{SG}), and this is apparently conditioned, in the Hull view, to the after effects of non-reinforcement in the stimulus-compound during training.

It has been argued that in extinction following partial reinforcement, the stimulus situation, by virtue of generalization, is more like conditioning than after 100 per cent. reinforcement. In extinction as opposed to conditioning, the cue pattern is changed greatly for the 100 per cent. group, but is reinstated for the partial reinforcement group.

Concept Formation

It should be recorded also that Hull (1920) carried out some experiments upon concept formation. He assumed that concept formation was the process of abstracting common features from any set of events, and that a particular word might be chosen to depict these events. This, of course, is how words are learned, and this is assumed by Hull to be the basis of concept formation.

The experiments themselves were carried out with sets of cards such that common features in each subset were associated with a particular name. There may be some differences of opinion as to whether this constitutes an analysis of concepts or of word learning, or whether both processes are more or less the same. What, however, is interesting from our point of view is that Hull, who is so much the molar learning theorist, should have thought it worthwhile to devote some time to human behaviour in the field of concept formation. Secondly, it is of interest that what he showed adds evidence – which we shall be gradually accumulating – that the input system and its associated processes are mainly processes of sorting or categorizing.

Neo-Hullianism

It is clear that Hull has had a great influence on other learning theorists, even to the extent that he has made a major and lasting contribution to learning theory. We shall now add some notes about some of the neo-Hullian theorists who have departed to some extent from the original Hullian ideas.

Sheffield and Roby (1950) tested the reinforcement theory by devising an experiment in which the reinforcement given was inappropriate to satisfying the equivalent need. For example, a sweet taste was rewarding in a situation even though the sweet taste had no effect whatever on the need for sugar which was set up in the rats used. Along the same lines, Sheffield, Wulff and Backer (1951) showed that male rats could be made to perform certain physical acts, such as leaping barriers, in order to copulate with female rats, even though no ejaculation occurred.

Results of this sort are reminiscent of Guthrie's results, and suggested to Sheffield a somewhat similar theory which he called a theory of prepotent responses, and which were used to support a contiguity theory of learning.

In fact, we should notice in passing that exactly the same objection could be made to these experiments, or rather their interpretation, as has been made to Guthrie's. In other words, they only demonstrate that what is an incentive to a rat in a particular situation may not be the incentive the experimenter has in mind; but this in no way demonstrates that incentive is irrelevant or even unnecessary. At the same time, it seems likely that if we say motivation is essential to effective learning, then we shall almost certainly mean this to be understood in a purely formal way, and therefore to include all sorts of circumstances where the motivation is only trivially relevant to the immediate learning.

The main work done on Hull's theory in recent years is that by K. W. Spence (1950, 1951, 1954). Although Spence's views are essentially in the same mould as Hull's, there are certain differences.

(1) Spence does not regard reduction in drive strength as necessary to reinforcement. Hull seems always to have assumed it was necessary, and that it was therefore a point of difference over the relevance of motivational considerations at *every* point of learning.

(2) Spence also follows the typically experimental tradition in keeping his theorizing more piecemeal, and closer to the empirical data, than Hull. He has criticized mathematical theorizing in psychology (1952), pointing out that mathematics offers nothing new in and of itself. This is indeed a point over which we might ultimately disagree, since one of the views put forward in this book is that the form of presentation of a theory, which involves the language chosen, is independent of the facts described. In practice we would argue that this is never wholly true.

It is for this reason that it seems likely that while Spence has done something to strengthen Hull's position by his work, his opposition, or relative opposition, to axiomatic methods and physiology, are not in themselves appropriate criticisms of Hull.

The fact remains that Spence has done a great deal of interesting writing on learning theory in a manner that is reminiscent of Hull, and some familiarity with his later writing will be found to be worthwhile (1955).

Spence himself may conveniently be quoted on his own reinforcement theory:

> The theory is, then, a reinforcement theory so far as excitatory potential is concerned, that is, the presence or absence of a reinforcer, and differences in its properties when present, do make a difference in the strength of the instrumental response. It is not, however, a reinforcement theory in the traditional sense of the term, for the habit or associative factor is not assumed to vary with variations in reinforcement.

This certainly distinguishes Spence's theory in some measure from Hull's, and it calls for a brief comment. Both parties agree that the strength of response is affected, but Spence is arguing that the associative strength is unaffected. Much the same sort of thing was in Hull's mind, apparently, when he modified his own theory in the way we have described in the present chapter. In Hull's newer theory he allowed motivation to enter into performance directly, and not indirectly through learning. The fact is that Hull also said that learning is a function of the number of reinforced trials, and we must agree with him that motivation must surely affect the strength of association in the organism, and not merely the strength of response.

Seward (1950, 1951, 1952, 1953) has also contributed significantly to the learning controversy, both as a critic of other theorists, and in his own right. We shall in fact be using a part of Seward's analysis at the end of the next chapter in comparing the theories of Hull with those of Tolman.

Other work has been done which shows influence by Hull, and undoubtedly more will follow. As far as this book is concerned, some more comments will be made on contemporary theorizing in learning, in the last chapter.

Basic Conception

The great value of Hull's theory is now largely historical. He has emphasized the importance of methodology, and his work will undoubtedly promote many more models and theories of learning in the future.

Perhaps the most important single basic concept of Hull's is that learning is made up of stimulus-response connections. Much learning is certainly of this form, and very much is like the response substitution learning envisaged by Thorndike. Now we should argue – and Hull seems to have been clear about this in his later theory – that learning can *also* be a matter of stimulus substitution, as envisaged by Pavlov. Indeed, we should now regard learning as occurring by means of both of these means; something similar was suggested by Mowrer (1950), although here the emphasis is no longer on two factors.

Learning is an associative process which may either involve the stimulus and the response, or stimuli with stimuli, and for that matter, responses may be associated with each other. More generally, we should perhaps talk about the association of organic states, but this would take us beyond the theory originally suggested by Hull.

The next chapter in effect carries on the same discussion, but primarily from Tolman's point of view.

Summary

Hull's theory has great historical importance for cognition. It was the first serious attempt to place learning theory on a rigorous and formal footing, and to that extent it must be regarded as a very successful theory. That it was less successful in terms of the more obvious criterion of predictability is a matter that should be regarded more as a measure of the complexity of learning theories than of inadequacy in this particular theory.

This chapter has dealt with Hull's work in a general way, and the summary cannot be regarded as complete without the many references in the next chapter.

Chapter 6

TOLMAN'S THEORY OF LEARNING

The principal contemporary opponent of Hull's stimulus-response theory of learning has been Tolman. This is not to say that there are only two contemporary interpretations of learning, but the various contributors to learning theory have tended to align themselves around either Hull or Tolman. There is some evidence, as we have previously observed, that this opposition has now become more imaginary than real, and there is in sight the possibility of an integration between the two views; but this was a possibility that always existed.

Historically, Tolman started from a broader base than Hull and, far from directly applying the findings of the conditioned response, his roots are imbedded in McDougall's hormic psychology, which emphasized the purposive nature of behaviour; Gestalt theory, which we shall be discussing in a later chapter; and in Brunswik's act-psychology.

Although the background is broader based, the theory has always had many features in common with that of Hull. They are both behaviouristic in so far as they are constructing a stimulus-response theory in theoretical terms that represent the unobservable aspects of behaviour, these theoretical terms being logically connected to the observable stimulus and response. Furthermore, like Hull's, Tolman's theory is "molar"; it deals with the observed behaviour of the organism-as-a-whole. This is not to say that neurological facts are irrelevant, but rather that they are not necessary to the development of the theory; in fact, as with Hull, the theoretical terms can be given a neurological interpretation. Perhaps the principal difference between Tolman and Hull lies in the fact that, whereas Hull thought of explaining the whole of learning in terms of a stimulus-response unit derived from the concept of a simple reflex, Tolman used a stimulus-response-stimulus unit, laying emphasis on the state that followed a response to the environment. It is in this way he hoped to deal with purposiveness and expectancies. It is, as some people have put it, an *S-S* rather than an *S-R* theory, in that learning is conceived of as sign learning process. This is the process of associating stimuli with each other rather than stimuli with responses.

Tolman's theory lays emphasis on certain principal features of human and animal behaviour that must be explicitly mentioned.

In the first place, behaviour is goal-directed; all behaviour involves doing, acting, going, and generally showing the characteristic of *purpose*. Animals are never purely passive victims of their environment, but effectually modify that environment and interact with it more completely than Hull seems to suggest in his theory.

In the second place, Tolman makes use of a concept that is rather similar to that of Guthrie; he thinks of maintaining stimuli, or environmental supports, that contribute as means-objects towards the specified goals of the organism. It is in this sense that Tolman's theory has sometimes been thought of, and described, as a "cognitive" theory, as opposed to the more primitive or simpler "telephone switchboard" theory of Hull.

Tolman makes use of a concept of least effort that helps the organism to use the shortest path to its goal – a matter that is clearly connected with the role of motivation in his theory. But above all he emphasizes the docility, or plasticity, of organisms, and by this he means their ability to learn and adapt actively to their changing environment; and that whereas the mechanical stimulus-response form, with its stereotyped reflex concept, is applicable at the level of the nervous system, it is docility and purposiveness that are most obvious at the molar levels of behaviour.

While Tolman's theory is concerned with "what leads to what" in the sense of what is a sign of what, there is the question of the acquisition of expectancies.

The acquisition is without doubt an explicit function of weighted experience and the details of how the acquisition takes place will be made clear by the MacCorquodale-Meehl formalization of Tolman's theory (see p. 111).

Motivation, in the form of drives, produces performance and learning occurs when drives produce a state of "tension" which precipitate a search for goal-objects.

Methodological Considerations

Methodologically, as we have already mentioned, Tolman's approach is similar to that of Hull. He calls his theoretical terms "intervening variables", but although this takes the emphasis off any premature interpretation in terms of physiological structure, it differs from Hull's logical constructs in degree only.

Some of the intervening variables that Tolman (1938) regards as central to his system are:

1. *Environmental Variables*
    M–Maintenance Schedule.
    G–Appropriateness of goal-object.
    S–Types and modes of stimuli provided.
    R–Types of motor response required.
    P–Patterns of preceding and succeeding maze units.
    $E(OBO)$–cumulative nature and number of trials.

$E(OBO)$ is a symbol that is meant to draw attention to the summation of previous experience.

2. *Individual Difference Variables*
    H–Heredity.
    A–Age.
    T–Previous training.
    E–Special endocrine, drug or vitamin conditions.

Now to each environmental variable a theoretical term is connected by a correlation: M is associated with *Demand*; with G is associated *Appetite*; with S, *Differentiation*; with R, *Motor Skill*; with P, *Biases*; and finally with $E(OBO)$ is associated the very central notion of *Hypotheses*, later called *expectancies*.

These intervening variables are to be given an interpretation entirely in terms of their definition, and are to be regarded as wholly behaviouristic terms.

We have seen in the development of Hull's theory the process of writing axioms and generating levels of formalization. This Tolman has never done. He has been influenced in his presentation by the topological work of Lewin and, as a result, has restricted his theory statements to informal ones coupled with quasi-topological models. This, of course, increases the difficulty of comparing the two theories, but some light has been thrown on this matter by MacCorquodale and Meehl, who undertook to formalize Tolman's theory for him, and although there is some doubt as to what extent they have modified Tolman's ideas in the process, it will be convenient for us to use their formalization for comparison purpose.

But before we consider the formalization it would be expedient for us to develop Tolman's own informal theory. For this purpose we must use some of his diagrams to illustrate his own way of thinking.

Typical of Tolman's own approach is the Cognition motivational model (1952) in which he put his concepts into diagrammatic form. For this model he postulated the need system, the belief-value matrix and a behaviour space in which the behaviour occurs.

The following three figures illustrate the development of beliefs about restaurants and foods to be eaten. Figure 6 shows the belief-value matrix for this situation.

Figure 7 shows the larger situation including the momentary stimulus state and drive conditions.

Figure 8 shows the results of the confirmatory process – the result of reinforcement, whether positive or negative.

This theory is in many ways accepted as part of the theory language to be discussed in Chapter 12, and one can also see how it is that Theory of Games, Linear and Non-linear programming are relevant to psychological problems. They are techniques that represent in a public way, processes which the organism approximates to, in a more rough and ready way. Thus we can compare the belief-value matrix to the pay-off matrix (von Neumann and Morgenstern, 1947).

It was of course a part of the Tolman campaign to try and make an effective link between conditioning theory and the broader based facts of human behaviour, as mirrored for example in Gestalt theory.

Tolman's aim is, in one sense, to emphasize the reverse side of Hull's coin; he wishes to make the organism a sign-follower to a goal rather than a reactor to internal and external stimuli associated with drive reduction. For Tolman, organisms learn sign-significate relationships; they show insight, and insight is something to be explained behaviouristically, and involves placing the emphasis on the storage system, and the ability to manipulate signs in storage without necessarily having to run off the responses in actual trials.

It is *relevant here to consider* a well-known experiment by Tinklepaugh (1928). A monkey was allowed to watch while a banana was placed under one of two inverted containers, and he appeared to have

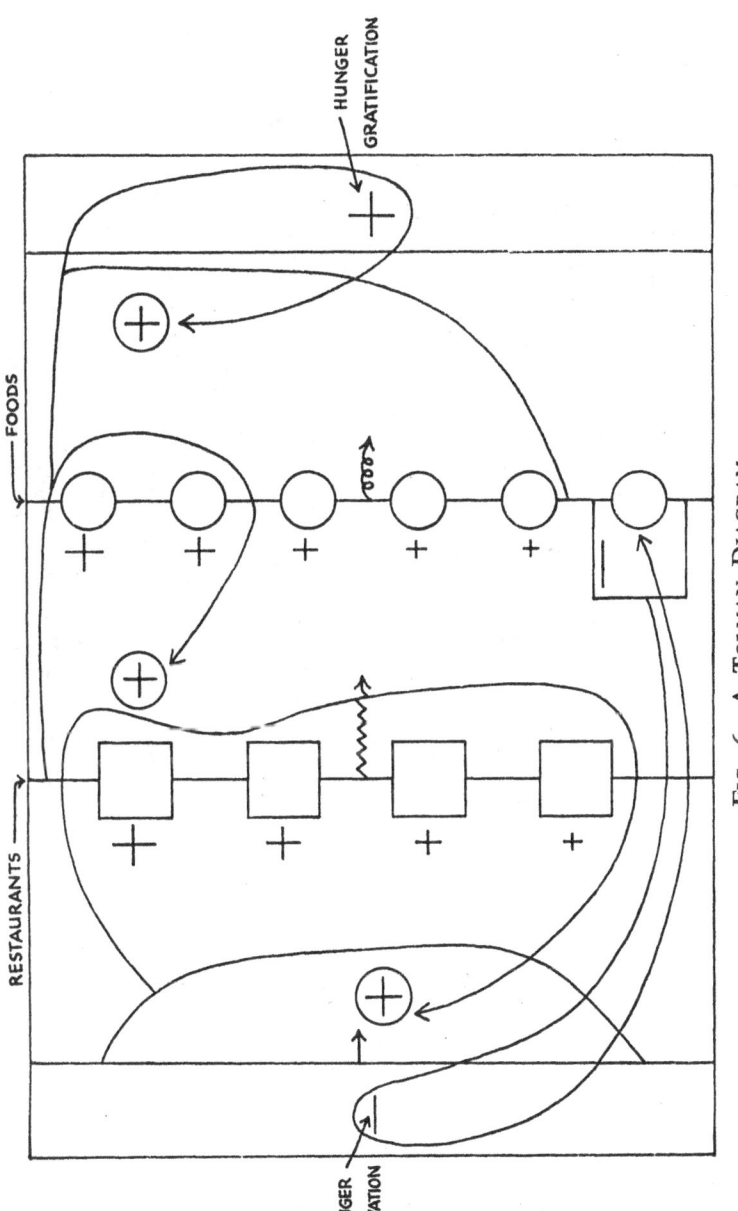

FIG. 6. A TOLMAN DIAGRAM
A belief-value matrix including values is illustrated here.

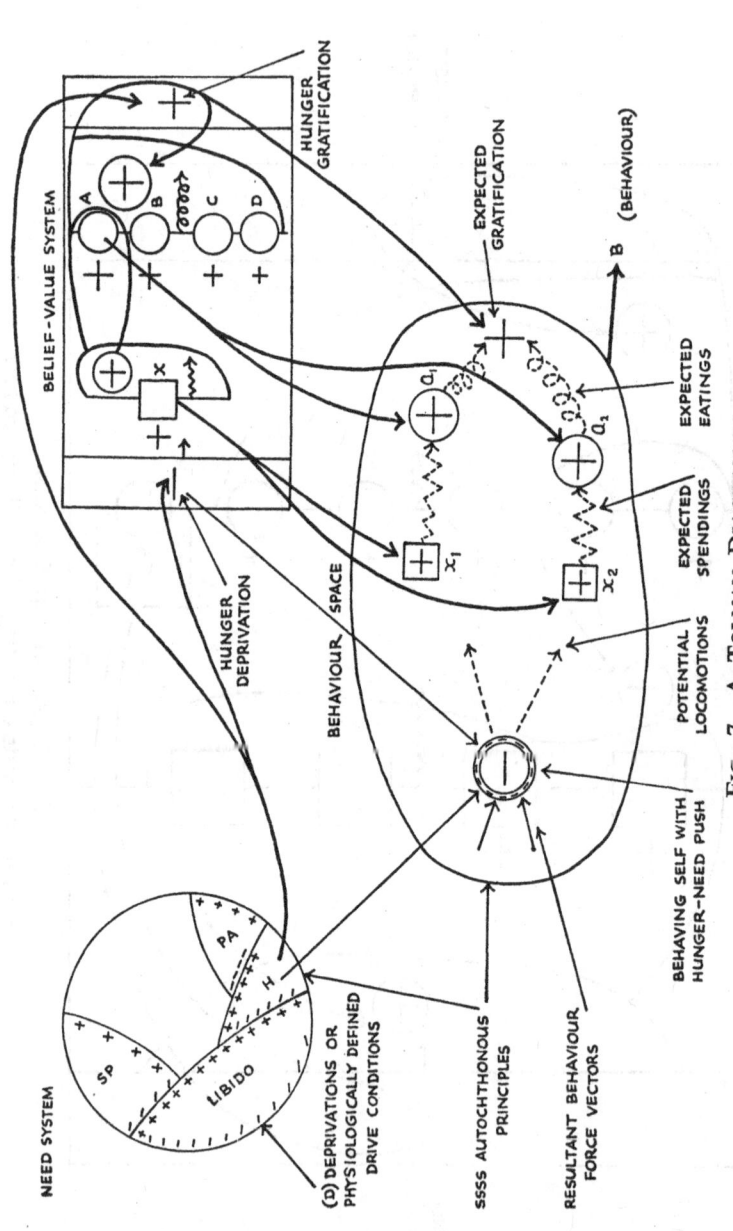

Fig. 7. A Tolman Diagram

A belief-value matrix, a need system and behaviour space.

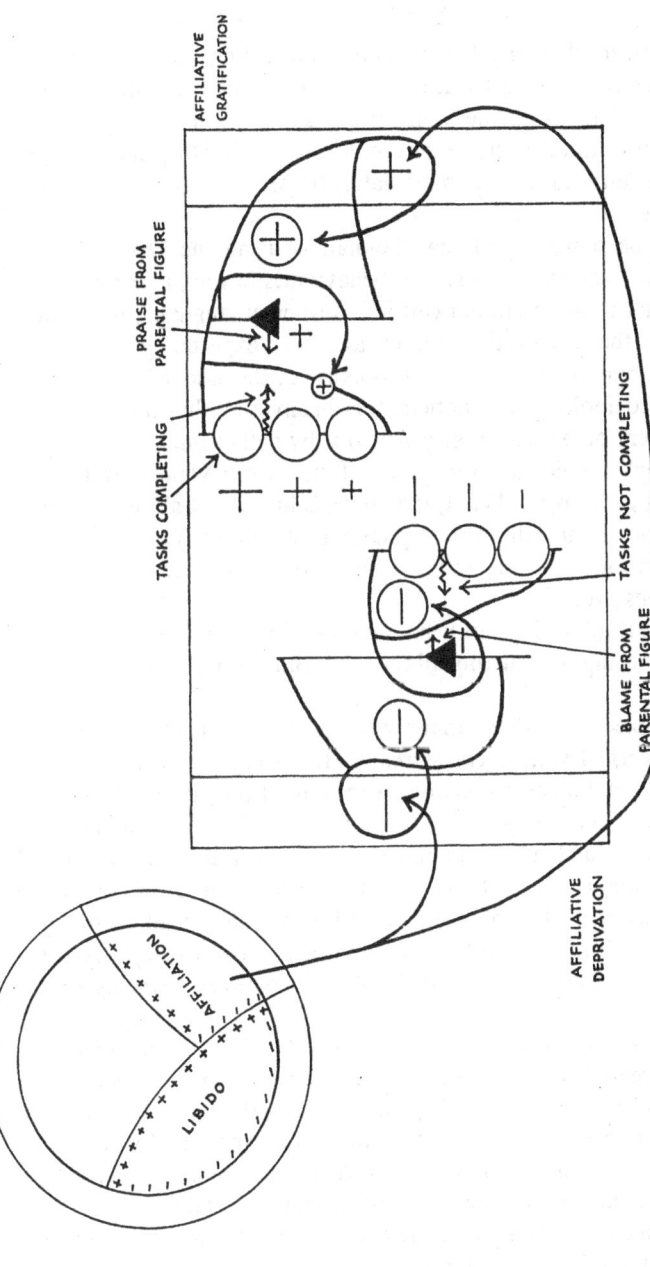

FIG. 8. A TOLMAN DIAGRAM

This diagram shows that completing tasks and failing to complete tasks are respectively a source of parental praise and blame. This leads to gratification and deprivation of the love (affiliative) need.

no difficulty in choosing the container concealing the food. After some successful trials, a lettuce leaf was substituted for the banana by sleight of hand, and the monkey was again given his choice. As in the previous trials he chose the container covering the food, but he rejected the lettuce leaf, and immediately began an obvious search for the banana.

It must be remembered that Tolman is using the central term "expectancy" (or hypothesis) in a behaviouristic way, and the look of expectation, as we should call it in ordinary language, has little bearing on the use of the theoretical term "expectancy" which – although it may have been chosen because of the associations it has with forward looking and anticipatory behaviour – has no meaning in this system other than that given to it by definition, i.e. roughly, "expectancy" implies a given piece of behaviour which results in achieving a goal object. What, therefore, is important about Tinklepaugh's experiment is that the emphasis must be placed on the event that follows the response, and not merely on the fact of responding to a previous event.

When we think of human behaviour we can be in no doubt at all that sign learning is occurring all the time. But we shall return to this point later.

The next piece of evidence that obviously supports Tolman's theory is that concerned with *latent learning*. His theory would appear to have no special difficulty in giving an account of this since it does not demand the S-then-R type of behavioural action, in which the responses have actually to be run off to reinforce the learning. Although latent learning is an embarrassment to Hull's older theory, his modified theory, as has been mentioned, can be made adequate by freeing both J and K from "habit", i.e. the gap can to some extent be bridged by differentiating more sharply between learning and performance.

Tolman's theory depends upon the existence of an expectancy that may be increased in strength *without the actual running-off process*. It can be achieved simply by increasing the strength of the expectancy, and this can occur by inference. The reader should pay careful attention to the fifth postulate of the formalized scheme, since this is an important key to the operation of Tolman's system. This is revealed again in the example at the end of the chapter where Hull's and Tolman's theories are compared.

Before we can actually compare Tolman's and Hull's theories, it is

Tolman's Theory of Learning

necessary to state the postulates of Tolman's formalized system. The following section contains the complete set as provisionally suggested by MacCorquodale and Meehl.

Tolman's Theory in Axiomatic Form

Tolman's theory has sometimes been called a map-control-room theory, in contrast, as we mentioned before, with the telephone-switchboard theories of Hull and Guthrie; this is merely a matter of metaphor and therefore of relevance only to the meta-language of the theory, and not relevant to a genuine comparison between the two views. The important points that characterize Tolman's theory have been pointed out by MacCorquodale and Meehl (1956). They argue that there are certain important aspects of behaviour which are *not necessary* to an expectancy theory (these include such vague and general terms as "Gestalt-configural stress", "perceptual field stress", "discontinuity in discrimination learning", and – perhaps more surprisingly – the distinction between "learning and performance"). Tolman's essence is in the fact that it is an S-S, rather than an S-R theory. His system anticipates increments in learning other than by an S-and-R sequence. The basic definition of "expectancy" has previously been quoted, and here will be stated the preliminary postulates as suggested by MacCorquodale and Meehl for the introduction of an "expectancy" postulate. These are, of course, essentially tentative.

POSTULATE *1. Mnemonization:* The occurrence of the sequence $S_1 \rightarrow R_1 \rightarrow S_2$ (the adjacent members being in close temporal contiguity) results in an increment in the strength of an expectancy $(S_1 R_1 S_2)$. The strength increases as a decelerated function of the number of occurrences of the sequence.

The growth rate is an increasing function of the absolute value of the valence of S_2. If the termination by S_2 of the sequence $S_1 \rightarrow R_1$ is random with respect to non-defining properties of S_1, the asymptote of strength is $\leqslant$ relative frequency P of S_2 following $S_1 \rightarrow R_1$ (i.e. a pure number). How far this asymptote is below P is a decelerated function of the delay between the inception of R_1 and the occurrence of S_2

POSTULATE 2. *Extinction:* The occurrence of a sequence $S_1 \rightarrow R_1$ if not terminated by S_2 produces a decrement in the expectancy if the objective S_2 – probability has been 1.00, and the magnitude of this decrement is an increasing function of the valence of S_2 and the current strength of $(S_1R_1S_2)$. Such a failure of S_2 when P has been $= 1$ is a *disconfirmation* provided $(S_1R_1S_2)$ was non-zero. If the objective probability P shifts to a lower P', and remains stable there, the expectancy strength will approach some value $\leq P'$ asymptotically.

POSTULATE 3. *Primary Generalization:* When an expectancy $(S_1R_1S_2)$ is raised to some strength, expectancies sharing the R and S_2 terms and resembling it on the elicitor side will receive some strength, this generalization strength being a function of the similarity of their elicitors to S_1. The same is true of extinction of $(S_1R_1S_2)$.

POSTULATE 4. *Inference:* The occurrence of a temporal contiguity S_2S^* when $(S_1R_1S_2)$ has non-zero strength, produces an increment in the strength of a new expectancy $(S_1R_1S^*)$. The induced strength increases as a decelerated function of the number of such contiguities. The asymptote is the strength of $(S_1R_1S_2)$ and the growth rate is an increasing decelerated function of the absolute valence of S^*. The presentation of S_2 without S^* weakens such an induced expectancy $S_1R_1S^*$. The decrement is greater if the failure of S^* occurs at the termination of the sequence $S_1 \rightarrow R_1 \rightarrow S_2$ than if it occurs by presentation of S_2 not following an occurrence of the sequence.

POSTULATE 5. *Generalized Inference:* The occurrence of a temporal contiguity S_2S^* produces an increment in the strength of an expectancy $S_1R_1S^*$ provided that an expectancy $S_1R_1S_2'$ was at some strength and the expectandum S_2' is similar to S_2. The induced strength increases as a decelerated function of the number of such contiguities. The asymptote is a function of the strength of $S_1R_1S_2'$ and the difference between S_2 and S_2'. The growth rate to this asymptote is an increasing decelerated function of the absolute valence of S^*.

POSTULATE 6. *Secondary Cathexis:* The contiguity of S_2 and S^* when S^* has a valence $|V|$ produces an increment in the cathexis of S_2. The derived cathexis is an increasing decelerated function of the number of contiguities, and the asymptote is an increasing decelerated function of $|V|$ during the contiguities, and has the same sign as the V of S^*. The presentation of S_2 without S^*, or with S^* having had its absolute valence decreased, will produce a decrement in the induced cathesis of S_2.

POSTULATE 7. *Induced Elicitor-Cathexis:* The acquisition of valence by an expectandum S_2 of an existing expectancy $(S_1R_1S_2)$ induces a cathexis in the elicitor S_1, the strength of the induced cathexis being a decelerated increasing function of the strength of the expectancy and the absolute valence of S_2.

POSTULATE 8. *Confirmed Elicitor-Cathexis:* The confirmation of an expectancy $(S_1R_1S_2)$, i.e. the occurrence of the sequence $S_1 \rightarrow R_1 \rightarrow S_2$ when $(S_1R_1S_2)$ is of non-zero strength, when S_2 has a certain valence, produces an increment in the cathexis of the elicitor S_1.

The increment in the elicitor-cathexis by *confirmation* is greater than the increment which would be *induced* (see preceding law) by producing a valence in S_2 when the expectancy is at the same strength as that reached by the present confirmation.

POSTULATE 9. *Valence:* The valence of a stimulus S^* is a multiplicative function of the *need D* and the *cathexis C^** attached to S^*. (This applies only to cases of positive cathexis.)

POSTULATE 10. *Need Strength:* The need (D) for a cathected situation is an increasing function of the time interval since satiation for it.

(Upon present evidence, even basic questions of monotony and acceleration are unsettled for the alimentary drives of the rat, not to mention other drives and other species. There is no very cogent evidence that all or even most "needs" rise as a function of time since satiation, although this seems to be frequently assumed. Even the notion of satiation iself, in connexion with "simple" alimentary drives, presents great difficulties.)

POSTULATE 11. *Cathexis:* The cathexis of a stimulus situation S^* is an increasing decelerated function of the number of contiguities between it and the occurrences of the consummatory response. The asymptote is an increasing function of the need strength present during these contiguities.

POSTULATE 12. *Activation:* The reaction potential $_sE_R$ of a response R_1 in the presence of S_1 is a multiplicative function of the strength of the expectancy $(S_1R_1S_2)$ and the valence (retaining sign) of the expectandum. There are momentary reactions of reaction-potential about this value $_sE_R$, the frequency of distribution being at least unimodal in form. The oscillation of two different $_sE_R$'s are treated as independent, and the response which is momentarily "ahead" is assumed to be emitted.

Hull and Tolman Compared

Tolman, as we have said, regards his intervening variables as in need of defining experiments. The difficulty here is that it does not appear possible to apply the usual form of linear experimental situation to define variables that will generally be non-linear; it is probable, in fact, that the so-called intervening variables should actually be regarded as full logical constructs, as Tolman himself now seems to suggest. This certainly indicates a further measure of rapprochement between the theories of Hull and Tolman.

It will be seen, then, that when the two theories are carefully compared, the differences tend to dissolve; indeed it is possible that the theories are interchangeable, provided that a suitable interpretation is given to the word "response" by the S-R (Hullian) school. If, however, it is insisted that this should be interpreted as an "effector" event, then it does constitute a definite non-verbal difference. From the methodological or cybernetic point of view the suspicion is again that the differences are at the level of the theory language, i.e. in the interpretation rather than in the model itself.

Like Hull's, Tolman's system is, in general, a molar behaviourism, but it tends to emphasize purpose in the theory construction in a way that Hull's theory does not. There is in Tolman no direct use of reinforcement; in place of it we find the notion of expectancy based on sign learning (cf. expectancy and effect). The strength of Tolman's theory can be seen most favourably in three situations: (1) Reward-expectancy; (2) Place learning; and (3) Latent learning.

The place-learning experiments, of which MacFarlane's (1930) work may be regarded as typical, incline to show that the actual process of running a maze is not a chain of S-R acts, but involves a knowledge of the maze-as-a-whole – a sort of insight.

The two almost classical illustrations of place learning and insight learning in rats are the experiments by Tolman, Ritchie and Kalish (1946) and Tolman and Honzik (1930).

Tolman, Ritchie and Kalish used a simple cross as a maze, with starting points at either end of one arm and food at either end of the other arm. This means that the rats can be divided into groups that always turn left or always right, or turn according to which end they start thus finding food at either of the two possible places. Under these circumstances the place learning of the second group was rather more effective than the response learning of the first.

The Tolman and Honzik experiment involved three pathways of different length from the starting box to the goal and the rats were trained to take the shortest first and then the next shortest and so on. Figure 9 illustrates the maze. Now when a block was placed at X the rats tended to run down the second shortest route but when the block was placed at Y, instead of again taking the shortest route they went down the longest route. This seems to indicate an insight based on a recognition of the general layout of the maze, or at least the significance of the point where the second choice path enters the first choice path.

Many people have tried to reproduce this experiment with somewhat varied results, leaving a doubt about the experimental facts – a state of affairs by no means uncommon in experimental psychology. Nevertheless there is some reason to believe that the sort of cognitive activities suggested by the experiment are ones that rats are capable of carrying out. Our question is simply as to the nature of the processes entailed.

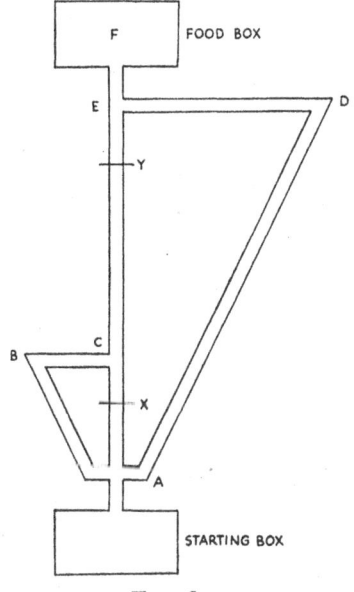

FIG. 9.
THE TOLMAN-HONZIK MAZE
This figure shows the maze actually used in the Tolman-Honzik experiment on 'insight learning' in rats. See text for description.

Latent learning supplies perhaps the strongest experimental evidence in support of Tolman's position as opposed to *the older* Hull theory.

A further experiment, carried out by Krechevsky (1932b), must suffice as an example of the type of hypothesis theory that is characteristic of the expectancy, or *S-S*, theorist rather than the *S-R* theorist. This example is an analysis of individual rat performance. The experimental situation involved the training of rats to discriminate between a path containing a hurdle, and an equally lighted path containing no hurdle. A multiple discrimination box was used, and the performance was documented in terms of number of errors, number of right turns,

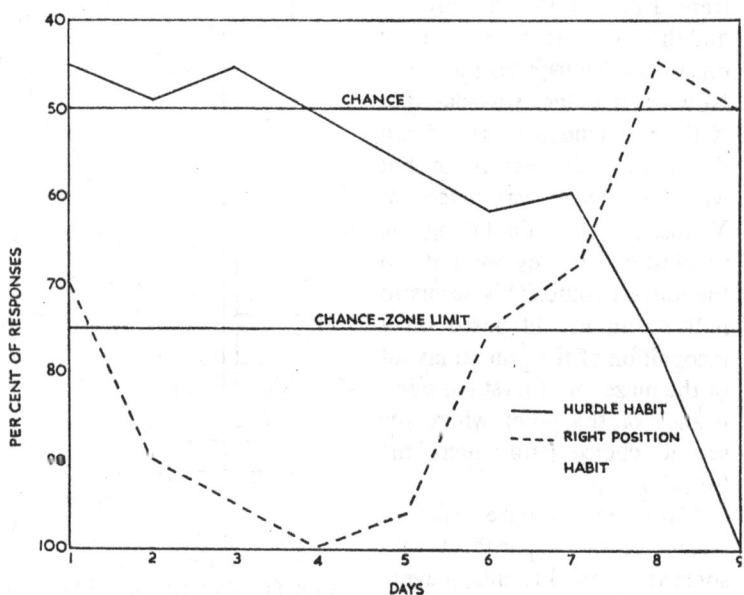

FIG. 10. KRECHEVSKY HYPOTHESES

This graph shows evidence from one of Krechevsky's experiments in favour of the formation of hypotheses ('insight learning') in rats. The rat is trained to discriminate between two paths, only one of which contains a hurdle to be surmounted.

number of left turns, and number of turns in keeping with an alternating scheme. On statistical analysis it seems that any response occurring above 73 per cent would almost certainly be a non-chance factor. The graph (Figure 10) shows the cases of greater than 73 per cent response-rate, and is thought to constitute evidence for hypotheses. The solid line represents the percentage of errors on successive days; the broken line shows the right-turning response of the subject.

Krechevsky (1932a, 1935) also averred that "bright" rats use spatial hypotheses predominantly, whereas "dull" rats are more prone to use non-spatial hypotheses (e.g. visual, in this particular experiment). Control rats appeared to be neutral in this situation. Krechevsky further reported that the number of hypotheses used by rats is decreased in discrimination learning. In the argument regarding "bright" and "dull" rats there exist the seeds of possible circularity in an objectionable sense.

The important fact about Krechevsky's work is the relation between learning and performance. Inevitably, the process is to observe performance and make deductions about learning, and here the notion of hypotheses does, in fact, appear to fit very well.

Some attempt has been made to decide between S-R theory and "field" (or cognitive or S-S) theory at the experimental level, notably, among others, by Humphreys (1939), who carried out an experiment on eyelid conditioning in humans. Conditioned discrimination was thought to be more rapid when subjects knew which stimulus of a pair was to be positive and which negative, rather than when 'experience" was a necessary prelude to prediction. Humphreys showed that a random alternation of reinforcement and non-reinforcement led to a higher level of conditioning, and a greater resistance to extinction, than if reinforcement was 100 per cent (this is a classical case of partial reinforcement, which was treated more fully in Chapter 4). Humphreys assumed that changing hypotheses accounted for this and, using humans in a study of verbal expectations, he appeared to get corroborative results. The actual study involved showing two lights to a subject and, when one light was switched on, asking the subject whether the other light would follow or not. Two groups were set up, one of which was always shown light 1 followed by light 2; the other group had a random distribution of light 2 or not light 2 following light 1. The second group guessed at chance level, as was to be expected. The second part of the experiment was the extinction of these responses, and this was seen to be much quicker in the first group. The results of these rather subtle experiments are, of course, wholly in favour of an expectancy theory, and the resemblance to Krechevsky's "hypotheses" will not be overlooked.

Another series of experiments was carried out by Loucks (1935), and has been quoted by Spence (1950). Using Spence's shorthand: S_c = conditioned stimulus A_1, A_2 = afferent processes, E_1, E_2 = efferent neural processes, and R_o and R_u are equivalent responses to

S_c and S_u where S_u = unconditioned stimulus (see Figure 11). Loucks' experiment omitted the S_u and A_2 stages.

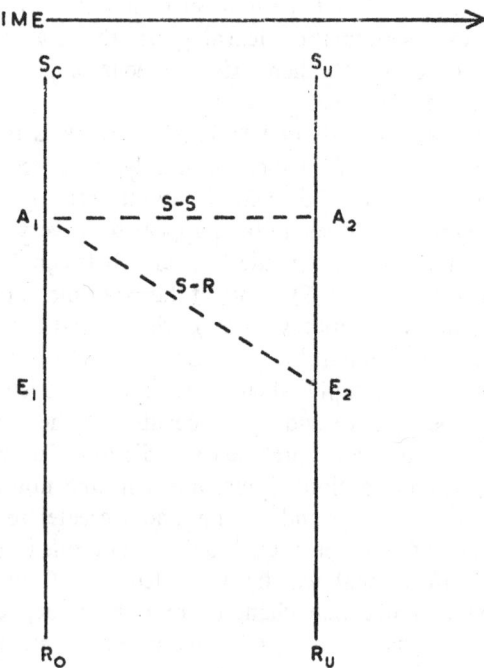

FIG. 11. NORMAL CONDITIONING

The association is set up between the conditioned stimulus and the unconditioned stimulus as well as between the conditioned stimulus and the conditioned response.

The unconditioned flexion response being elicited, by applying faradic shock directly to the appropriate area of the motor cortex, no conditioning took place.

This is shown diagramatically on page 119.

In the next stage of Loucks' experiment, the leg flexion was followed by food presentation, and conditioning took place. This has sometimes been interpreted as favouring an *S-S*, as opposed to an *S-R* theory of reinforcement, but this is utterly denied by Spence who says, merely, that there was no reinforcement in the first part of the experiment, and there *was* in the second. Figure 13 shows the position.

Returning to the more direct comparison of Tolman and Hull, one or two tentative statements may now be made. Tolman tends to place emphasis on the organism dominating its environment, while for Hull, the emphasis is on the environment's domination of the organism. But although it may only be a matter of different emphasis, this divergence can be traced back to the dissimilarities in philosophical

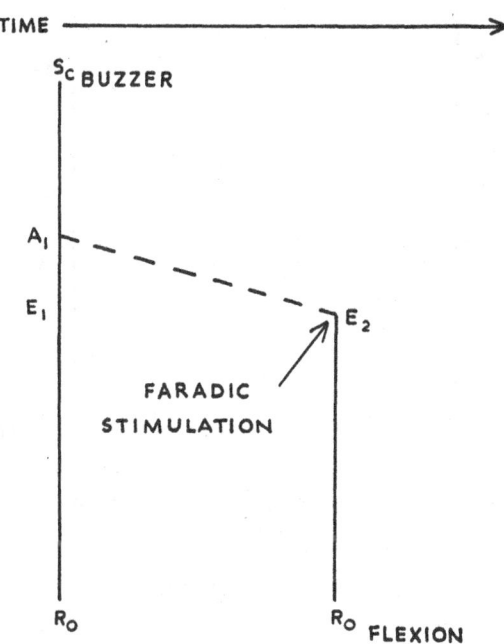

FIG. 12. LOUCKS' CONDITIONING – STAGE 1
An electrical stimulus is applied directly to the appropriate area of the motor cortex and no conditioning occurs.

directives accepted by their two viewpoints. They are modern variations on the well-known mechanistic-idealist controversy.

We shall now show how Tolman and Hull would derive an inference in their respective postulate systems. We shall consider a situation where the steps involved are: (1) to learn that $A \rightarrow B$, (2) to learn that $B \rightarrow C$, and (3) granted that $A \rightarrow B$ and $A \rightarrow D$ are both learned equally strongly, to show that, because of (2), the organism will be able to infer $A \rightarrow C$ in spite of the equality of $A \rightarrow B$ and $A \rightarrow D$.

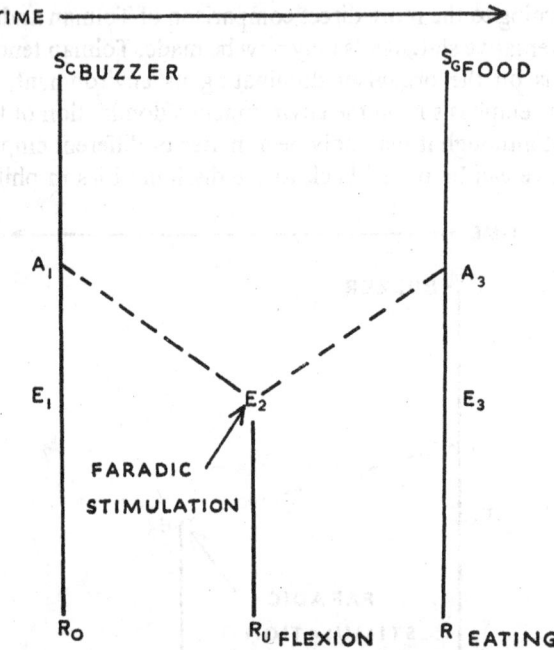

FIG. 13. LOUCKS' CONDITIONING – STAGE 2
The electrical stimulus now being followed by the presentation of food leads to the appropriate conditioning.

Tolman's derivation is fairly straightforward. In the first place we have, by his first postulate, using X for A when B follows, and Y for A when D follows,

$$(S_X R_X S_B) = (S_Y R_Y S_D) > 0 (A \to B . A \to D)$$

Then we have an *induced cathexis* with respect to S_B because of the reward involved in achieving C from it (the $B \to C$ step is highly "rewarded").

Therefore by postulates 1, 6 and 7 we derive:

$$C_{S_B} > C_{S_D}$$

and by postulate 9 we get

$$V_{S_B} > V_{S_D}$$

The final step involves (by postulate 12)

$$S_X E_{R_X} = (S_X R_X S_B) . V_{S_B}$$

and

$$S_Y E_{R_Y} = (S_Y R_Y S_D) . V_{S_D}$$

Tolman's Theory of Learning

which leads to $\quad S_X E_{R_X} > S_Y E_{R_Y}$ (by all the above)
and this implies the probability of the appropriate response $A \to C$.
Hull's derivation (after Seward) reads for the first stage:

$$_{RS_X}E_{r_B} = D.K_B.V_{RS_X}._{RS_X}\bar{H}_r$$
$$_{RS_Y}E_{r_D} = D.K_D.V_{RS_Y}._{RS_Y}\bar{H}_{r_D}$$

by use of postulate 10 and postulate 8 corollary 3A (see last chapter), and where $_sL_R$ is the reaction threshold.

The second stage, involving the $B \to C$ step, is achieved by the arousal of antedating reactions (anticipatory goal responses) to the reward at C.

This gives $\quad _{RS_B}E_{r_G} = D.K_G.V_{RS_B}._{RS_B}\bar{H}_{r_G}$

by use of postulates 10 B and (corollary 3A) again, given a somewhat liberal interpretation.

The final step involves S_X producing an end-box surrogate rS_B where r_{S_B} arouses r_G. If we assume that the antedating reaction potentials can be summated, we get

$$_{S_X}E_{R_X} = c(_{RS_X}E_{r_B} + RS_B E_{r_G})$$
$$_{S_X}E_{R_Y} = c(_{RS_Y}E_{r_D})$$

by use of $\quad _sE_{R_d} = c(_{RS}E_{r_G})$
where $\quad _{RS}E_{r_G} = D.K.V_{RS}._{RS}\bar{H}_{r_G}$
and finally by the above step

$$_{S_X}E_{R_X} > _{S_Y}E_{R_Y}$$

which achieves $A \to C$.

This argument is necessarily somewhat compressed here, but as in any case it will be very much a prototype for a part of our subsequent discussion of *thinking*, and we shall leave it for the time being at this point, with the mere comment that the rapprochement implied by these two arguments seems fairly complete and the two theories differ primarily over terminology. It has to be admitted though that both theories have an extremely ugly notation and often unsuitable terminology.

Olds' Theory

In this monograph, little has been or will be said about Hebb's theory (1949) although references to it will be made from time to time. The value of Hebb's work lay largely in drawing attention to the urgent need to build from the known behavioural facts to neurological data. This aim, as far as the writer is concerned, is wholly laudable, but does come rather outside the context of the present work.

As a result Olds' (1954) attempt to integrate Tolman's theory with the cell-assemblies of Hebb is not perhaps a central theme of our book either. What is worth mentioning is that this represents an alternative approach, partly cybernetic and partly neurological, to cognitive theories.

Olds provided for associations between cell assemblies. In his own words:

> After an associational relation has thus been formed between cell assemblies a and b through the response control unit r_1, the firing of a will tend to arouse reverberation in b, and reverberation in b (aroused from some other quarter) will add to the motive force of a and a's further antecedents.

Olds further assumes that cell assemblies have two thresholds, one for stimulation and one for motivation and both these must be achieved before activation occurs.

A particular point of Olds' theory is to cater for latent learning. So that if there is a change in the value of the outcome there will be a change in the value of the preceding responses without further actual responses having to be made.

Milner (1956) has also modified the Cell assembly theory of Hebb, from a more neurophysiological point of view. The interest in both these works is the clearcut attempt to supply an effective model for a theory of learning. Olds achieves a certain integration not previously achieved, but still does not carry Tolman's theory through to the necessary degree of precision nor link it adequately with our new cybernetic knowledge of stochastic processes. In saying this though we are anticipating the ultimate findings of the book.

Chapter 7

PHILOSOPHY, INTROSPECTION AND COGNITION

Following on our pattern of analysis of learning, we now turn to a philosophical analysis of the methods and languages to be used, and something of the findings of philosophers where these are relevant to the science of cognition. Once again, considerations of space impose the compression into one chapter of matter that might usefully be extended to a whole book. However, we have dealt in advance with learning, and shall next be dealing with perception and the other cognitive processes, and may now treat the philosophy of cognition *en bloc*.

We might describe our problem now as one of explaining human behaviour from simple, common-sense beginnings, where we pose our questions and give our answers in ordinary language. Firstly we ask, "why does a human learn?" or "how does he learn?" and we try to say what we mean by "learn" in sufficiently simple terms to permit of a simple answer in the same terms. This, of course, is *not enough* for scientific purposes, and we are therefore led into using more specialized terminology and other specialized methods; but the preliminary, and in some respects the final, steps of application are tied to ordinary language, and this is how our philosophical analysis begins. We use the word "philosophical" here loosely, to apply to intuitive and introspective approaches to cognitive problems, usually with a view to a clearer understanding of what the processes of cognition entail.

The hierarchical nature of the behavioural sciences – i.e. degrees of complexity in description – suggests that one might expect to find equivalent problems turning up at different levels of investigation, and this we do in fact find. Philosophically, the problems of learning and perception certainly exist, and text-books on philosophy include references to memory and other branches of behaviour that are also treated by psychology. Perception and learning as philosophical problems can be to some extent separated from their psychological and physiological equivalents, but the relationship necessitates the inclusion of the present chapter in the book, and incidentally gives us the opportunity to explore our subject in a detailed and careful way.

Perception goes under the same name at all our principal levels of investigation. Learning at the psychological level is, with perception, called "theory of knowledge" when dealt with by philosophers. Strictly speaking, neither "learning" nor "perception" are terms used in physiology, but it is increasingly clear that the concepts which physiologists handle must ultimately be used in the scientific explanation of learning and perception.

It is clear, of course, that the concern of philosophers with learning and perception has a somewhat different motive from that of the scientist; but it does not by any means follow that what the philosophers have discovered will be unimportant to what the scientists are doing.

It is generally admitted that there is current in psychological circles a distrust of philosophy in general. It is really a distrust of arm-chair theorizing; but whatever is amenable to logical analysis in science *is* an arm-chair activity, and it should be mentioned here that psychologists and other scientists have frequently failed to distinguish between theories that directly describe empirical facts, and those that only describe other theories, or symbolic models.

We might ask again now what the word "learning" means. Experimental pscyhologists usually reply that only an approximate definition can be given, and that a rough indication of what learning means can be gleaned from a working, or glossary, definition, and that furthermore a precise definition is unnecessary – a view previously accepted in this book. Whether such an answer is justified, however, is still a matter of debate, and we should try, therefore, to analyse further the need for precise definition. The acceptance of a vague, glossary type definition is obviously consistent with a philosophical view that suggests that it is not the definition of important terms, such as "meaning", "truth", and here, "learning", that we need, but a clear idea of what these terms mean, whether or not we can express that meaning in words. This would seem to be a dangerous attitude, and we should perhaps first *try* to express a precise definition of "learning".

The difficulty in defining "learning" lies in the problem of finding a definition narrow enough to exclude a penny-in-the-slot machine activity, and broad enough to include human behaviour. Failure to find such a definition might have the important consequence of suggesting that learning, even in humans, is not fundamentally different from the activity of a system that follows a penny-in-the-slot principle. Such a view is, in fact, consistent with the behaviourism commonly espoused today.

As with a single term's meaning, so with a whole set of sentences, we have the problem of interpretation; and the way we interpret such sentences is very closely bound up with the sort of linguistic framework we accept, which really means the ontology and the epistemology we accept. The problem is, then, what sort of ontology or epistemology *should* science accept. But, perhaps more immediately, we smust consider the sort of frameworks that have been suggested, with special reference to perception. Their importance for us rests mostly in the attitude they inculcate towards our scientific material. Is it, for example, an attitude of awareness of the many pitfalls – often due to lack of empirical knowledge – that can entrap the scientist? Obviously we must commence by analysing some of the philosophical approaches to cognition.

Naïve Realism

The first philosophical system we shall consider purports to be the common man's philosophy: The world is just what it seems to be. This view, which is on the whole rejected by philosophers, needs a careful word of explanation. This is particularly important because many scientists seem to start (and often complete) their investigations almost entirely in the implicit background of naïve realism, and it frequently appears to be quite sufficient for their purpose.

Perhaps the simplest statement of naïve realism is the belief that there exists a real world in which we all live, and that people and houses, trees, mountains, etc., exist in the ordinary independent sense of being "really there". It is a world of "things". The world is independent of the organisms in it; it existed before the people were upon it, and it could quite well exist if there were no longer any people upon it.

The world of things outside ourselves is essentially independent of the ideas of those things we have inside us. For many purposes this view is indeed sufficient.

The criticisms of naïve realism spring largely from the very field we are interested in investigating, the field of cognition, and in particular, *perception*. But before we launch explicitly into the naïve realist's account of *perception*, let us pay attention to what are essentially the general difficulties.

The first sort of problem the naïve realist runs into is that of a substance and its changing properties. If he is asked, "Is that the same cloud as you saw last week?" he will answer in the negative. If you ask the same question about a mountain, he will answer in the affirmative. And if you ask how he knows either of these things, he will answer either that it is obvious, or more carefully, there there is evidence from meteorology or geology that makes it extremely unlikely that the cloud is the same or that the mountain is different. Here, then, our first big problem arises. There is no clear understanding of what the question *means*. What is the *same* cloud and the *same* mountain? This is an old philosophical problem, and we believe an answer can be given in the sense of relatively invariant characteristics in a world of change. The problem of the invariant nature of substances is closely bound up with the philosopher's objections to scientific explanations being regarded as legitimate in philosophy. They (scientific explanations) themselves are subject to the same ultimate perceptual standard, or to put it more bluntly, they are themselves dependent on perception. This argument becomes vital as soon as we consider perception itself, which is in a sense prior to a study of knowledge.

The question of illusion in perception is usually regarded as being the final death-stroke to the naïve realist. We appear to acquire all our knowledge either by virtue of sensory perception or by inferences made from such sensorily given information (learning); so if we want to track down perceptual illusion we must have some standard by which we may judge it. In practice we correct false perceptions by comparison with other perceptions, but what makes us believe that some are false and some correct? and more precisely, what does it mean to talk of a false perception? Clearly the only answer must be that we make a judgment based on what we have learned from other perceptions over a long period of time. We must therefore examine more closely the naïve realist's view of perception.

In putting forward a form of naïve realism, it is intended to neglect, as yet, the analysis of words such as "perception". We are, however, involved to some extent in verbal matters when we use a term like "perceptual consciousness". This is used in Price's analysis of perception (1932). By *perceptual consciousness*, Price means the non-sensuous mode of consciousness, and this is intended to indicate the processes of which an observer is conscious, and which do not depend on immediate sensory input. This is difficult to delineate with any great precision; indeed it is a vague concept over which we have every reason to be suspicious. Perceptual consciousness is closely connected with sensing, but is to be distinguished from it. The main question that might be asked of our perceptual consciousness is, "what is its relation to sensing?" If we add Price's second question, which enquires of the relation of sense-data ("appearances") to a "material thing", then we can characterize the main points of naïve realism.

For a naïve realist, perceptual consciousness is "knowledge about", or "apprehension of" an object. It is knowledge in a strong sense, and not a belief in a weak sense. It is knowledge that there exists an object to which the sense-data now sensed belong. Naïve realists believe, in the case of Price's second question, that a visual sense-datum "belongs to" part of the surface of some material object – a material object being a commonplace three-dimensional body having certain well-known spatio-temporal properties.

Let us now briefly consider the established criticisms of this viewpoint. The best known argument against naïve realism is that called the *argument from illusion*. An illusion, for this argument, is a sense-datum which does not represent the surface of a material object. The argument is perhaps sufficiently established by pointing to hallucinatory or wild perceptions, such as the many cases reported in psychological literature of sense-data which are clearly not connected with material objects. There are also various examples of colour vision where, for example, the case of contrast appears to be a sort of illusion. The well-known case of a stick partially immersed in water is another example, and one we shall return to later.

The so-called causal form of the argument from illusions says that sense-data vary with variations in the medium between the observer and the object. Further, it argues that the existence of sense-data depends on the central nervous system which generates them, and no sense-data can exist without a concomitant cerebral process. Both arguments from illusion are open to the logical objection that they seen to assume the correctness of the view they are designed to demolish. If, for instance, we deny that a sense-datum belongs to a material object, we must be basing the argument on our knowledge that such material objects as we do perceive are not present when we have a wild sense-datum. It will be appreciated that argument on these lines involves a commitment to a *criterion of physicality*, which means an independent statement of what constitutes a physical object. This appeal, which is necessary to either side of the argument, is rooted in a complex and not easily comprehensible background, and we shall pursue this matter no further here.

Before considering the conceivable modifications of naïve realism, it is worth reminding ourselves of the possibility that our statement of naïve realism has not been a fair one; have we set up a "strawman"? There are some scientists and philosophers who would prefer to keep their interpretations of nature as near to naïve realism as possible.

We shall be in some measure anticipating a typical psychological viewpoint if we reformulate the foundations of naïve realism. Such a foundation has been proposed by Hirst (1950):

1. The public assumption of individuals and public interacting entities must be made.
2. Perception is direct.
3. Things may look different from what they are since we have various *views* of the *same* thing.
4. It is possible to obtain the *real* nature and character of material objects although several acts of perception, etc., may be necessary for certainty.

This statement shows a healthy, empirical starting point, and makes the necessary distinction between what is learnt and what is perceived, but there are difficulties. It is true that it appears very reasonable to say that a circle will look circular at one angle and elliptical at another, indeed it would be impossible to identify a circle at all if it did not look elliptical from most of its possible viewpoints. This seems fair; but is the claim, then, that sense-data are quite public? The answer to this appears to lie in the fact that we do not *need* to accept a sense-data language; we may even deny that it is a language at all Ryle (1949) George (1957).

The next question arising concerns the reasons why phenominalism (which is our second methodology, to be considered shortly) is supposed to offer us a better language than sense-data language, i.e. a language of appearances. It may be for either philosophical or psychological reasons, and it is essential that we should separate the two *if possible*. Philosophers are interested in perception as the foundation of empirical knowledge (in the sense that the epistemologist is interested in the reliability of perception as a source of knowledge of physical facts), and in this connexion it is worthy of note that the argument of Price and other phenomenalists seems to depend on the strict certainty of sensing. Psychologists, on the other hand, are interested in an interpretation (explanation), and a predictive theory of perception. It seems possible that a predictive theory could be made to rest on a *model* wihch would have little explanatory value. This is relatively unusual, and yet seems to be at the bottom of the many arguments between philosophy and science.

The question of certainty in perception will be returned to later. The statement of Hirst (above) comes near the conditions of physicality which have been frequently laid down, and seems to be in essential agreement with them. The problem of the exegesis of existing philosophically inclined writings on perception is complicated by their own internal inconsistencies and changes, with time, of viewpoint.

The naïve realist has a model of much scientific usefulness, and he may reasonably proceed to formulate a viewpoint like Hirst's, and deny the privacy of sense-data. Indeed, the whole *idea* of private experience may be taken to be impossible and nonsense, and therefore not a suitable starting point for any form of either scientific or philosophical analysis.

Phenomenalism

It has already been said that it is difficult to delineate the various philosophical viewpoints in a very precise manner; nevertheless we shall now attempt to give a broad interpretation of the phenomenalist's view. We know that there are at least two phenomenalistic views, both of which accept the fact that our knowledge is limited to phenomena, both physical and mental. They differ in that the first of these two views – the view called epistemological monism – denies any *reality* behind the phenomena, whereas epistemological dualism accepts the reality but denies that it is knowable, or may deny that it is knowable other than by description or inference.

The point here is brought out by C. D. Broad (1923) when he says that we may gain our criteria of physicality by categorical means, or means that do not *directly* depend on our phenomenal perceptions. It would be of great interest to have a much clearer statement of what these categorical means entail and from whence they spring, but we may guess that they represent precisely what has been *learnt*.

The monistic view seems to be supported by Berkeley, among others, while the dualistic view has the support of Kant, Lewis and many modern thinkers.

It should be remembered that such monistic and dualistic views cut across the phenomenalist-realist controversy. Locke, for example, although an epistemological dualist, was not a phenomenalist (or was so only in a special and limited sense). We shall take Berkeley's views as representative of phenomenalism; his philosophy is a monistic one, and is usually referred to as subjective idealism. This category again – as we have seen – cuts across the phenomenalist-realist controversy.

The most extreme, and also the most lucid, statement of the phenomenalist position is that made by Ernest Mach. This position regards the world as personal to the individual, and as that which is observable at each moment of time. It is the totality of observed phenomena that marks the beginning and end of the individual world. "There is nothing but what I observe." This extreme view has a great many difficulties attendent upon it from the logical point of view, and indeed Mach's view comes near to the fictionalism of Vahinger. However, this is not the place to evaluate the logical difficulties inherent in the reducibility thesis, and the rather arbitrary use of induction made by the phenomenalists, and our most profitable plan would seem to be to take up and expand the two views which we shall hold as representative of phenomenalism.

Berkeley's Idealism

It would be fruitless to try to separate Berkeley's general philosophical position from his strictly perceptual views; they are more or less inextricably entangled. Furthermore, it will be appreciated that Berkeley, like other philosophers, did not necessarily hold the same views all his life; indeed, many people have pointed out that the later Berkeley was not himself a "Berkelian". In this short survey we shall, as with our representative views, ignore, or smooth out, such inconsistencies as may be apparent.

Berkeley seems to have based much of his philosophy on the one hand on the refutation of Locke, and on the other on the belief that, "the *esse* of things is *percipi*".

Locke's dualism distinguishes primary (objective) and secondary (subjective) qualities. He considers that the real objects of the world have certain qualities, and that there are further qualities that may be added when these objects are perceived. Berkeley's attempt to upset Locke's view was based on denial of the existence (at least in Locke's sense) of primary, or objective qualities, and on the claim that they all existed in the mind. What the phrase, "a given quality . . . exists nowhere but in the mind" means is not, however, easy to decide. If it means that the observations of "external" conditions depend on the state of the observer, no one would disagree with this in itself. If, on the other hand, it is suggested that there is nothing other than a "mental state", almost nobody would agree. Is "redness" a sensation that bears no relation to some "external red object"? Berkeley seems here to have confused sensations with the objects of sensation.

Having demolished the Lockian distinction between primary and secondary qualities, Berkeley then proceeded to reject the notion of material substance. "What is in a substance other than a set of qualities?" he asked. What he is intending to infer is that a physical object is really an infinite set of possible perceptions. "I perceive everything there is. 'Everything there is' are *ideas* in my mind, and the notion of 'matter' is just a device to try to explain how the causal relations work with respect to sensation." If matter causes sensations, then we are committed to a mere tautology, since sensation is now simply that which is caused by matter. This, as it stands, is indeed an inadequately circular definition.

It would be useful now to compare the Locke approach to perception with that of Berkeley. If I say, "I see an orange on the table," both would agree that I can have the *idea* of an orange on the table whether there *is* one or not. But whereas Locke would evoke the causal theory – a scientific view which has its own difficulties, since it is difficult to distinguish a real orange from a non-real orange – Berkeley's alternative was to make further sensory tests, and thus have further ideas which make for *certainty*.

It is clear that, as expected, Berkeley's view implies no distinction between appearance and reality. Indeed for Berkeley (and perhaps in the same way for any other phenomenalist) it is difficult, if not impossible, to take the step from private to public knowledge; i.e. to be able to say, "There *is* an orange on the table." Berkeley would interpret this as meaning, "There seems to be an orange on the table"; he could not get beyond that, and that of course is in a sense all we can ever reasonably say.

General Phenomenalism

The ideas expressed somewhat briefly by Berkeley have been given a more detailed analysis by modern philosophers.

Modern Phenomenalism has been in revolt against the epistemological dualist's concept of matter, but at the same time it rejects Berkeley's "*esse est percipi*" principle. It may be described as the view that holds that the material world consists of causally-characterized families of sense-data, and indeed there are some advantages in such a view, the main one being – according to A. J. Ayer (1936) – that it is a convenient language.

Phenomenalism is a modification of idealism (e.g. in Berkeley's form). The material objects of the world include all possible as well as all actual sense-data. However, there are certain "if . . . then" operations which can now be performed in corroboration of one's perceptions.

We need not waste any time asking whether sense-data are substances. According to Price, sense-data are *events*. For Ayer, they are parts of a useful, descriptive language. They are not physical, mental or cerebral events, but they are related to the psycho-cerebral compound. Sense-data are part of sense field, and all non-wild sense-data *belong to* external objects. A sense-datum is a private item of knowledge, but families of sense-data are part of public knowledge, and it is of interest that Price disputes the full phenomenalist identification of material things with families of sense-data. He also criticizes the causal theory for its identification of the material thing with the physical object. Sense-data families, for Price, seem to have the potential status of theoretical terms, but they also seem to have more than this – an ontological status – in that they are physical objects.

Let us now turn to the phenomenalist's treatment of the problem which appears to upset naïve realism. His test for the reality is essentially a test of coherence. A real *perception* will be followed by correct predictions or expectancies of the "if . . . then" kind. It may be that many confirming tests have to be made before the real, or the illusory, nature of the perception can be ascertained, and this in itself is an objection that may be raised against phenomenalism, for since there may be an infinity of such "non-terminating judgments", how can we ever be sure that, if we go on long enough, a disconfirmation will not occur?

In discussing Ayer's verbal thesis it has been pointed out that, on the basis of his accepted criteria of physicality, it follows that there is a commitment to verbal usage that does not allow us to translate freely from one language to another. Indeed many other perceptual views, including naïve realism, not only become unacceptable translations of sense-data language, but are also unacceptable by virtue of a commitment to the criteria of physical objects. One feels drawn to the conclusion that the contention, in Ayer's thesis, that the import is linguistic, is a tenable one, but that nevertheless this is not the whole of the matter. For how, after all, do we arrive at our idea of physical objects in the first place? We may take it that we do so by long-forgotten assumptions, and that this leads us directly towards an empirical attitude.

There are some semantic points, about "sensing", "seeing", "perceiving", etc., which we must now take up. Pap (1949), the American philosopher, says:

> But how is it possible to perceive anything unreal? If it is perceived, must it not be so far real? This paradox, like so many others, vanishes upon analysis. The phrase, "An A is perceived, but this A is unreal", is to be analysed as follows: something is perceived but incorrectly analysed as an A. What is perceived exists, but it is erroneously identified as an instance of the kind A. In other words, we are never mistaken in what we perceive, but in the inferences drawn on the basis of our perceptions.

This paragraph reveals the belief that perception is indubitable. Again, Pap says:

> What makes, then, a perception illusory is an erroneous inference drawn on the basis of a law of association of sense-data that has been verified in the past and is hence expected to hold for all future occasions.

Pap claims that in a case such as a stick half immersed in water, our experience leads to expect that our tactual experience will be of a *straight* stick, just as the sense-data of elliptical coins imply tactual sense-data of circular coins. In a sense, therefore, the illusion does not lie in the perception, but rather in any erroneous inference I might make about the *real* shape of the stick or coin with respect to that perception.

The above suggests that *sensing* and *perception* are being identified as they appear to be in Ayer. Against this, Price takes the process of *sensing* as indubitable, and the process of perceiving as being liable to illusion. From this it follows that wild sense-data are not taken to be a failure of sensation; they are perceptual illusions in that they imply the existence of objects, substances, etc., which do not, in fact, exist. The semantic question, or question of usage, is important since it is true that naïve realism, for example, cannot be shown to be true or false if sensing alone is under consideration. Now if sensing is identified with perception, then it is clearly still true that naïve realism is inviolable; but any translation from sense-data language involves (as we have shown) assumptions of physicality and this, of course, is *not* merely a matter of perception. We are therefore brought back again to the point where it seems important to draw a rough distinction between the process of sensing and the process of perceiving. This point must be analysed much more fully later on, and in more psychological (or cybernetic) terms, for it seems that a great deal of confusion lies at this very place in perceptual theory. But let it be said in the meantime that, roughly speaking, we shall differentiate sensing from perceiving, and say that the problem of illusion is primarily a problem of perception (we reserve the right to question the indubitability of sensing).

Returning once more to the general viewpoint of phenomenalism, the extreme position taken up by Ryle (1948) against the phenomenalists should be noticed. He regards the position held by them as palpably false, basing his criticism essentially on the confusion of sensation and observation. Ryle puts his finger on the fundamental difficulty of attempts to preserve an indubitable element in sense-datum statements, or protocols as they are sometimes called. Simply because they are sense-statements they cannot be sensibly described as true or false, and in the same way as they cannot be true or false, neither can they be *factual*.

The sense-datum theory which is so closely (although not necessarily) associated with phenomenalism is based on very much the same confusion of sensation and observation. Ryle says some interesting things on this point.

> Two-dimensional colour patches are what I see in the strictest sense of "see"; these are not horses and jockeys but, at best, the looks or visual appearances of horses and jockeys.

The reference is, of course, to the glimpses (sense-data) we have of a horse-race. The advantages of a sense-datum are admitted, but the obvious point is that the use of the term "sense-datum" does not necessarily involve us in the whole of what is now called the sense-datum theory.

If logical considerations seem to require that having a sensation shall not be on all fours with descrying hawks, or gazing at horse-races, so much the worse for those considerations, since having a visual sensation certainly is a non-inferential discerning of a particular sensible object.

The views expressed by Ryle in this matter are essentially in accord with our own.

Now to the general considerations. Phenomenalism is plainly unsupportable as a philosophical thesis in its reduction assumption, which seems to be completely untenable. It is not part of the present intention to give evidence for our belief in the manifest failure of phenomenalism. The biggest problem of its advocates is to show how one may get from a private sense-datum language to a public physical-thing language. They are, in fact, desperately near to the impossible viewpoint of solipsism.

What value, then, may the phenomenalist have? Generally, of course, any opposition has the advantage of sharpening the approach of the thinker who, from lack of it, may get slovenly. In particular, realism has gained enormously from the criticisms of phenomenalism. Ayer's analysis, especially, has had a very valuable influence on the semantic aspects of our perceptual theories; for although we believe that Ayer's view, that the problem of different perceptual views is entirely verbal, is false, it is near enough to the truth to be of the utmost value. It seems perfectly possible to preserve the notion of a *sense-datum*, provided that these are regarded as analytical tools and no more, for while they are not indispensable, they appear at this stage to be a convenient way of talking about perception. The question of tactics in philosophy, and the contrary dogmas that assert a particular point of view and deny all others, have obscured the fact that many problems can be reconstructed in a variety of different ways; it would therefore be unwise to deny certain merits to phenomenalism, which may yet be able to defeat its critics. But as we have said of naïve realism, our view is that phenomenalism, in all the forms known to the writer, still labours under considerable difficulties which seem, on the whole, to be best avoided (or handled) by a form of critical realism.

It might be wondered, at this stage, what the effect of philosophical thought has been on the psychology of cognition. There seems to be nothing that can be *directly* said about philosophical help, except that philosophy has tried to suggest information as to the appropriateness of one model rather than another. It is really more to the molar levels of psychology that our philosophical discussion is useful, that is to say, in the determination of *ultimate* choice of models. In fact many people – such as Charles Morris – who are interested in behavioural semiotic and pragmatics, claim that our models should be capable of explaining those same philosophical differences which we have just been discussing; and this is an aim which we should always bear in mind.

Critical Realism

The meaning that is intended here by the term "critical realism" is perhaps a little different from many usages. The viewpoint is roughly in keeping with what the American philosopher Charles Peirce meant by *realism*.

The issues that the critical realists (at least as the writer sees it) wish to carry are: (1) the denial of the narrowness and unnecessary obscurity of extreme phenomenalism; (2) the belief that a *sufficiently critical* phenomenalism is indistinguishable from a sufficiently critical realism; (3) that naïve realism, while stated over-simply, is essentially correct, at least as part of a wider framework of scientific questions; and (4) that "theoretical terms" and the use of hypotheses about the empirical world justifiably imply the use of a *real-world* assumption.

Reichenbach (1938) has presented one type of the realism we would support. He takes observed physical things as the basis of knowledge, instead of sense-data, and, although the problem of illusion still looms as a difficulty, he would want to say that sentences in a natural language, of the form, "that is a table", are reducible only to the level of sentences about observed physical things. Observation sentences are the basis of his argument but, just as for the phenomenalists, some of the same reductionist difficulties occur. Here we are hovering near the well-known difficulties involved in dealing with unobserved objects; and we are also, at this stage, on the fringe of *the problem of induction*, and its justification.

Another slightly different rendering of a critical realism can be made by virtue of the assertion of the independent existence of the things (referents) to which theoretical terms refer. Lenzen (quoted by Feigl, 1950) says:

> In general the dualistic (realistic) theory may be viewed as a scientific hypothesis which explains and predicts perceptions. Contemporary physical theory is characterized by the dominant role played by con-

structive hypotheses. Assuming for the moment that everyday things are directly given in perception, knowledge of the entities of atomic physics consists in the acceptance of hypotheses from which it is possible to deduce consequences that can be tested by experiment. The energy levels of the atoms are objects of hypotheses from which one can predict the positions of spectral lines on a photographic plate. . . . In all these examples there is no direct perception of the entities considered; confirmation of the hypotheses consists in the explanation of past phenomena and the prediction of future phenomena. . . .

This view, similar to Reichenbach's, and that of the probabilistic realists, is not committed to justification by means of inductive probability, but shares the other's belief in existential hypotheses.

In the view of realism adopted by Peirce (1931-5), the indubitable elements in knowledge (which was part of Cartesianism) are rejected, and he insists on the fallibility of all our beliefs. Belief is a basic term which characterizes a *disposition to respond*. He argues that we know *when* we are believing because of our readiness to *act* on what we believe.

From his other epistemological views we see that Peirce would not deny that every man's thoughts are private to him, but he would deny that the immediacy and privacy of a man's thoughts in any way serve to account for his knowledge of them. Indeed, immediacy and privacy cannot be taken as a criterion of *all* general knowledge, and in this Peirce follows up a view which is in the spirit of modern science, and is near to *common sense*. Indeed he frequently says that there is only one genuine or trustworthy method of enquiry, and that is the method of science. Science for him is a public method of systematic enquiry which produces discoverable answers to all genuine questions, and to which all rationalist observers would, ultimately, subscribe. This, of course, is reminiscent of Peirce's pragmatic theory of truth.

For Peirce (1931-5) the conception of inference is the essential function of the cognitive mind and he sees, and in his broad notion of inference he includes, an hypothesis as a piece of inferential reasoning. The perceptual for him is essentially analogous to the other thought processes, such as the inquisitive, scientific, etc.; they mutually support each other in interplay with the various inferences we make. Perceptual judgments are inferential judgments, only they are unconscious and therefore uncontrollable and, as Peirce says, "not subject to logical criticism". If we recognize the colour or shape of any object that we see (sense), it is through the process of hypothesis and inference. All such perceptual judgments which we are unable to doubt at the time they are made, involve necessary consequences. Peirce gives this example:

> If one judges that an event C appears to be later than an event A, one is thereby committed to maintaining, as a necessary consequence, that any other event standing in this relation of "apparent subsequence" to C must stand in the same relation to A also. But one would be *justified* in making this inference only on the supposition that the perceived event "C subsequent to A" embodies all the necessary or defining properties of the relation of apparent subsequence; and to suggest that one actually sees this in making a particular perceptual judgment is surely quite absurd.

This absurdity is explained by Peirce by the assumption that we habitually draw such inferences, and that the process is unconscious and uncontrollable; he gets out of the subsequent difficulty of explaining how habits of inference find occasion for exercise other than by virtue of non-inferential perceptual judgments, by appeal to *unconscious inference*.

Peirce concludes that our perceptual judgments in general are adequate, but that any individual one may be in error.

This brand of realism is of a kind similar to that of many other scientists, and amounts to a statement that there is no reason to doubt the existence of the (external) real world; it is much as it appears to be, and the common beliefs to which enquiry leads are the truth about this real world. Peirce's views are essentially those that we wish to foster in experimental psychology.

In the writer's view, the philosophic directives to be accepted in the construction of any scientific theory are those of realism, at any rate for as long as realism can be maintained. Matters of ontological and epistemological significance are generally only of interest to philosophers, although occasionally it appears that such questions confront the scientist (e.g. Quantum Mechanics, and many other problems in modern physics and in experimental psychology). An awareness of the philosopher's problems seems to be necessary to the modern scientist for, at the very least, philosophical analysis may clarify the problems of science; at times it can give valuable directives, and in perception it has, if no more, the power to tell us whether or not theories are logically tenable.

Philosophically, although it does not appear possible to start with a directive about the nature of reality when it is the nature of reality that we are trying to investigate, yet in fact ontological assumptions are at the basis of most philosophical theories, and do act as directives – a fact which gives philosophy some common ground with science, in practice. Nevertheless the differences which tend to earmark the philosophical problem, in contradistinction to the scientific problem, remain generally unreconciled. The rule that should be observed here, in the writer's opinion, is that of keeping as near as possible to common sense. This elliptical statement really implies the sort of simplicity with which Occam's Razor is informed, but it leaves us with the problem of deciding what the nature of common sense is.

It may be argued that the *common sense* view of perception is naïve realism, and indeed, if we can state, in language, an acceptable (internally consistent) view of the world in such terms, our problems are solved. Certainly the common sense view of the world is realistic, with no doubt of the existence of material objects. The fact that I can touch, taste and, in general, sense material objects (as can other people) is essential to what is meant by a "real world". The difficulty for philosophy seems to be to find a language to express this view. A. J. Ayer and others have suggested that this is the only difficulty, and that diverging views of perception are relative to language; but surely, unlike problems in the philosophy of science, where the philosopher's job is the analysis of scientific language, here the problem is to construct a language with respect to non-verbal acts in which, inevitably, assumptions (not necessarily verbalized) about the nature of reality will also be a variable into which error may creep. Furthermore, we believe that facts are relative to language, in such a way that we cannot reorganize our language without a consideration of the facts that language describes. These are the bases for the belief that the *purely* verbal theory of the problem of perception is incorrect.

Let us now glance at some historical aspects of our problem. Philosophical empiricism first separated *sensation* from perception, and sensation became, for people such as Wundt, the subject of empirical investigation; later, Külpe and Titchener began to decompose *sensation* into dimensions of consciousness. For Locke, Berkeley and Hume, psychology was still a part of philosophy, and we have, then, the important question as to why psychology broke away from philosophy. The answer is seen to be that some aspects of perception are open to experimental investigation and, when these are abstracted, what remains is, in essence, the philosophical problem. This is supported by Price's (1933) insistent claim that empirical investigations cannot help the philosophical problem, because such investigations themselves depend upon it. Perhaps the answer to this is that the restriction is perfectly justified by the way the problem is stated or (at the least) intended; the idea being, in part, that we cannot investigate empirically until we know what is being investigated, and if the problem is merely to clarify what is being investigated, then to talk of experiment does not make sense. One answer to this, for science in general, is that the role of experiment is bound up with linguistic clarification in so far as the application, or construction, of languages is relative to non-linguistic data. More knowledge of the data to be described is surely some aid to the construction of the necessary language. This matter has been put, perforce, altogether too briefly, but it is the foundation of one aspect of the need for a pragmatic reconstruction.

The above point leads us to suppose that the statement of a philosophic problem often has the effect of excluding that aspect of the problem which might help in a solution. It may be admitted that empirical science (especially psychology) cannot, in and of itself, solve a philosophical problem, but it *can clarify* it and prepare the way for its solution.

Our interest in philosophy ends here, and psychology, as a representative of science, now takes over, although in fact we return to discuss some of these problems again in the chapter on language. Our earnest hope is that psychologists will remember that their work emanates from these philosophical beginnings, for our belief is that science can now do the job of finding a science of cognition without losing contact with what is, after all, an aspect of common sense.

Chapter 8

PSYCHOLOGICAL THEORY OF PERCEPTION

The previous chapters have summarized some of the principal variables of what has been called "learning", and while there seems to be a great deal to be said for breaking down our analysis, description and explanation of behaviour into such terms as "learning" and "perception", we shall do well constantly to bear in mind that these divisions are to a great extent arbitrary; indeed, even the most precise definition of either term yet attempted involves a good deal of vagueness.

We shall assume in this chapter that the reader is fairly familiar in a general way with what occurs between the covers of books on *perception*, and we shall not attempt anything approaching a careful analysis of the term until later in the book. In the meantime we can go so far as to say that "to perceive" is something more than "to sense" and something less than "to know", and is concerned with the way we get information about the world around us.

Some General Considerations in Perception

Several suitable texts have been published for the reader who wishes for a detailed description of the history, and of the varied aspects, of the problem of perception as it has been dealt with in psychology (Boring, 1942, Gibson, 1950, Vernon, 1954). Here, space allows only a selection of what seem to have been some of the most important questions.

A theory (or theory-language) of *perception* (coupled with *learning*, and making up the bulk of *cognition*) will be proposed, at least in outline, in Chapter 12. The present chapter will discuss general items of perception already fairly well documented and, to some extent, understood.

Some further reference is necessary at this point to the mind-body problem. Briefly, the writer believes that this problem has arisen largely from the denial, by many philosophers, of the relevance of empirical science to philosophical problems, for it involves the quandary as to what terms are to be used for philosophical explanations. However, the question is not – or should not be – a problem for psychology, and we shall leave it at that, except to say that it seems clear that psychological data is directly dependent on physiological states as well as on environmental stimuli, logic and language notwithstanding. The plain fact is that psychology has been able to proceed by making these assumptions, for the way the mind-body problem enters psychology is in correlating introspective evidence with neurological, general physiological, and externally obtained evidence. We have no intention here of entering further into the logical difficulties over behaviourism; the big problem of modern psychology is to find large-scale relations between psychology and physiology.

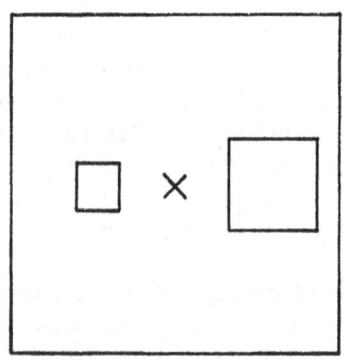

FIG. 14. FIGURAL AFTER-EFFECT – THE INSPECTION FIGURE

This is the inspection figure which is fixated, at x, by the subject for a period of about two minutes prior to fixating, Fig. 15, below.

The above point leads directly, in perception, to the physiological job of reinterpreting the evidence collected within psychology in physiological terms. Current evidence is against the view proposed by Lashley (1929, 1950), who said that *perception* cannot be represented by any sort of *specific* neurological processes. There is no reason to believe that specific behavioural acts are not directly correlated with specific neurological states. Neither is there any evidence to support a field theory of the type suggested by the Gestalt school of psychologists.

Let us consider some specific problems of visual perception. The figural after-effect, which has been of special interest in this respect, is illustrated in Figures 14 and 15. Figure 14 is presented to the subject, and he carefully keeps his eyes fixated on the fixation point, indicated by X, for about two minutes. If he then transfers his fixation to the cross in Figure 15, he will tend to see the circles as unequal in size. The circles are actually of equal dimensions, but the effect of the first figure is somehow to disturb the perception of the second.

The use of the *optic chiasma* has been a standard method of distinguishing *central* from *peripheral* phenomena. The optic chiasma is the point behind the eyes where one half of the fibres of the optic nerve from either eye cross over to the other side of the brain, so that each of the two parts of the visual cortex at the back of the head contain information from each eye. If a red light is shone for a few minutes into the left eye of a subject and then, for the same eye, a white card is substituted for the light, the card will appear to be green. The subject is then asked to look at the card with his right eye only. If the card still appears to be green, the effect must occur somewhere behind the optic chiasma. If not, as is in fact the case, the effect is presumably occurring in the retina. This particular effect is one of a series of after-images.

In this case, then, since no cross-over effect is discovered, the colour after-image is retinal; but the figural after-effect, in the previous experiment, is central. If Figure 14 is presented to the left eye and Figure 15 to the right eye, the distortion still occurs.

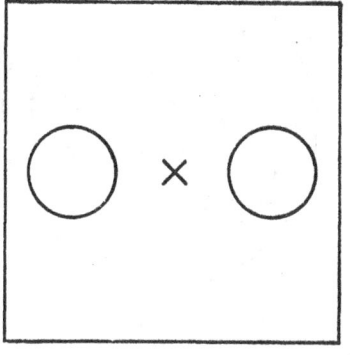

FIG. 15. FIGURAL AFTER-EFFECT – THE TEST FIGURE
After the inspection period the subject immediately transfers his eyes to the point x and fixates steadily. He should then get the after-effect. This is called the test figure.

Most after-effects of the after-image kind can be shown to be primarily peripheral and thus primarily a function of physiological effects in the retina, or eye-ball, itself. The central effects, such as the figural after-effect, and the closely related Plateau spiral effect, are interesting since they involve the "higher interpretive" levels of the central nervous system.

The Plateau spiral is shown in Figure 16. When rotated, it appears to unwind towards you, or to wind away from you, according to the direction of rotation. If you fixate the centre of the spiral as the figure is rotated, and continue to fixate it when the rotation stops, an apparent motion in the opposite direction occurs. Readers will have noticed many other such movement after-effects when, for example, looking from the window of a moving train. When the train stops there is a sense of motion in the opposite direction.

The lateral geniculate body, which is another pathway on the way to the brain, is one anatomical location which still holds some "unknowns", but generally these so-called "central" phenomena are thought to be cortical. In the closely associated problems of perception of movement, *apparent* movement (as in the cinema), and *real* movement (as in life), are very near to each other. The pendulum effect, also, is closely related to apparent movement.

The pendulum effect is shown by an apparatus which demonstrates ordinary apparent movement. Two light sources are presented, in a darkened room, a few inches apart, and a foot or two from the eye, and the lights are switched on alternately. The impression received is of a single light moving to and fro from left to right and back. In one of the many variations on this experiment the pendulum effect is intensified by accompanying the alternating of the light flashes with clicks. Under these circumstances observers claim that the apparent movement is curved, as though a single light source was fixed to a pendulum.

FIG. 16. THE PLATEAU SPIRAL

If this figure is rotated about its centre point, it appears to unfold away from, or towards, the observer according to the direction of rotation. If the subject continues to fixate the centre of the spiral when it is suddenly stopped, an apparent motion occurs in the opposite direction to the original movement.

It has been found that intermittent illumination of the static spiral of Figure 16 gave "apparent rotation"; it also gave after-effects similar to that associated with an actual rotation. There is, of course, no difficulty in accepting the idea that our eyes, and our senses generally, can record certain external events, and cannot, if certain clues are suppressed, distinguish different cases that depend solely on having those certain clues. It is clear, therefore, that "apparent"

Psychological Theory of Perception

and "real" movement are visually the same, and can only be distinguished by means of inferences from contextual clues. This leaves open the question of central after-effects, but it is believed that the explanation of the effects depends upon the cortex. It is surely in the *central interpretations* of the cortex that we see the function of experience in the form of beliefs and expectancies.

One of the problems throughout this sort of perceptual work is to deal with different levels of explanation, while being aware that the process is a function of the organism-as-a-whole. It does not seem wholly reasonable to talk of uninterpreted recordings in the visual system alone, and then of their interpretations in various cortical areas, e.g. area 17 alone (the visual cortex area); the occipital areas alone; the cortex-as-a-whole. However, we can in some respects reconstruct a set of theories with these crude distinctions in mind.

There are many experimental problems of perception yet to be understood, and this is surely one fruitful field for amalgamated work by perception-psychologists, sensory-physiologists and neurophysiologists. We shall make no attempt in this book to summarize the very considerable (but still very inadequate) evidence that has been collected by neurophysiologists and other biologists with respect to perception, but we shall search, primarily, for psychological, or molar, models, although in Chapter 13 we shall discuss some part of the physiological model making.

From the molecular approach to *perception* we turn now to another useful path, which is through so-called molar experiment and theory alone. Three or four recent outstanding contributions in this field come immediately to mind.

Professor Boring has stated a view that regards perception as being related to the constructed space of science on the one hand, and the subjective space of the observer on the other. Boring is interested in the invariance, or unchanging factors, among the variables, or changing ones.

Some of the principal results of these molar experiments can be profitably mentioned. Perceived size of an object is constant with change of distance with free binocular vision, provided that sufficient of the normal cues are present. If these normal cues are inadequate, then perceptual size depends more and more on the retinal size of the object, and less and less on "object-size". This sort of relationship, which has been brought out by work on what has been called "constancy", poses no serious problem, since it is the way one would expect an "inference-making" organism to respond under such circumstances.

The effects of constancy can be illustrated in the case of colour by the fact that we say that we see, or believe, a shirt is white, even though it is in the shadow of a tree and has, at the moment, a grey appearance. Indeed, no one looking at the shirt through a reduction screen (which is simply a tube) would call the shirt "white". A similar constancy can also be observed with respect to size and shape. Reduction-screens are simply a means of reducing some or all the *cues* to the holding of a correct *belief* with respect to some object, or more generally, some stimulus state.

Perception poses a semantic problem as well as an experimental one, as is shown when we say that a six-foot pole close at hand and a similar one a hundred yards away are such that, "the far-away pole looks just as big although it looks smaller". This is no paradox; it simply reflects the ambiguity of the word "looks". We may either, "look in the sense of by literal-retinal-equation", or "look in the sense of believe". This matter will be treated semantically in Chapter 12.

One other well-known problem is that of the relation of size and distance when celestial distances are involved. Up to some limits, the relation between size and distance is approximately linear, but over a sufficient range it would seem to have a much more general relation where phenomenal size falls off much less quickly with distance. If asked why this is so, we can only confess ignorance; but there is some datum-line (the bow-and-arrow, or the box-dropping level) for all investigations, and perhaps the empirical relation, if it were known, would prove sufficient. The question of constancy has given the moon a special interest; writers have used data on it "for" and "against" both empiricism and nativism as interpretations of perceptual effects (Chapter 9 discusses the Gestalt nativistic theory, and Chapter 10 the Transactionalist empiricist theory). There is also the interesting relation between the degree of size-constancy and the angle of viewing, which is illustrated by the well-known case of the "horizontal moon", the moon when near the horizon appearing much larger than the moon at the zenith. One suggestion is that this depends on the elevation of the eyes in the head; but it could be a function of non-euclidean dimensions of *perceived* space, or it might be a function of *experience*, either in the central or non-central sense, or it might be a function of all these factors together.

Psychological Theory of Perception

A vast number of experiments on the constancies, in addition to their own intrinsic interest, seem to the writer to support the empiricist view of *perception*, and inversely, they themselves should be explained in terms of *experience*. This is, of course, not a denial of their immediate and essential dependence on the visual system, but it does seem unlikely that the visual system works in any sense independently of the inferential (cortical) processes; the general evidence is surely against such a nativist view.

To return to the question of size-perception – for it is a topic well adapted to illustrate the scientific problem of perception – it has been suggested by some psychologists that *objects* are primary and *sensations* secondary. A dualism of this kind has its own problem, in that the question of the primacy of the object or of the sensation is one to which it is difficult to ascribe any significance; it is a matter of words and not of empirical fact. What is perhaps noteworthy in this view is that it allows *attitudes* to play a part in the perceptual process; a fact which is now fairly established.

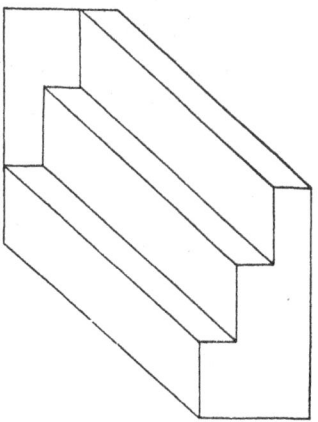

FIG. 17. THE SCHRÖDER STAIRCASE

An example of an ambiguous figure that can be seen as stairs as viewed either from above or below.

One of the dangers we have to face in the piecemeal reconstruction of perception is the fact that these various problems of size-perception, apparent movement, and so on, are not sufficiently independent. There can be little doubt, for example, that *motivation* modifies perception, perhaps by change of thresholds in nervous tissue, and the danger is that we seek part explanations for certain phenomena that are only explicable when the organism is treated as-a-whole.

It would be easy to multiply many times over the number of perceptual effects we have just studied, but since a list of these effects can be found in any standard textbook on the subject, just two more problems will be mentioned here.

The first is the problem of ambiguous figures, or "illusions", as they are sometimes rather misleadingly called. Figure 17 shows what is known as the Schröder staircase. This picture of stairs can obviously be regarded as being looked at either from above or from below. Figure 18 shows the Neckar cube, which also has the effect of being seen either from above or below. In each of these cases there is the problem of why it is that the figure can be seen in two different ways and, furthermore, can only be seen in one of those ways at any one time.

Some part of the theory that answers these problems has already been suggested, and more will be said later about these ambiguous figures; but from the point of view of the Nativists they represent a serious problem which involves, perhaps, the point of fixation of the eye at the moment the figure is first looked at. For the empiricist they are also a problem, but the manner in which you are likely to see them will certainly be a function of the way you have seen such figures in the past.

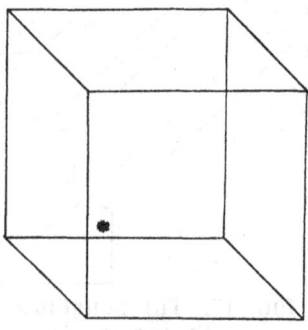

FIG. 18. THE NECKAR CUBE
Another ambiguous figure that can be seen as a hollow cube, viewed either from above or below.

What we can be fairly sure about at this stage is that the interpretation is an essential feature of the perceptual act, and operates in something like the manner described in the case of the Pendulum effect.

The last problem is rather more general, and is connected with what have been called the psycho-physical methods. This collection of methods has been used by experimental psychologists for many years, and can be characterized by such techniques as paired comparisons, the limiting method, and the method of just perceptible differences.

These are all straightforward, common sense ways of describing the relation that is presumed to exist between the objectively defined stimulus and the sensation that it gives rise to in the individual. The problem here for behaviourists is that we are assuming that one is some sort of measure of the other, which brings us into apparent conflict with such facts of behaviour as selection of stimulus and *set*. "Set" means that, from all possible stimuli in the environment, we tend to select, and often to expect, certain ones to occur. This purposive aspect of human behaviour has often been used as an argument against behaviourism, but is now thought to be evidence in favour of the fact that human beings are not merely passive victims of their environment, but active participators in it. Such a view has influenced the Transactionalists in perception, and the followers of Tolman in learning, without in any way impairing the essentially behaviouristic attitude adopted.

O'Neil (1958) has tried to categorize the various points of view in perception in the following way. Discrimination theories, which include that view that talks in terms of primary perceptions or sensations and secondary perceptions or interpretations and this is perhaps represented best by Osgood and Skinner among modern theorists in the field of perception. The second group is called Phenomenalists and includes the Gestalt theorists (see next chapter), Gibson and Michotte, and finally the Judgmental Theorists who include Brunswik and Bruner.

The first view is obvious enough and is essentially the one proposed in this book. The second is concerned with the appearances of things and one that has already been mentioned in philosophical terms, and the third is a view that directly relates perception to thinking.

Drever (1960) adds a fourth category which he calls Adaptation theories which includes the work of Helsen and Kohler, and the view taken up in this book is that this is a typical example of different interpretations of the small perceptual facts all contributing something towards the general understanding of what the process entails. They are not mutually exclusive theories and all can operate at different levels of the perceptual process.

O'Neil's categories are mentioned because they do draw attention to interesting distinctions within the field of perception which thrive on precisely the sort of semantic confusion that is discussed later in Chapter 12.

Before concluding this general consideration of perception it should be made clear that there are other problems, such as that of colour vision, night vision, and dark adaptation, that need to be accounted for to complete our picture of the relation between the well-established facts of physiology, and the psychological data about seeing colours.

There is clearly no hard and fast division between physiology and psychology, but rather a difference of emphasis that characterizes two groups of scientists; one working towards the problems of behaviour from what might be called a synthetic point of view, and the other from an analytic viewpoint; two groups building a bridge from opposite sides of the river, and hoping to meet somewhere in the centre.

The problem is essentially one of how human beings interpret their input, and to what extent is there an interaction between input and the information already in store. All this is bound up with the way we recognize shapes and forms, and we shall be discussing it in some detail.

Chapter 9

GESTALT THEORY

With the growth of behaviourism there was an inevitable contrary movement which opposed the cruder materialism of Watson's and Thorndike's views. In some respects this was represented by introspectionists and others whose objection was vocal and vehement. But a more moderate, though no less emphatic, opposition was offered by the group of psychologists who have become known as the Gestalt school of psychology. Those described by O'Neil (1958) as Phenomenalists and by Drever (1960) as Adaptation theorists.

The initial opposition of the Gestalt school to behaviourism was with respect to the idea, suggested strongly by Thorndike, that learning was a trial-and-error procedure. They believed it to involve what they called "insight". They emphasized the perceptual aspects of learning, labouring the point that much of the learning or problem solving of the higher organisms showed a set of responses that was by no means random, and was very much dependent upon the manner in which they perceived their environment.

Gestalt theorists further emphasized that we perceive our environment not as made up of individual bits and pieces, but as-a-whole; we perceive patterns, the parts of which are meaningless in themselves. Their emphasis was on the meaning that situations had for active, purposive organisms.

Regarded from an historical viewpoint, it seems that the Gestalt school had a far-reaching and liberalizing effect on the development of experimental psychology in the field of cognition. It seems all the more strange that their positive contribution to psychological thought retains so little current potency; for this is only partly explained by the fact that the best of their ideas have been integrated into the current theories of cognition.

Apart from various summaries, Kurt Koffka's *Growth of the mind* (1924), Wolfgang Köhler's *Mentality of Apes*, and very much later, Max Wertheimer's book *Productive Thinking* (1945), remain the only lasting contributions of the Gestalt school, and these are read less with each succeeding year.

Nevertheless, the work of Köhler (1925), carried out on apes on the island of Teneriffe during World War I, has become a classic, and his results are as important to modern experimental psychology as if they had been performed by a behaviourist.

Köhler's principal results were in the field of problem solving, especially in the problems of stacking boxes, and using sticks, to reach food that was otherwise out of reach.

The box-stacking problem required that one box be placed upon another in order to reach food that was out of reach if one box alone was used. The apes found this problem difficult to solve, and Köhler admitted that some of their attempts were of a trial-and-error kind; however, he also believed that the idea of understanding that one box needed to be on top of the other was something they achieved by having insight into the physical relations that were needed to solve their problem.

The better known problem, which we have already noticed in a previous chapter, and which involved the famous ape Sultan, required that two sticks be joined together to form a longer stick in order to reach a banana that was previously out of reach. The apes succeeded in solving this, but only after a long time, and after some of the apes had had an opportunity to observe how the solution was performed; again the point about insight was brought out. It is a fact, of course, that human beings regularly exhibit this sort of behaviour, which we call "insightful".

The point that learning and problem solving may involve some operation of insight is now widely accepted among experimental psychologists; what is less clear is the nature and detail of insight.

In attempts to explain insightful behaviour and, especially, to put forward a clear picture of perception – which was thought to be vital to insight – Köhler and Koffka and others carried out a comprehensive series of experiments. Some of these will shortly be described, since they represent an alternative approach, through perception, to the problem of learning. The reader should note that, while he may disagree with behaviourism, especially the narrower kind, and even agree with criticisms by the Gestalt school, it does not on that account follow that he will agree with the alternative theories suggested by them.

The Gestalt View of Perception

One view propounded was that the perceptual field emerged in stages. First, the bare recognition of the fact that there was something in the environment to be aware of; then the awareness of shape and form, which later divided into two classes, that of the figure and that of the ground. This figure-ground hypothesis has been elaborated upon by many writers, and the following conditions have been suggested by Wever (1927).

1. There must exist a degree of heterogeneity between the figure and the ground, each of which tends to form a whole of its own.
2. There exists a minimum brightness difference between the figure and the ground, which gradually leads, with 1, to the emergence of the figure.
3. When stage 2 reaches a certain level, there emerges a clear region of separation between the figure and the ground which becomes the contour line around the figure.
4. The shape or form of the figure emerges before the contour is completely defined.
5. Protusion of the figure out and away from the ground may also appear.
6. The figure may be localized fairly specifically in depth.
7. There is a tendency to refer to the ground as having a "surface texture", and the figure as having a "filmy texture".
8. There may exist a halo effect around the figure, which is dependent upon the contour line separating the two.

The halo effect may be emphasized by what is called simultaneous contrast; this merely means that white is emphasized on a black ground, and vice versa. More generally, contrast effect is concerned with the relational effects of emphasis between colours and shades. This last point is a matter of great importance to the artist.

Some important experiments by Werner (1935, 1940) should also be mentioned. Werner used two figures, one a black disc and the other a black ring on a white background. It was found that if the disc was presented to the observer, and followed sufficiently quickly by the ring, then the disc was never given form at all. It was thought by Werner that this was due to the fact that no contour was formed with respect to the disc, and when the ring appeared it immediately took over the contour line of the disc.

This particular experiment – and there are others that bear on the same point which are mentioned later in this chapter – brings out the fact that shape and form perception is closely bound up with contour formation, which is itself a particular stage in the differentiation between figure and ground. We shall develop this subject from a cybernetic point of view, at which stage we may come to doubt the importance, not of the facts of figure and ground and contour formation, but of the Gestalt interpretation placed on these facts.

Experiments have been carried out by Rubin (1921) and many others to show that the figure-ground division of our perceptual environment is a reality.

Rubin himself prepared a number of figures by cutting cards into two pieces by means of an irregular line. Then he projected a half of the card on to a screen so that one area looked green and the other black.

With many repetitions of each figure he first instructed the subjects to see the green part as figure and then repeated the operation instructing the subjects to see the black part as figure.

Finally the set of nine cards used in the first experiment were shuffled up with nine new ones and the subjects told to take a "passive" view of the figure-ground relationship. This though entailed reporting which appeared as figure and which as ground.

The results showed that there was a tendency – it cannot be stated more strongly – for a form once to be seen as a figure to be seen again as a figure.

Some of the work on contour formation, which will be discussed again later in Chapter 13, is of relevance to Gestalt theorizing.

Galli and Hocheimer (1934) showed, as indeed Rubin also showed, that when two parts of a field are separated by a contour, the parts may appear very different in shape. And this is true even though they have exactly the same contour.

Galli and Hocheimer cut rectangular cards in two with an irregular line. These two pieces which were black were mounted on a white card with a gap in between the cards. Figure 19 illustrates some typical samples.

The total figure was now presented to the subject tachistoscopically and the subject was asked to reproduce the contours with pencil and paper. It was abundantly clear that for every subject the contour shape "perceived" varied according to whether it was the left-hand or the right-hand contour that was "perceived".

Schumann (1904) also demonstrated the presence of "subjective" contours, by taking a figure made up of concentric black and white rings and cutting it into two semi-circles and then placing it so that a square area of white separated them. This had the effect of creating an impression of contour lines enclosing each semi-circular figure. Figure 20 demonstrates the point.

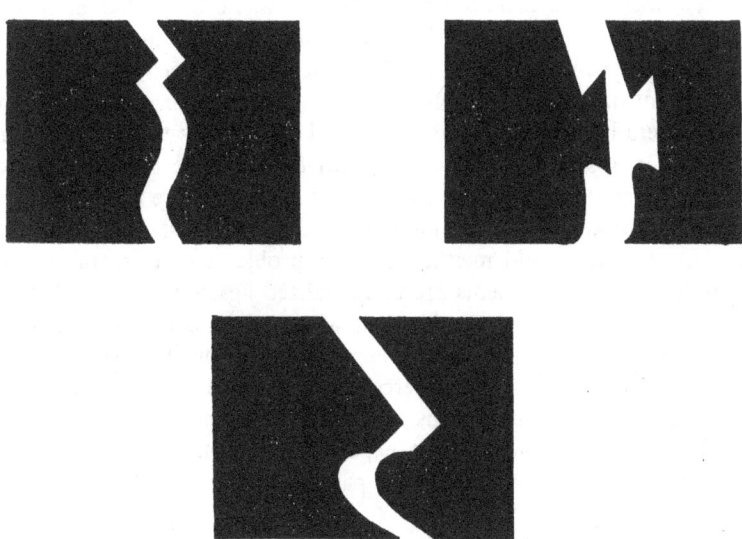

FIG. 19. GALLI-HOCHEIMER FIGURES

Some of the pieces of black cardboard were cut by Galli-Hocheimer with a double contour. The figures were presented tachistoscopically and the subject was asked to reproduce them with a pencil.

FIG. 20. A SCHUMANN FIGURE

This figure shows a 'subjective' contour so that in the gap between the two parts of the roundels, a broad white stripe appears.

Another set of experiments, or demonstrations, which came in for review by the Gestalt school, was that of the so-called Schroder staircase and Neckar cube mentioned in the last chapter. The Gestalt view was that *apartness* or *togetherness* was exaggerated in seeing the figure as-a-whole, and for example in the case of the Muller-Lyer illusion, where two equal lines appear unequal because they have different size appendages on their ends, the effect is brought about by the overall difference in size which makes the lines themselves seem of different size. An obvious alternative is that the two lines could be seen as being in three dimensional space, and are therefore subject to the combined considerations of size and distance.

Lastly one should mention various problems that are presented by figures. The problems are like idealized jigsaw puzzles and their solution seemed to depend on the actual given configurations and are solved, not on the basis of experience, but on the insight which amounts to a "seeing" or "perceiving" of the given properties.

Again it is difficult in this last example to understand how such insight could occur without experience, although the experience could be generalized rather than particular to the figures concerned in the experiment.

Before proceeding to give further experimental evidence which bears on other Gestalt views, let us consider the general principles of perceptual organization which were thought by them to operate.

The Law of Pragnanz is a central concept for Gestalt theory. This law suggests that perceptual events have a certain direction, and that they always move towards a state of goodness, a goodness that is dependent upon the circumstances in which perception is taking place. The goodness – a vague concept in some respects – is characterized by such properties as regularity, simplicity, and stability.

If, for example, we see a shape that is almost circular but not quite, we remember it as a circle. If we see a shape that is complex in design, we simplify it, and its form becomes more symmetrical in our memory. There are criticisms of this concept, particularly of the way in which it is said to operate in memory, but we shall leave this until after the elaboration of the other general rules of perception, sometimes called Wertheimer's generalizations.

The first rule concerns similarity; it is one that is necessarily included in any attempt to explain human or organismic behaviour. Here it is used to explain the way we perceive elements in space;

elements would appear to fall into groups according to the degree of similarity they have to each other.

The notion of similarity is, of course, difficult to define, but it obviously includes such cases as the classifying together of a set of objects of the same colour and the same shape, and so on. There is no doubt that this is fundamental to the working of the special senses.

The second rule is the rule of proximity. This is closely allied to similarity, in that it refers primarily to the fact that elements near each other are inclined to be classified with each other. It is in these terms that we talk of clusters of objects, and distinguish one cluster from another. This law is closely related to recent work on perception by Michotte (1946) in Belgium which points out, with experimental evidence, that our concept of causality springs from the manner in which we perceive our environment. Things that occur at the same or immediately adjacent points in space are said to be causally related, especially where they behave in a manner that is consistent with our idea of the way in which they should behave.

The third rule is the rule of closure. Closed areas, it is argued, have a greater degree of "stability" than open areas; they are more easily perceived and more easily remembered. This particular rule is less obvious than the first two, and more open to criticism, for in fact many unclosed areas are clearly remembered, and indeed it may be the very property of being non-closed that makes them easy to remember.

The rule of good continuation states that it is expected that there will be stability in shapes in the environment, so that a straight line will remain straight, a circle remain circular, and so on. This, like some of the earlier rules, can be applied directly to learning; it is simply placing emphasis on the homogeneity of the environment. Our learning is more effective and more lasting when the environment changes only slowly, or not at all.

Another rule, that the elements have a "common fate", is another way of saying that there will be a similarity, not necessarily in the elements themselves, but in their behaviour; for example, all the elements moving to the right are grouped, all those moving to the left are grouped, and so on. This could be regarded as yet another illustration of the fact of sensory classification of the environment.

It should be said that most of the rules are assumed to apply to the learning situation, where the organization of the perceptual field was seen to be important. In the Köhler experiments, for example, they apply in deciding the method of solution, and whether or not a solution was arrived at.

Closure operates in a manner to bring stability to the organism with the completion of tasks. Zeigarnik (1927) carried out some experiments in which tasks were allocated to subjects, but the subjects were not allowed to complete them. The tasks were of interest to the subjects, and when they were taken away, uncompleted, they became a source of irritation, for the subjects would continue to think about them, and showed symptoms of "frustration".

The next rule deals with "set". This simply means that a human being can actually overcome to some degree the requirements of the rules of proximity and similarity by the strength of his anticipation of a specific configuration. The strength of what is expected by virtue of the context in which these events occur is thus a perceptual influence.

The role of past experience was not wholly denied by Gestalt psychologists, but it was played down to a minimum because they felt that perceptual explanations should be accounted for, as far as possible, in terms of the characteristics of the perceptual equipment itself.

The work of Gottschaldt (1926, 1929) is relevant to the matter of experience. He showed that the occurrence of a familiar pattern some hundreds of times did not increase the probability of recognizing that pattern when it occurred within a more complex pattern. For example, showing a triangle many times will not increase the probability of its recognition when it is a part of a complex geometrical figure. On the other hand, experiments have shown that the familiarity of a pattern, say, a piece of a jigsaw puzzle, will increase the probability of its being recognized as part of a pattern.

The Gestalt theorists applied the same rules to memory as they applied to perception. They argued that a figure that was remembered went through a phase of evolution in memory towards the "good figure". This implies that a shape which is not, as it were, balanced between two of their limiting "good" shapes will tend towards one of the limits.

Some of the experiments that have supported this theory have been open to criticism on the grounds of the method used, that of successive reproductions. By this method, an observer is shown a pattern for a few seconds and, after some lapse of time, asked to reproduce it, then to reproduce it again and again, in each case without being able to see the original pattern or his previous attempts. The subsequent simplification and symmetry shown more and more in succeeding reproductions is not, in fact, so much a matter of a tendency towards a good figure, but rather the result of information being lost in the serial process.

Another type of Gestalt experiment which, they claimed, supported their views, is that of the hidden figure. We are familiar, of course, with the shapes of the letters of the alphabet, but when one of them is mixed up in a complex pattern of lines, then we no longer see it as a letter. This sort of example, however, has a particular difficulty for the Gestalt school; it was never explained by them how it was possible, once the individual letter was isolated, to see it clearly as a letter.

The whole problem of creative thinking has been tackled by Gestalt theorists, and they lay constant emphasis on the organizational, the purposive and the creative nature of thought. In so far as their emphasis is on insight we can accept the importance of what they say without in any way relinquishing our grasp of firm behaviourist principles.

The question arises, for the whole of Gestalt theory, as to whether they are offering us anything that is contrary to a behaviourist view, and it is probable that the majority of psychologists would now agree that they are not.

A great deal of neural theorizing has been done by Gestalt psychologists, and though their other views by no means stand or fall with their dynamic or field theory of the nervous system, it is perhaps somewhat weakened by its apparent failure.

Their neurophysiological viewpoints are not stated here mainly because there is now much evidence that their concept of large-scale field effects of an electrical kind going on in the brain seems to have little or no support from empirical evidence.

Chapter 10

EMPIRICISM AND TRANSACTIONALISM

Empiricism is opposed to the Nativism which is supported by the Gestalt theorists. As a particular form of empiricism we will now consider the views of the school called Transactionalists.

Transactionalism is a brand of empiricism with special views on the nature of visual perception, yet having wider philosophical implications. It is a viewpoint that has recently evoked some interest in experimental psychological circles, and it demands careful analysis.

Our plan for a critical analysis of Transactionalism is first to summarize the most important of the so-called Ames demonstrations (Ames, 1955, Kilpatrick, 1952) around which the theory has been constructed, giving, at the same time, a brief résumé of the general inferences that the transactionalists draw from these demonstrations. Then we shall come to the more general theory for science, and analyse this in the light of our earlier analysis.

Since it is impossible in this chapter to review each of the demonstrations carried out in America by Adelbert Ames, Junior, we shall discuss five representative experiments which will be grouped as follows:

1. Introductory experiments involving uniocular vision. Example: The Chair demonstration.
2. Experiments involving the perception of distance. "Objects", "brightness", etc., and "thereness", "thatness", "togetherness", and so on.
3. Irreconcilable clues and assumptive implications.
4. Aniseikonic lenses. (These have the effect of distorting the environment, e.g. by making an ordinary room seem distorted, at any rate to people with normal eyesight.)
5. Perception of motion.

Plate I. The large distorted room showing the same two people having changed over corners.

PLATE II. The small distorted room in which it is impossible for subjects actually to stand up, but in which they can make manipulations, such as striking at mechanical mice with sticks. This is a task which turns out to be extremely deceptive, but with which there is a marked improvement with practice.

Empiricism and Transactionalism

The first demonstration involves the setting up of various empirical shapes made from string, such that the retinal image produced in the observer suggests a chair. The implications of this experiment must now be discussed.

The central implication is that what is in your *visual awareness* does not necessarily correspond to what is in the external world. Thus, what is not in the external world and is in your awareness is given by you. This is a fairly general state of affairs, and typical of all the demonstrations. Transactionalists would add, however, that the similarity of what you are perceptually aware, must be related in turn to the similarities of the stimulus patterns which, in turn, are related to the similarities in light ray bundles to your eyes, and retinal images in your eyes. In other words, we bring to the situation much that is our own, and what is "out there" only partly determines our perception.

In the second group of experiments we have certain phenomena, which include demonstrations by star-points, balloons, etc., showing that, everything else being equal, a brighter object looks nearer, and also a larger object looks nearer; and that other clues or cues relative to size and distance are differentially weighted when in conflict. It should be mentioned that Gibson has made the point that brightness is not an "indicator" (clue) of distance. The point here is that the subjective impression due to "change of brightness" is to create an effect of movement. (This point itself requires further investigation.)

The general inferences from these experiments are as follows:

(1) You yourself contribute to your perceptual awareness, and even when two stars, or balloons, are equi-distant from you, their respective distances will appear different to you if they are not of the same size. (This is demonstrated uniocularly, i.e. looking with one eye only.)

(2) Size and brightness can work together to increase this effect and, if there is a conflict between them, more weight is given to size than to brightness.

(3) In 2, if we include the parallax and overlay clues put in conflict, the importance of the clues has the order:

overlay, parallax, size, brightness,

there being a dependent differential between overlay and parallax.

(4) The assumption made by the observer is regarded as his contribution to the situation, and this directly affects his perceptual

awareness. The nature of one's assumptions about size, for example, is brought out by a demonstration of the uniocular viewing of projected articles such as playing-cards, leaves and rings.

The third case is built on the rotating trapezoid; this is the most complicated demonstration so far mentioned, and one that has aroused considerable discussion. The trapezoid is like an ordinary window-frame except that it is shaped as a trapezoid, which is the way an ordinary rectangular window looks when viewed from the side. In the demonstration it is suspended and rotated, and it then appears to oscillate backwards and forwards from the points where it is perpendicular to the line of the observer's vision, although actually it is rotating. Now consider the case in which a rigid rod is placed through the framework of the trapezoidal window. When the trapezoid is rotated, the rod appears to bend as though it were a rubber tube while the window is "perceived" as oscillating, and the problem is: where did the event of the bending and elongation of the rod come from, and why. The transactionalists conclude that the observer's experience of windows, rods, etc., gives him assumptions about the world which are offended by inconsistency. Thus the observer is, as always, himself contributing to his own perceptual awareness. His assumption that the window is rectangular in shape (which, of course, it is not) is the datum by which all the other perceptual judgments are made. This effect can certainly be effective binocularly (at least, within limits) as well as uniocularly.

The distorted room demonstrations, which are also effective in both uniocular and binocular situations, add nothing essentially new. The binocular cases for all these perceptual demonstrations admit of a slightly broader interpretation, which says that what you are perceptually aware of binocularly is not solely the observer's contribution, and depends on physiological and environmental phenomena.

In the case of the distorted rooms it will be appreciated that they look normal from only a small range of points, in fact at roughly one position with respect to each room. The assumptions, and the egocentric reference brought to the situation by the observer, are intended to explain the perceptual awareness of the observer.

The aniseikonic glasses demonstration seems in many ways to be a case apart from the remainder of the Ames demonstrations. Here there is a differential suppression of binocular and uniocular cues. The weighting of the differentiation, however, is regarded as being dependent on experience.

Nothing further need be added to the question of perception of motion. The general inferences in the case of both radial (movement away from the observer and towards him) and tangential (movements across him) motion are that the observer's perceptual awareness is not in accordance with the environmental events. For "perceived radial motion", perception is based on the "subjective estimate" of the size of the moving object. The perceptual awareness of direction and speed of tangential motion is based on the assumption of the size of the object and its constancy. The awareness of motion is based on definite objects, and assumptions as to varying distances and directions.

Many more experiments have been undertaken than those briefly alluded to here, but the same general findings have been made in each case.

Some other experiments must now be mentioned which, while not regarded as being part of transactionalist experimental approach, lend credence to the belief that *experience* plays an essential part in perception, and thus supports empiricism in perception. Certain relatively simple objects were used, such as triangles and squares, and subjects were tested monocularly in distance localization with respect to these shapes against a binocularly viewed background of references. The subjects were then employed in tasks requiring the manipulation of sets of these objects, members of which sets differed from each other only by small amounts. They were retested within about three weeks on the initial situation. Controls were used in the form of groups who did not perform the intermediate manipulations but merely performed the initial and final test. Another control was employed in terms of a comparison between judgments of two forms, one which was *not* utilized in the "experience" session, and one which was. The results were statistically significant in supporting an "experiential" explanation with respect to these tests. It has been inferred from these experiments that *experience* is essential to *perception*, but the manner of its working needs much more discussion.

Other data, which will not be quoted in detail, purports to show that *action* ("the doing of something") in the perceptual situation modified the perceptions of the observers. This view seems to gain further, though somewhat oblique, support from an experiment with three distorted rooms, and involving comparisons made by observers before and after *action* in the rooms. In these experiments evidence was found for two kinds of "learning", which were called "formative" and "organizational". The only unpredicted aspect in the experiment was that the *action* apparently did not need to be carried out *by the subject*; carry-over was obtained even when the experimenter performed the actions for the passive observers. It was, in fact, to this extent only that support for the work in these experiments was oblique (Kilpatrick, 1953).

The next experiments are in keeping with, and indeed have largely contributed to, transactionalist literature. Two experiments were conducted with respect to continuous size-change, as an indication of continuous radial movements. A further experiment has also been done on size as a cue to distance, and three experiments, or demonstrations, on movement, all of which yielded the same generalized results as those already mentioned. They form the bulwark of the transactionalist case. The fact of *continuous change* should be noted here; it is clearly of interest in the other perceptual matter of *real* and *apparent* movement, for these are only distinguishable by matters of continuity.

Taking a general view of these experiments and demonstrations, one would say that the Ames demonstrations are extremely effective, and there can be little doubt that they are a challenge to the explanatory powers of psychologists. The only possible misgiving is on the question of whether, *in principle*, they offer anything new to explain, for empiricists of one kind and another have considered such problems as these for a long time; but from this doubt we would certainly exclude the demonstrations with aniseikonic lenses.

The general demonstrations seem to be an elaboration of examples that have been used previously to support an empiricist viewpoint, and while they are brilliantly designed and carry conviction, they do not, it seems, in and of themselves, affect the position of perceptual theory. Let us now consider the general theory that has emanated from these experiments.

Transactional Theory

There are two aspects of the transactionalist theory; one is a general theory of science and scientific behaviour, and the other a more or less specific interpretation of the Ames demonstrations, their own experiments, and the general field of perception.

First let us digress for a moment from the psychology of perception and consider the general transactional philosophy. It has been based, to some extent, on the pragmatism of Dewey, and is not intended as a complete philosophy of science.

The emphasis of the general view is on the transactions between the observer and *his* world. It repeats many of the axioms of scientific method and enquiry, which the writer would expect no one seriously to doubt. Scientific enquiry has two major functions: firstly to provide "scientific facts" which, when interpreted, permit of prediction and control; and secondly, to instigate improvement in the conceptual reorganization of knowledge about our environment and, in the process, *naming* it. In brief, understanding as well as prediction is part of the job of scientific enquiry.

The more strictly philosophic aspects of the argument can be traced back to the work of Dewey and Bentley (1949), who represent an approval of a certain type of descriptive pragmatics. This is not intended, apparently, to take the place of the formal investigations of philosophers, but is merely part of a prescription for an approach to science.

To pursue a detailed analysis of this philosophy of science is not within the scope of this chapter, and the few comments and criticisms to be made will be reserved until their particular theory of perception has been stated.

The transactional theory of perception emanates from the general transactional view of philosophy, but does not lean very heavily on what are, after all, relatively vague generalizations. To supply the needed theory it will be necessary to generalize, systematically, the inferences that transactionalists draw from the demonstrations which we have briefly noticed.

Picking up the fragments from various sources, an attempt will be made to put the generalizations together.

They have attacked Gestalt psychology in the following terms (quoting from Kilpatrick, 1952):

> Gestalt psychology is hardly a theory of perception at all; it is, in a sense, the modern nativism in which the percept is a "given" based on a natively determined isomorphic relationship between the properties of the thing perceived and the properties of a physiological brain field.

This helps to clarify one dimension of the theory. They say, further:

> It is apparent that the locus of the problem of understanding *why* perceptual processes operate as they do is not to be sought in the physical stimulus-configuration. A different approach is suggested in the philosophies of James, Dewey and Whitehead. Perceptual knowledge is an

apprehension of the relatedness of things, according to Whitehead, who has termed this relatedness of things "significance" ... Adelbert Ames, Junior, has extended this orientation into investigations of visual phenomena.

And again, quoting this time from Dewey and Bentley (1949):

> Each transaction of living involves numerous capacities and aspects of man's nature which operate together. Each occasion of life can occur only through an environment, is imbued with some purpose, requires action of some kind, and the registration of the consequences of action. Every action is based upon some awareness of perception, which in turn is determined by the assumptions brought to the occasion. The assumptions are in turn determined by past experience. All of these processes are interdependent. No one could function without the others.

Now let us look at some of the more immediately relevant generalizations. The chair demonstration is reckoned to make clear the fact that you don't see what is "out there"; indeed all the Ames demonstrations make this point over and over again. They make it plain that different stimulus-conditions can achieve the same perceptual response (or the same perceptual awareness). Transactionalists do, of course, admit the relevance of physiological and environmental factors, but they make their main stand on *experience*. In the case of the distorted room, the question is, "Why do you not see it as a distorted room?" The answer is that you have associated such cues in experience with normal rooms, and you therefore see this room as normal. This is, in fact, the case even when clues in the form of two empirically equal-sized humans are placed in two corners of the room and look incredibly disparate in size.

A more difficult question for the transactionalists is, "How is it that 'action of a kind' allows you ultimately to see the room as normal?" They would answer that this was the result of new *experience* which was changing our perceptual awareness; new assumptions that had become formed and part of your new *perceptions*. As Kilpatrick (1952) says:

> Perception ... is that part of the transactional process which is an implicit awareness of the probable significance for action of present impingement on sensory receptors ... perception may be altered simply by altering assumptions.

The transactionalist view, then – and it is repeated in all their writings – may be summarized as saying that organisms are a part of their environment; they construct their own worlds through their perceptions, which are the result of assumptions based on experience. They claim that their demonstrations and experiments show that the point of experience, assumptions, and indeed all that is brought to the situation by the perceiver, is overwhelmingly clear. But too much space has already been lavished on this interesting set of experiments, and the time has come for a critical analysis.

Critical Analysis of Transactionalism

It is clear that transactionalism is a form of empiricism in the nativist-empiricist controversy, although it does not share exactly the philosophical directives of certain other forms of empiricism. But this may not be relevant to the actual content of the perceptual theory.

It should be said at this point that the writer is in general agreement with empiricism, and therefore largely in agreement with the transactional viewpoint, so that, to him, there are many aspects of their philosophical background which seem wholly laudable. They quote Einstein and Infeld (1938) as saying, "The formulation of a problem is often more essential than its solution." There can be no doubt about the truth of this, and what is especially heartening to the writer is the realization of the valued help in clarification and understanding that can be given by some aspects of philosophy. Particularly agreeable is the quotation from Hadley Cantril *et al* (1949a, b, c):

> ... the idea seems to be that if one only gathers enough data, possibly with the use of new gadgets or apparatus, one must sooner or later come out with some sort of scientific result.

This idea is indeed the scourge of modern psychology. The general position of transactionalism, both in the wider and in the narrower sense, seems to me to be essentially correct, and any adverse criticism that this chapter contains should be understood only within the framework of this support. And here we must turn to the less pleasing business of supplying some of the adverse criticism, and ask, in what respect is transactionalism deemed to be inadequate?

It is inadequate on one or two general points of philosophy of science which we must now consider, without entering into some minor criticisms. It would seem that the neglect of a more detailed philosophical analysis of some of the crucial points, both of their theory and the empirical facts, may appear to give an impression of superficiality. In particular, the choice of Dewey and Bentley as principal philosophical patrons is unfashionable, philosophically.

This in itself is not very serious except that it tends to keep certain otherwise interested philosophers at a distance. Dewey and Bentley's work on pragmatics, while being probably adequate to the extent that it is used by the transactionalists, is in itself open to criticism, and it is to be regretted that they have departed from the great pragmatic tradition of Charles Peirce. Many of the views expressed in *The Knowing and the Known* seem peculiarly unprofitable philosophically.

The next criticism, phrased as a question, has already been alluded to in passing: Are the Ames demonstrations (except aniseikonic lenses) novel *in principle*? The answer is that they offer no new philosophical or scientific problem of explanation, although they do highlight the existing problems in a very interesting way.

The truth is that transactionalism is not, in itself, a complicated theory, indeed, it is a quite simple principal which can be incorporated into a theory. It is altogether too easy to become confused over words like "sensing", "perceiving", "seeing", "believing", etc., and the writer thinks that the main problem that transactionalists have neglected has been the semantic analysis – the careful, logical clarification – of its verbal explanations, and this is where philosophy is so important to scientific problems. This fault, however, is universal. The nativist-empiricist controversy, as it has been called, is primarily a confusion over terminology.

It will be appreciated by now that the word "perception" is many-meaninged and essentially vague, and therefore requires a deal of clarification. In one of the main transactionalist's manuals, no explicit definition of "perception" is given – not even a glossary definition – although, of course, the word is in general use. This is surprising in view of the obvious semantic consciousness of the transactionalist movement. As an instance, they make the distinction between "what is in your visual awareness" (what you are "subjectively" aware of) as opposed to what you are looking at in your environment. This seems an admirable start, but it is not good enough in that it assumes a distinction between two states, or processes, which cannot be shown to be differentiable. Indeed the whole point of transactionalism comes perilously near the logical rocks on precisely this point. How do we know when we have a correct perception? The problem is not insoluble, but some of the transactional writing falls into the trap of suggesting that the observer constructs his own world, on one hand, and is yet able to appeal to the real-world, on the other. A quotation will help to clarify this point (Kilpatrick, 1952).

... perceivers do affect the what, where, when and how of that which they perceive. As long as we can keep on thinking of the mind that perceives as purely "subject", and that which is perceived as purely "object", we shift back on to the horns of a dilemma: one being solipsism and the other, mechanistic materialism.

In situations where what we see and what is out there do correspond, we cannot identify any evidence to the effect that the perceiver contributes anything to the qualities or characteristics of that which he perceives.

This calls for logical criticism. How can we know what is "out there" other than by making further perceptions? This passage, and others in their writings, reads as if there were perceivers with perceptions on one hand, and observers with "inside knowledge of what was really there" on the other. Is this the claim? If so, it should be brought out into the open and clarified, especially in view of the philosopher's difficulties over just this point. This transactional assumption might well be thought to lead to plain inconsistency. There can be no people (experimenters included) who transcend the situation, and who do *not* transact with their situations in their worlds.

This problem is again brought up in the next paragraph of the same reference, so it can be no casual slip.

On the occasions when the two do *not* correspond, however, there appears to be identifiable evidence that what we see is determined not only by whatever is "out there" but also by what we contribute through our own activities of looking and seeing.

Some light may be shed on this by a quotation from Kilpatrick (1952):

Perception is that phase of the total process which is an implicit awareness of the probable consequence of purposive action with respect to some objects. Man can never know more of the external world than those aspects which are directly relevant to the carrying out of his purposes. Each man's perceptions are therefore his own, unique and personal; common perceptions become possible in so far as common experience and common strivings are shared among individuals.

This statement highlights the fact that *perception* means something broader to transactionalists than it does to nativists, or gestaltists, for example. However, we should notice that the implication, once more, is clear that there is an *external world* to know something about, and therefore the view is clearly a brand of realism. Nevertheless, we cannot know more than a certain amount. How, one might ask, do we know that there is more to know about, than we know about?

No purpose would be served by carrying this part of the analysis any further. Enough has probably been said to cast doubt on the clarity of the transactionalists. The writer is left with the suspicion that they are trying to get the best of both the phenomenalists' and the realists' worlds, and it cannot be done this way. This is perhaps not too serious a criticism, and all could be made well by a clear statement of philosophical directives, ontological assumptions, etc., but it does remove some of the slight air of mystery that surrounds the transactionalist movement.

To return now to the explicit question of perception, it is abundantly clear that *perception* is closely related to the total adaptive organizing behaviour of the individual. The word "perception" can be used, of course, how we please, and it has certainly been used more narrowly by many other philosophers and psychologists. To take the extreme case, Ayer (1936) uses "perceiving" as synonymous with "sensing".

We may agree that the transactionalist's idea of "perception" is a good one, and our own theory makes use of a somewhat similar idea (see Chapter 13). However, as will be shown in Chapter 12, there should be no quarrel with nativists over whether experience comes into *perception* or not, because the word "perception" means something different to each group.

Parenthetically, it should be noticed that experience may enter *perception* in two different ways: either by central influence, or through modification of the activity of the visual system itself. This last point is still in need of further investigation, but its possibilities cannot be overlooked.

There are one or two further points about the Ames demonstrations that should not be forgotten. The "chair" demonstration does not really carry conviction (note its similarity to the distorted room cases), since the underlying facts are rather too obvious. No one would (or should) say that it *is* a chair, on looking through the peephole, unless he means, when he says, "that is a chair", to be understood to be talking in an *expressive* language. If this is the case, no surprise will be occasioned by finding that what *appears* to be a chair, under rather restricted and artificial conditions, turns out not to be; conjuring has been so much a part of every child's world, that the adult is hardly likely to be surprised at this. However, this experiment does perhaps shed light on the transactional view that what is really "out there" is not what is *perceived*. Without entering further

Empiricism and Transactionalism

into this rather confused question, it will be easy to see that this will be false if "perceived" were taken, as it would be by some, as *expressive* of a sense-datum, or by others for plain *sensed*. We have no reason to doubt that the observer correctly "sensed" ("perceived", for many) what was out there, but he is only incorrect if he thinks that what is "out there" can be sat on and used in the usual manner of what is called a "chair". This significant error, for transactionalists, comes about because of the wider use of the word "perception".

These same comments are more or less applicable to all the demonstrations; they simply remind us that there are semantic and other philosophical points that transactionalists, and empiricist psychologists generally, have not made sufficiently clear.

Let us consider again briefly the trapezoidal windows. It should be observed that a careful, analytic observation (by selection of a special fixation point) can more or less eliminate the effect and, rather like the Neckar cube, it may be found that one can "switch-in" or "switch-out" the effect, at any rate to some extent, "at will". Presumably the effect was gained by elimination of many of the clues that misled the observer about the actual rotation of the window. No doubt there is a two-way Neckar Cube system here, such that the trapezoid may be seen in two ways, which we will call A and B, and when A dominates, other visual (illusory) effects A' occur; and when B dominates, effects B', (non-illusory) occur. The trouble here is that it is difficult to *prove* that it is a matter of conscious, or unconscious (central) experience that does the trick, rather than differential adaptation of the visual system which manifests experience.

No doubt the answers to these questions awaits physiological investigation of the visual system. In the meantime, however, it is consoling to remember that the central factors can hardly be altogether absent from any visual activity; the problem is to find the dominant variables. The trapezoidal window experiment depends for its success – as do the experiments in distorted rooms – on suppressing the usual clues, and leaving the organism to behave (by experience) as if the usual clues were there. This supports an empiricist interpretation, and the writer believes that empiricism is the right (more sensible) interpretation of *perception*, relative to a language.

An interesting point that we have not yet considered is the distinction often made between "seeing" and "believing". This topic will be discussed in Chapter 12, but in the meantime it may be said that, for the transactionalists, the gist of the argument is that "perceiving" includes "believing", and, I think, rightly so. Further, there is no reason to suppose that, for the observer, differentiations are possible as between *seeing, sensing,* and *perceiving*. The question as to whether the observer really does *see* the distorted room as different, after "action" has taken place in it, can be answered only (unless the opposite can be convincingly shown) by the admission that he cannot certainly separate *seeing* from *believing*, and therefore it is not a sensible question. He does *perceive* the room differently (apparently), but this is only true in the transactional sense of *perceive*.

As a last note on this matter, there is a question that one would very much like to put to the people who organize these demonstrations: are they themselves *perceiving* the distorted rooms as distorted, or not?

The case of the aniseikonic lenses has not received a sufficiently full treatment here. In some of its aspects it seems to stand apart from the remainder of the Ames demonstrations, and it should certainly receive further close analysis in the future.

As in the case of the philosophical theory, it seems to the writer that there are many approaches to perception, and transactionalism represents one of them. Stripped of its philosophical and logical vagueness, it would be a good version of modern empiricism (with respect to perception) in a background of critical realism. Trouble starts when there is thought to be only one possible reconstruction, but it is difficult to doubt that this particular one has many advantages for behaviour theory. This, let it be noted, is an *external question*, however, and not an *internal question*, i.e. a question about what sort of linguistic framework to use, and not about inconsistencies within that framework, if we may borrow Carnap's (1952) convenient terminology.

It should perhaps be added that there may well be other grounds both for supporting and opposing the transactionalist movement, apart from the reasons for doubt given here, but it seems that what is most fruitful and most useful in transactionalism should be amended at the level of the linguistic formulation of the theory. That it also needs to develop in the other direction, towards an ever more precise statement of what the theory predicts, goes without saying, and we may look forward to work in the future that will formalize transactionalist theory.

These same arguments and methods of analysis could, and should, be applied to all theories of cognition.

Chapter 11

ETHOLOGY AND COGNITION

Preliminaries

In this chapter it is intended to supply, in general terms, a biological background to the specialized study of cognition, both at the molecular and at the molar levels. Work in this field has been done mainly by ethologists, or biologists who have studied animal behaviour. Space forbids that we should explore these remoter levels of cognition other than in general terms, but the psychologist must be familiar with what is being done in allied fields of endeavour, and constantly bear it in mind.

Our picture of cognition, so far, suggests that the organism is born with certain inherited properties, or capacities, and then proceeds to be modified, and changed in a complex manner, with respect to its environment. The psychological discussion has surrounded the problem of learning, and now it is important to try to fill in some part of the gap, it being assumed that there is no complete discontinuity between primitive cognition and highly complex cognitive processes.

The first step is to consider some general principles of organic development. C. M. Child (1921) has insisted on the essential unity of the organism in its environment; this is sometimes called the "organism-as-a-whole" principle, within which take place the essential organic principles of specialization and differentiation, all being part of the organized pattern of behaviour of an individual organism.

First we shall consider the notion of "organismic pattern". If it is assumed that a plan or order exists in the constitution of the unity of the organism, then it is this that constitutes the pattern. Necessarily dynamic in form, it establishes a series of changing processes which are a function of the organism's own changes with respect to its environment. According to Child,

> ... organismic pattern is an order, plan, unity or integration of which a protoplasm constitutes the material substratum.

Protoplasms are irrevocably connected with "organisms" in nature. There are numbers of different forms of protoplasm, and a study of protoplasmic properties (under obscure subject names, such as "colloidal chemistry") is indispensable to the study of life.

If protoplasm is regarded as a physico-chemical system in which dynamic changes of a certain kind take place, than an organism can be regarded as a system of protoplasms. A start can be made to this essential study in the simplest organisms by a consideration of such simple facts as radial and bilateral symmetry, and the relative selectivity of semi-permeable membranes, which allow certain substances to pass through them, and not others. The nerve impulse operates on such a principle where sodium and potassium gradients exist across the surface of the nerve membranes. No study of behaviour will ultimately be complete, in any sense, without an exhaustive study of chemistry, especially the chemistry of protoplasm.

The organism is regarded, then, as a system of protoplasms, and from a genetic standpoint, it has the latent capacity for behaviour which is evoked by external stimulus, and subsequently guided by the complex relation of external to internal change. To some extent the differentiation and specialization of the organism is an adjustment of internal conditions to external conditions.

Speaking in comparative terms, it is noticeable that organismic patterns are much alike for very different forms, the general principles of symmetry, and polarity, being perhaps dominant at some level. However, as differentiation, etc., takes place, more and more emphasis is placed on the difference between their protoplasmic characteristics. In the integrated resultant of overt molar behaviour, the important distinction is between the dominant and the recessive functions. An important question now arises as to what extent, in any particular, does energy-transfer dominate specific chemical transfer, and vice versa. The factors of dominance, and recessiveness, are of special importance in excitation-transmission gradients, and are of special interest in cases of neural transmission. A complex co-ordinated activity (e.g. a neuro-muscular "skill") is mainly composed of dominant-recessive excitation patterns. Thus the particular organismic pattern is a function of the species, and of the protoplasm in which the pattern is worked out (these are obviously not necessarily independent).

The physiological correlations suggested above involve the integration of dominant and recessive factors. There may be local physio-

Ethology and Cognition

logical differentiation which may or may not be dominated by the overall physiological state.

Material correlation is an important aspect of physiological correlation, and involves transportation between parts, e.g. the breakdown of carbohydrates, salts, fats, and so on, in blood, lymph, and various systems, where osmotic pressures, or semi-permeability, act as differential selectors.

During the transport of these materials through the body, many changes may occur in the electrical, chemical and mechanical conditions, and there are also the sub-effects of surface tension, ion-concentration, etc.; however, there remains some correlaton between the change and the states produced. There may be a range of variation in material correlation, involving great specificity of effect, or, on the other hand, great generality, in which the substances transported may undergo very great (in the case of specificity), or very little change. A hormone change, such as abnormal thyroid output, may be taken as typical of material correlation, in which the effects appear to be, to some degree, specific, and yet will have recessive characteristics under certain circumstances; indeed it is clear that no understanding of thyroid output can be made independent of other endocrine or exocrine products, and perhaps even the state of the organism-as-a-whole, although a degree of approximation may be arrived at by neglecting certain features at certain levels. It is also clear that the material correlation is a function of the organismic pattern.

As opposed to material correlation there is dynamic correlation, which involves the transfer of energy (pressure and excitation) and will be in a dominant-recessive relationship with material correlation. From the energy viewpoint, "life" may be regarded as differing in its entropy equations from the "non-living". A simple, pictorial energy model is a flowing river in which little, isolated whirlpools of water move for a while against the general direction of the stream. A small organized energy entity, with temporarily positive entropy, is "life", in its transcience, in the background of the "non-living".

This particular picture of the energy world as being made up of the transportation of particles bears an interesting relationship to the concept of information and information theory. The measure used for information is the same as the measure used in statistical Thermodynamics to describe entropy. This identity may have no more significance than is clearly implied by having the same measure, although it could be that the concept of choice and observation are what are inevitably common to both processes.

However we shall not pursue this matter further in this book and return to the biological generalizations that are preliminary to ethological studies.

The mechanical relations of pressure and tension affect growth and differentiation; that is to say, the structure of bone, the differentiation of connective tissue, etc. The general excitation-transmission pattern is the basis of "physiological gradients", as has been suggested by Child. These gradients are common to all living tissue, but here the concern is essentially with organisms. As has already been mentioned, the symmetry, or geometrical organization of an organism, is of primitive importance, and spherical symmetry, axiate-radiate forms, axiate-bilateral forms, spiral, asymmetric, and so on, all involve certain differences. The simplest example of spherical symmetry is found in the Amoeba. Temporary asymmetry can be introduced, in the form of pseudopodia, by external stimulation which brings about a gradient of excitation from the point of stimulation, and so bringing to light a simple organismic pattern from the protoplasmic potentiality. Changes in the amoeba's behaviour may be induced by changes in the chemical concentration of the medium; or a change of pH (acidity) may be sufficient.

It was shown as long ago as 1911 that placing an amoeba in distilled water induced marked and characteristic, as well as enduring, changes; similar changes, it should be noticed, may be effected by the chemical Lactase. The importance of an organism-in-an-environment has been continually emphasized, and in this connexion the world-famous biologist Jacques Loeb (1911) has shown that, even in the presence of active spermatozoa, the sea-urchin could not fertilize eggs without the presence of certain chemicals. Contrarily, Loeb was able to bring about artificial fertilization in a sea-urchin's eggs.

The notion of a physiological gradient is associated with organized body forms, even of protozoa, possessing a definite anterior end. The anterior end is more sensitive to external stimuli, and this is connected with the differential response in a homogeneous medium. Jennings (1906) devoted much attention to this matter, particularly to the avoidance reaction of *Paramecium* which involves differentiation to local disturbances, and is dependent upon regional sensitivity.

The Organism-as-a-whole principle has its interesting examples, one of which is the marine planarium. If it is placed on its back it will soon right itself, and if the brain is removed it will still right itself, but more slowly. This is, of course, analogous to the well-known Yerkes T-maze experiment with worms, which was mentioned at the beginning of this book.

Two other examples concern experiments which are worthy of note. The first one showed that a beheaded moth is able to live as long as a normal one; it can mate, and produce the normal number of eggs, *but* it will not lay eggs spontaneously, nor select the proper kind of leaves on which to deposit the eggs. The second experiment showed the vital part played by diet in a large number of different ailments, and irregularities of behaviour. For example, a rat – normally an adequate parent – if kept deficient of some vitamins will destroy rather than nourish her young.

Large numbers of such experiments from the endocrinological field have been summarized by Beach (1948) of Yale University. He showed that a deficiency of one hormone-output, or a change in, say, the Androgen-Oestrogen ratio, will markedly change the behaviour of the organism-as-a-whole, as well as affect some specific organic functioning. The whole of the work of Beach is essential to the molecular theorist; it represents one of the early stages in the huge programme of describing behaviour at the biochemically organic level we have been considering.

For students of cognition, the origin and development of the nervous system is of special interest to our enquiry. It is most important in playing a major role in the behaviour of the complex organism, and has been studied by many outstanding workers.

Some of this work at the more general level has already been discussed in Chapter 3. Child (1921) sees the nervous tissue developed and differentiated, in terms of physiological gradients (lines of diminishing intensity). Primarily, the nervous system is built on a chemically mediated foundation. The development of specialized nervous tissue with partially specialized functions, such as receptors, effectors, analysers, and perhaps the brain-as-a-whole, may be regarded as a centre for sign-activity dealing in scanning, codes, etc. All this has been built up in a complex of hereditarily-given protoplasm, subjected to the environmental flux, and which has been discussed in a general way in terms of physiological gradients. The comparative studies of nervous systems, and their relation to behaviour-as-a-whole, and the embryological approach, are ultimately necessary to fit together the essential pieces in the picture.

But this matter must be left temporarily, while we return to our more general approach to the subject.

The nervous system is assumed to have certain properties: irritability, excitability, and transmissability. These properties are common to all protoplasm, but they are especially developed in so-called nervous tissue; it is thought, also, that they are basic to organismic integration, and it will be remembered that they have already been discussed under physiological correlation. Although our detailed knowledge of excitation and transmission is meagre, it is clear that it will include a picture of specialized physiological gradients. No attempt will be made in this chapter to discuss the basic properties of neural transmission, for, although they must ultimately be taken into consideration, it is doubtful if they are immediately vital to behavioural considerations.

In steering a course towards behaviour theory, the regulation of pattern in organisms must be taken into account. Child puts the matter succinctly:

> Investigation of the functional activities of organisms, particularly the higher animal and man, could not proceed very far without becoming aware of the existence of various mechanisms and processes which serve to control, order and adjust the various activities to varying conditions, in such a manner as to maintain the physiological unity and harmony of the organism in the changing environment to which it is subjected.

Normal states of organism are to be thought of as states of internal equilibrium which may imply a state of steady change, and not necessarily some fixed state. The physiological gradients – the excitation transmission gradients – may be regarded as fundamental regulatory processes; to put it more generally, excito-motor behaviour is regulatory in character. A particular form of behaviour, and one which is associated principally with the work of Jacques Loeb, at least in the initial stages, is that of tropism, which has, of course, been mentioned previously. The actual notion of tropism is vague; it is, as one might expect, a word which has been used in a variety of different ways. However, in Loeb's terminology, certain orientation responses to light, gravitation, etc., investigated by him in relatively simple organisms, are referred to as tropisms, and the term now usually implies the presence in the organism of an effective integration pattern, although in another usage, due to Jennings, this pattern is not necessarily pre-determined, or inherited.

It is probable, as Tinbergen (1951) has said, that the tropism is only a very special case of orientation behaviour. The Loeb-Jennings controversy over tropisms is in many ways similar to the Hull-Tolman controversy over molar theory: both are partly correct, but both are arguing from particular cases.

The tropism, for some experimenters, is described as "oriented behaviour in an energy field", though this seems rather too general a definition to be useful. However, many experiments with respect to tropisms in rat behaviour have been carried out, and Crozier and Pincus (for various references, see Munn, 1950) who are two of the principal contributors, were able to show much tropistic behaviour in rats with respect to light, stimulation with respect to touch, and gravitation. There is, in fact, little reason to doubt that a tropism is a particular case of unlearned activity, which becomes dominated and integrated into the rat's whole behaviour pattern as development takes place. This work emphasizes a point of considerable importance: that such unlearned behaviour does exist; and it throws much needed light on the nature of internal organization. It is probably true, however, that the simpler organisms show more tropistic behaviour than the higher forms.

The next stages in the investigation involve the modifiability of behavioural patterns, and take us to comparative behaviour proper: "instincts", "reflexes", and so on. Child's work, especially, shows the value of the notion of activity in gradients involving continuous variables, and that such a model allows more easily for dominance and recession.

Ethology

The work of ethologists (those, principally zoologists, who make a comparative study of animal behaviour) has recently developed very considerably, largely on the lower levels of vertebrate and invertebrate behaviour. These fundamental levels are regarded as vital in the clues that they give to the developmental aspects, and underlying principles, of all behaviour.

Before considering some important ethological findings in the field of instincts, it is of methodological interest to consider one of their representative's criticisms of experimental psychology. Tinbergen (1951) has, I think justly, made the following points:

1. Psychologists are not genuinely comparative in their work.
2. Psychologists have studied the behaviour of only a limited number

of species, in a limited number of often artificial situations (Mazes, Puzzle-boxes, etc.).
3. Psychologists have, all too often, neglected the "Organism-as-a-whole" principle, and have often been biologically naïve.

With respect to 2, Tinbergen illustrated his case with a discussion of Hunter's (1913) delayed reaction experiments. These multiple-choice apparatus experiments are very well as far as they go, but how, asks Tinbergen, would they show up the complex case of the digger wasp (*Ammophila Campestris*), investigated by Baerends (1941)? Briefly, this is what Baerends observed:

A female wasp digs a hole when about to lay an egg, then she kills or paralyses a caterpillar, carries it to the hole and deposits an egg on it. She then digs a second hole and repeats the whole performance in this, and may be in a third hole, and then feeds each of the holes in turn. Each subsequent morning, before the daily "hunting" trip, the wasp visits the holes and feeds each of them, but she is *only* influenced by the *first* visit, as Baerends showed by altering the amounts of food in the holes; he found that, after the wasp's first visit, the alterations had no effect on the amount of food brought at later visits. This experiment involved a delay of 15 hours in the wasp's response-patterns, and the comment on delayed-reaction experiments is clear. It showed, said Tinbergen, that the basis for generalization in behaviour theory had been much too narrow, and his conclusion is incontestable. The arguments of Loeb and Jennings over tropisms, and of Hull and Tolman over reinforcement, well illustrate this important point.

The approach followed out by the ethologists – particularly as far as Tinbergen and Lorenz have been concerned – has been the study of instinctive behaviour. They have produced some important results, and gained some quite fascinating information, but from the psychological viewpoint they are open to criticism on the grounds of a certain naïvety. It is difficult, for example, to accept that the stickleback's zigzag dance, and the response to the swollen belly sign, and to the red belly sign, are wholly instinctive, and in no way a product of environmental circumstances. Not, of course, that ethologists would deny the necessity for environmental factors (that would be nonsense), but they do not appear to consider the question of adequate reinforcement as a factor of a very vital nature. Their explanation lies in the assumption of an "Innate Releasing Mechanism" (IRM) which is released by suitable sign stimuli. This must be

Ethology and Cognition

recognized as one more molar type theory; indeed it is one which has a certain cogency at some levels of behavioural organization.

In discussing external stimuli, Tinbergen makes some interesting points that are worth the closest attention on the part of psychologists. One concerns the relative independence of certain auditory stimuli, as shown by the domestic fowl. It was found that a hen reacted to the *sound* of the chicks' calls, even if they were out of sight, but paid no attention to obvious distress calls by a chick close to and in front of her, if she (the hen) could not hear the calls. This points to a need for the study of the "selector activities". The need for studying chain activities in organisms has also been stressed, by both Tinbergen and Lorenz.

According to Tinbergen, the only way to find out what part of behaviour is innate, and what is acquired during an individual lifetime, is to raise individuals in isolation, and to observe the different effects of various environments, but this is an extremely difficult guide as to what behaviour is "innate" and what "learned". Indeed, as Tinbergen himself says, IRM's can be modified by "experience". It is interesting to note, as Lorenz has pointed out, that Wallace Craig, the famous naturalist, had previously exploded the myth of the infallibility of instinct by showing that organisms do, in fact, discharge "consummatory actions" that may not be in the interests of survival.

The essential factors of the ecological norm (normal environment for particular species) have been the subject of a considerable amount of work, for the study of ecology is quite vital to the understanding of behaviour. This last point is mixed up with the question of The Theory of Natural Selection, and one cannot avoid the feeling of growing verbal confusion and even possible circularity. How, precisely, can one separate instinctive from learned behaviour, in the complex of "behaviour-as-a-whole"?

Tinbergen, unlike many molar psychologists, does see the vital necessity, in the discussion of the spontaneity of much of behaviour, for consideration of the internal aspects of behaviour. The central nervous system is probably the principal internal mediator of behavioural patterns, but the endocrinological aspects of behaviour, as well as the chemical aspects generally, obviously cannot be ignored; they call for a specialized treatment and, ultimately, inclusion in the general framework outlined here.

Another factor which may be usefully considered now is what is called "maturation". Coghill (1929) was able to show, in his classical work on salamanders, that large general patterns of behaviour may become differentiated into particular units, and that the postnatal period starts a process of structural development, upon which the functional development may be entirely dependent. The earliest responses, according to Coghill and others, show that the earliest tactile and neural movements are essentially functions of the organism-as-a-whole, and that the development of particular, or specialized, movements is a part *within* the total system, and is dependent on the making – in the case of the salamander's swimming activities, for example – of certain neural connexions.

Here, we are once again faced with complications, particularly of the verbal sort. To begin with, in the investigation of the organism's performance there arises the difficulty of distinguishing the learned from the maturational. It seems clear that certain behavioural patterns will, in their generalized form, be largely maturational, and immediately dependent upon structural development. It is, in fact, obvious that function and structure are never wholly separable, and that the growth of a particular structure will, by virtue of its shape, form, etc., suggest the function which it must perform; but the particular series of patterns capable of being performed by any set of individual organisms will be a function of the particular environment as well as of the innate aspect. The development of locomotor patterns in eels is illustrative of the sort of complications that may arise in one particular aspect of this complex subject. It was found that the locomotory movements are a result of simultaneous peripheral stimulation of the somites of the trunk. Weak stimulation of the organism causes the animal to adopt the undulatory posture, and an increase of the stimulus strength causes the rhythmical simultaneous activities of all the somites. Tinbergen considers this sort of locomotor activity to be parallel to instinctive activity, and he thinks that it gives the lie to a purely Hullian theory of learning. There is room, he thinks, for spontaneity and reactivity. The reason why spontaneity has sometimes been suppressed is perhaps, as Tinbergen has suggested, because of a philosophical confusion over "free will". More recently, Pribram (1960) has also given reasons derived primarily from neurology for regarding the Hullian type theory of reinforcement as being too simple.

In ethological studies of invertebrate behaviour patterns, a few general remarks of Pantin (1950) are of special interest. Comparison of *Actinian* and *Stentor* show that different organisms aiming at the same goal do not always utilize the same physiological systems; and conversely, the same systems may be used by different organisms aiming at different goals. This, again, warns the theorist against narrow-based generalization, and the ignoring of species differences.

In spite of these sorts of warnings, Pantin does see many complex neural patterns in "higher" organisms, mimicked in the "lower" organisms, but he insists on the fact that there is not, generally, only one physiological mechanism for learning. This sort of proposition is made more difficult because there is not a sufficiently definite statement of what Pantin means by learning. However, with some slight reservations, it is easy to accept his general thesis. To quote his own words:

> At no stage may we jump to the conclusion that the machinery of uninvestigated complex behaviour utilizes only the properties of systems utilized in simpler activities already investigated.

This quotation certainly puts a point worth a little further consideration. The word "only" is perhaps the key here, for the fact is that, for example, more complex neurological tissue may dominate and somewhat modify, the function of the simple tissue from which it sprang. This must be continually borne in mind.

For Thorpe (1950), "learning" was originally defined as "adaptive change in individual behaviour as a result of experience". He rightly points out the faults attendant on the lack of intelligent co-operation between different groups interested in behaviour. Thorpe has himself devoted some time to distinguishing different types of behavioural modification; for example, he distinguishes "habituation", which he defines as:

> an activity of the central nervous system whereby innate responses to certain relatively simple stimuli, especially those of potential value as warnings of danger, wane as the stimuli continue for a long period without unfavourable results.

Konorski (1948), the neo-Pavlovian, calls attention to the similarity between "habituation", and "extinction by internal inhibition". For our purposes it is easy to see that the name "habituation" refers to a subset of stimulus-response behaviour, in which the repetition of a stimulus ultimately leads to the absence of response by virtue of internal changes. This is of special interest in developing both molar and molecular theories on both psychological and physiological levels.

One or two other terms in the ethologists' vocabulary, such as "imprinting" and "displacement activity", should be mentioned. Imprinting is a special case of learning, and Thorpe (1956) makes the following generalizations on it:

1. The process is confined to a very definite and very brief period of the individual life, and possibly also to a particular set of environmental circumstances.
2. Once accomplished, the process is very stable; in some cases perhaps totally irreversible.
3. It is often completed long before the various specific reactions to which the imprinted pattern will ultimately become linked are established.
4. It is a supra-individual learning – a learning of the broad characteristic of the species – for if this were not so, and the bird at this stage learnt (as it can easily do later) the individual characteristics of its companions, the biological effect would be frustrated.

Lorenz (1950, 1954) and others claim to have observed this phenomenon in birds, fishes, and other organisms, and a recent writer on "displacement activities" maintains that this activity has reached its highest point of development in birds. He says that displacement activities arise when conflict or thwarting of drives takes place. This sort of activity appears to be familiar to psychologists: particularly to clinical psychologists.

We cannot complete this chapter on ethological development without a consideration of Tinbergen's synthesis. This synthesis suggests a conceptualization of the hierarchical nervous organization underlying "instinctive" behaviour. In doing this, Tinbergen has drawn attention to Weiss's (1956) suggested levels:

1. The level of an individual motor unit.
2. All the motor units belonging to one muscle.
3. Co-ordinated functions of muscular complexes relating to a single joint.
4. Co-ordinated movements of limbs as a whole.
5. Co-ordinated movement of a number of locomotor organs resulting in locomotion.
6. "The highest level common to all animals", the movements of "the animal as a whole".

Tinbergen points out that 6 can be expanded to a number of different levels. His own suggested scheme envisages the dominant instinct (for the moment) at the top, subject to homeostasis, which thus elicits appetitive behaviour. If this leads to the relevant external

Ethology and Cognition

stimuli, the internal releasing mechanism removes the block to further endogenous movements which are of the instinct. He suggests, again, that the causal factors controlling behaviour are both internal and external, the internal, in general, determining the threshold of response to external stimulation; and he refers to motivation as a function of hormone factors, internal stimuli, and intrinsic impulses. Obviously these internal states may be affected by external stimuli. An interesting comparison is made with Beach's central excitatory mechanism, and Tinbergen stressed – a really very important comment – that Beach's model lacks the necessary hierarchical organization.

In viewing the work of the ethologists as a whole, it is clear that here is a movement of great psychological importance, and one which is complementary to the work of the animal psychologists. The value of their comparative approach has already been mentioned, and this is but one of many advantages. The main consideration for the future is not so much to point to the various differences and weaknesses of many of the approaches to behaviour, but rather that an effort should be made to appreciate the similarities, the potential meeting-grounds, in the hope that these varying approaches may at some stage become integrated.

Chapter 12

A THEORY LANGUAGE FOR COGNITION

From what has been said so far, it is clear that any science must start from a plain description of the facts as observed. This is not so easy as it may seem, since an apparently plain description really involves all the inferences that have been accumulated into the language that is used for the description (George and Handlon, 1956, 1957).

Notwithstanding these difficulties, in order to construct scientific theories and models – such as cybernetic models which we shall study in the next chapter – we need to have some fairly close knowledge of what it is we are to model. This perhaps implies that we should use an existing theory of learning, such as Hull's or Tolman's, or even start from a more general account of behaviour such as that given by Hebb (1949). In fact, we shall outline a language which, while it is eclectic, and more nearly neutral than those other languages committed to theories, yet incorporates their most important features It must be remembered that a language is much like a scientific theory, and they go together; the scientific theory being usually more specific in its domain, and more specialized than a language, and that is all.

It would seem that initial attempts to explain or describe cognition should rest on the most common-sense terms of ordinary language, and we should therefore start to describe human beings in terms of their immediate physical properties, and discuss their behaviour in the same terms. We would say that Mr. Smith is a friend of Mr. Jones; that Mr. Williams is unhappy and ill-tempered, but Mr. Stewart is happy and good-tempered, and so on.

If we started in this way we might well be able to produce a very valuable description of human behaviour, and eventually of cognition, which would be useful for many practical purposes, although for the sake of generality we would soon have to introduce general

A Theory Language for Cognition

statements, rather than refer continually to particular individuals. Furthermore, we should still find a certain amount of unwanted vagueness in our statements. When we use a phrase like "is a friend of", we feel that some further explanation of this is necessary. What are the conditions for making friends? What types of people, under what circumstances, are most likely to make friends?

It is because of these difficulties of vagueness and generality that we shall seek to formulate a more precise theory language. For reasons of space, many of the intervening steps will inevitably be left out.

This brings us to the sort of language system that has described most of the basic aspects of cognition in terms of explicitly defined theoretical terms. The nature of the definitions is necessarily limited to what have been termed "glossary definitions", though they can mostly be rigorously reduced to the two undefined terms "stimulus" and "response", where these two terms require special consideration.

But it is essential for an approach to cognition that a more complete molar basis for behaviour should first be laid, from which perception and learning should be *abstracted*. In other words, we need a theory language at least sufficient to fairly systematically earmark the general problems of behaviour as viewed from a *molar* point of view.

The language proposed is intended to meet criticisms of lack of rigour, and is, of course, liable to constant revision. The complete language will also involve a rigorous formalization of the present language, and also a detailed *molecular* model that is supposed to underlie it. At this stage it is possible to give an interpretation to the problem of cognition. The theory language (as we shall call it) will be laid out in the form of glossary definitions, with a necessarily brief word of explanation that is indefinitely expandable, in that any degree of detail can be filled in, in accordance with the nature of the questions it is attempting to answer.

The word "stimulus" will be used both for internal or external sources of excitation, which will imply a change of state of the organism. Externally, we can easily think of a stimulus as something *acting upon* the organism, but in fact we must distinguish between those things capable of acting and those that actually act or are *effective* in their action. This distinction depends upon the active, selective role of the organism, and we shall therefore talk of "activating stimuli". From the internal point of view, the distinction between stimulus and response becomes, in some respects, obscure, and we may think of internal stimulus – response activity as a succession of *states*. The obvious motor activity of the organism is the basis of a response, but equally, every response is also a stimulus, or rather evokes a stimulus. We must therefore treat these two words "stimulus" and "response" with great care. The theory language, which we are now to describe briefly, is a characteristically scientific project. It is a part of what has been called "black-box theory". We are seeking to find at a molar level, convenient terms to describe the behaviour of the black-box by reference to internal operations whose mechanisms or relations we do not wish to specify in detail. There must be a memory store, a method of input, and a recognition process which compares input with information stored. There must also be a motivational system which differentially reinforces the associations set up, an output system, and perhaps more besides, especially by way of detail.

Sooner or later we may wish to open the black-box and proceed from molar to molecular methods. Indeed, cognition is already bound up with neurophysiology, so our language should be couched in terms which make for convenient redefinition and interpretation at other levels of development.

We shall use the word "belief" as a theoretical term for a relatively permanent state of the organism which represents the association, through experience, of the activating stimuli with a "means-outcome". Implicit in this definition is the suggestion that there may be many associations involved in the acquisition of beliefs.

There may be associations between the means, or response to a stimulus, and the outcome or next stimulus; and associations between the activating stimuli and the means of association between the activating stimuli and the outcome; and there may even be association between the activating stimuli and the means-outcome taken together.

To put it in its broadcast terms, beliefs are stored associations which specify all the possibilities which might be expected to occur if certain behaviour was performed under certain stimulating conditions. We may distinguish between beliefs that are involved in general behaviour and those involved in the purely perceptual behaviour of the organism. This draws attention to the distinction sometimes made between learning and perceptual learning (Drever, 1960).

A Theory Language for Cognition

In general, given a particular stimulating condition, the belief is concerned with the probable outcome of certain responses, the probable amount of effort entailed in achieving this outcome, and the probable amount of reward to be attained by this outcome. As might be expected, that aspect of beliefs concerned with anticipated reward (or "value", as we might call it) and anticipated effort is closely related to the *motivational* aspect of the activating stimulus state. Certainly we shall want to accept the idea that *needs* form stimuli (these may be usually internal to the organism and perhaps should be called states) that impinge on the organism. "Valence" is said to be the amount of anticipated reward invariantly associated with a stimulus, where the value is the anticipated reward that also takes into account the needs of the moment. It thus varies from occasion to occasion.

For a perceptual belief, given a particular stimulus condition, the belief content is concerned with the appropriate categorization of the activating stimuli. We might guess that, for perception, the anticipated effort and anticipated reward play a smaller role in the selection of a category than does the *strength of the belief* regarding the appropriate way of categorizing particular activating stimuli; but there are perceptual occasions where valence and value may be important, for example, in ambiguous stimulating circumstances.

The *acquisition of beliefs*, we shall say, takes place through knowledge by acquaintance or knowledge by description (these may be subsumed under the phrase "through experience"). The two processes may be distinguished roughly by noting that knowledge by acquaintance involves direct experience with the relevant stimuli and responses, while knowledge by description involves indirect experience with these events through the mediation of *signs* which, the organism has learned, *refer to* these same events. We should note here that there is not a firm distinction between a stimulus acting as a sign and a stimulus acting as a stimulus only, simply because signs acquire their significance by association in experience. Thus all stimuli are potential signs. We have already discussed this briefly in Chapter 7, and will be returning to it again in Chapter 17.

In the acquisition of a belief by description, the organism is not exposed directly to the sequence of events, rather it is exposed to signs which have come to represent such events; otherwise the processes are the same, and are normally overlapping. At the human level, the signs used to express the sequence of events that make up our beliefs are often language signs, or simply languages, and these signs may vary in the degree of directness with which they represent events. For example, the representation may be quite direct and explicit, as when a mother warns her child, "If you touch something hot you will be burned." On the other hand, the representation may be very indirect, such as the statement, "Mazamet is a small town in the south of France." Here, there is no direct statement as to the outcome of a particular response under particular circumstances, but it does tell the organism, by implication, what to expect if the statement describes actual geographical conditions. That is, if the signs are meaningful to the organism, and if the organism accepts the statement as being true, then, by virtue of this belief, it will be prepared to act in a certain way under particular circumstances in order to attain a desired outcome. That is to say, having this belief about Mazamet, one would look at the appropriate map (a pictorial sign) in an atlas if one wanted to learn of Mazamet's exact location. Obviously, the number of such beliefs regarding behavioural possibilities that an organism derives from such a statement is a function of past experience, and of the degree to which it is able to apply this past experience to any present situation.

The acquisition of *perceptual* beliefs may also, of course, be brought about through the use of signs; that is, through knowledge by description. In fact, much of education consists in the learning of what is the appropriate way to categorize particular activating stimuli (signs).

The difference between the acquisition of a belief and the strengthening, or weakening, of a belief, should be carefully noted; this is similar to the distinction between *learning* and *having learned*. In the latter process the final response will determine, given a certain stimulating circumstance, whether the belief that a particular reponse will lead to a certain outcome is *confirmed* or not. If the belief is confirmed by the outcome, then this belief will be strengthened; if not confirmed, the belief will be weakened. However, the degree of confirmation or disconfirmation will be determined by the organism's own perception and interpretation of that outcome.

It will be noticed that the discussion of signs – so essential to our theory – acts as a link between the philosophical and the psychological aspects of cognition. However, we must not pursue this interesting point here; it should be understood that this chapter is not intended to give a complete or rigorous account of a theory

A Theory Language for Cognition

language, but rather to be sufficient to illustrate the method, and to clarify the subject in anticipation of the next chapter, which deals with cybernetic models.

Motivational Terms

A few terminological decisions should be made about motivation. First we will define "motivational stimuli" or "motivational states" as a sub-class of the class of all stimuli, internal to the organism, which derive from needs and their associated drives, and which have become associated with particular beliefs.

These stimuli are those such as hunger states which manifest themselves in chemical changes, and movements of the stomach muscles, and which have previously been associated with beliefs, – beliefs in hunger and related problems in this case. These stimuli may also be thought of as acting on, and being constant "energizers" of, all the sequential steps of cognition.

There is a further complication to be noticed. The motivational state of the organism is, at any time, capable of being influenced by either internal or external stimuli. The beliefs associated with them may feed back directly into the organism and modify, to some extent, its needs. Sometimes, for example, we no longer want something as much as we did, after thinking carefully about it and its implications.

It is important to note here that not all stimuli which impinge upon the central nervous system, from either external or internal sources, are capable of becoming part of the activating stimuli. It is therefore necessary that we distinguish, as Hull does, between stimuli as physical events which *may* come to play a role in behaviour, and those which *do* play such a role. In general, only those stimuli which are first perceived (categorized) are capable of becoming part of the activating stimuli. In perception itself, it makes no sense to say that a stimulus must be first perceived before it can be perceived, so we shall say that it is only necessary that the S_1 or activating stimulus has been previously associated with a perceptual belief.

The next two motivational terms to be defined are: First, *drives* which represent specific needs of the organism, both primary and secondary, which manifest themselves in the motivational stimuli. Secondly, *urgency*, which is a special state of the organism which manifests itself in the motivational stimuli.

Primary and secondary motivations contain primary and secondary drives, respectively. Those drives which are for the most part unlearned, such as hunger, thirst, sex, etc., are called primary while those which are learned are called secondary.

The effects of motivation on cognition may now be stated in chronological order:

1. Motivational stimuli have, through past experience, been associated with particular beliefs. Thus, when a particular drive is present it will, in conjunction with other stimuli, help determine which beliefs will be converted into actions.

2. Motivational stimuli conjoin with the external stimulus to form the activating stimuli that initiate behaviour. It is the activating stimuli which constitute the factor that transforms beliefs into active beliefs and actions.

3. Motivation, through drives, acts directly on the scanning process (we have yet to discuss this, but in the meantime it may be said that it involves looking through the set of beliefs aroused by activating stimuli). For example, increasing urgency will tend to decrease the range of the scan, while increasing drive will tend to increase the range. The scanning process is also affected by the degree of urgency and drive such that the speed of scan varies directly with urgency and inversely with drive. Further, as urgency increases, the anticipated reward (value) becomes more influential, and the anticipated effort less influential, in the selection process.

4. Finally, the speed of selection, which ends the scanning, has precisely the same relationship with motivation (drive and urgency) as does the speed of scanning.

We shall call the process of scanning beliefs for selection, the period of *rehearsal*.

This scanning activity may be thought of as a reviewing of the set of activated beliefs in order to "evaluate" them in terms of the valence, value, and the strength of beliefs. Such a reviewing leads to the selection process.

The selection is a process by which the organism selects a particular response in terms of the maximum value and the maximum strength of belief correlative with that response.

Scanning activity is, perhaps, best thought of as being a part of the motivational system in which the selection of an active belief, and the response that automatically follows, is dependent upon the "discovery" of the active belief which has the greatest value and the greatest strength associated with it. The conditions under which beliefs become activated, and which beliefs are selected, leading to particular actions or responses, form a most interesting study, but it would be inappropriate to press the matter further at this point.

The kinds of responses ultimately possible are, of course, extremely varied, and may include overt motor responses, and covert responses such as the categorizing response of perception, and the responses having to do with the conceptual process involving storage, and this may increase the range of beliefs activated.

In general, the greater the degree of motivation and urgency involved, the greater will be the strength of the response elicited. Response strength is also influenced by the amount of value and the strength of the belief selected to act upon.

The response leads to the outcome, or goal, ending a particular item of behaviour, except for the feedback of confirmation or falsification which leads either to the strengthening or weakening of the appropriate belief. No doubt the process is in fact continuous and integrative.

Perception

Let us now turn our attention to the perceptual process and note, first of all, the various ways in which it differs from the conceptual one described above.

In order that activating stimuli may activate a belief, it is first necessary that the stimuli be *perceived*. By *perception*, we mean the action of the categorizing response which, as we shall see, is the response to an immediately preceding perceptual act. That is, for a concept to take place it must be preceded by a percept. On the other hand, in the percept, in order that a stimulus may activate a perceptual belief into a perceptual expectancy, it is *not* necessary that the stimulus be first perceived; indeed, if in the present model this were necessary, we should be involved in an infinite regress.

Now since there may be more than one perceptual belief associated with a given stimulus, the question arises as to *which* of the beliefs activated will be selected; such selection leading automatically to the categorizing response which is here considered to be identical with what is usually called *perception*. A second difference now becomes apparent between the operation of perception as compared with conception. As we have seen previously, the selection of a belief is a joint function of its value, and its strength, while in perception the latter probably plays the more important role. This does not mean that value may not be important, especially where the stimulating circumstance is ambiguous and motivation is strong; but on the whole, the strength of the perceptual belief is primary in its selection, in most conditions. By strength of perceptual belief we mean, simply, the degree of association between a particular stimulus and a particular belief. What the conditions are that lead to the strengthening or weakening of such associations will not be discussed here.

We will now examine some of the details of the perceptual process a little more closely. We may define the activating stimulus state as: that state of the central nervous system which is capable of transforming beliefs into activated beliefs. But we shall find it useful to introduce some further terms.

"Cues", we shall say, are a sub-class of the class of activating stimuli which stem from objects or events, either internal or external, which are being apprehended directly through knowledge by acquaintance.

Cues from external events may be modified by internal motivating stimuli stemming from concomitant motivational states. Conversely, cues from internal events may be modified by external stimuli. For example, a motivating stimulus signifying to the organism that "I am hungry", may be modified by a disrupting external event such as the sound of an approaching fire siren.

"Clues" will indicate a sub-class of the class of activating stimuli which stem from the context, ground, or surround in which the apprehended object or event, either external or internal is imbedded. The apprehension of a clue is direct, i.e., through knowledge by acquaintance. Both cues and clues are really subclasses of signs.

Unlike cues, clues are not apprehended in and of themselves; when they are experienced at all, it is in conjunction with cues. Clues may exert an influence upon the apprehension of the concomitant cue, and vice versa. Here, again, it is felt necessary to repeat the warning that the use of such words as "apprehended", "experienced", "perceived", etc., does not necessarily mean to imply *consciousness* on the part of the organism.

While the separation, through the categorizing responses, of figure from ground probably occurs rather early in any perception of an object or event, it is not by any means always the first categorization; indeed the first categorization is most likely to be that of an object- or event-as-a-whole, and the separation into figure and ground comes

A Theory Language for Cognition

later. Obviously, before this figure-ground separation has taken place, we would consider all the activating stimuli to be *cues*.

Clues, then, are activating stimuli which inform the organism about some events or objects other than themselves and will not occur *within* the immediate framework of the object recognized. This information may have to do with objective matters such as size, colour, shape and the location of objects, as well as such subjective matters as pleasantness, attractiveness, harmfulness, etc. The information given by clues may or may not, of course, be veridical.

Knowledge *about* cues, clues, and signs, we can now say, may be acquired either through acquaintance or description; but the object or event about which cues and clues convey information can only be experienced directly, while the objects or events about which signs convey information can be experienced either directly or indirectly.

The breaking down of activating stimuli into the above sub-classes may often turn out to be a rather arbitrary matter; nevertheless, it is believed to be a convenient way of describing the various functions of the activating stimulus state.

In perception, when we apprehend an object or event we are often not able to categorize it completely or fully at the first attempt. Instead, we may commence by categorizing it one way, then another way, then a third way, and so on, often making use of further information from the object or event itself, or by examining our past experiences in order to try to remember what this object or event might be. Finally we may arrive at a categorization upon which we are prepared to act in so far as we are relatively sure that our categorization is a correct one. That is, we may make several *provisional categorizing responses* before we make a *final categorizing response* which will then become the activating stimulus for the subsequent behaviour. Of course, this series of categorizations leading to a final categorizing response may take place extremely rapidly; in fact, it is only on relatively rare occasions that such a series is so slow, and perhaps so difficult, that we become consciously aware of the process.

It is therefore necessary, for any complete description of the perceptual process, to make allowances for such a series of interpretations, leading to a final interpretation, as to the nature of the object or event apprehended.

From what we know of the perceptual process, those categorizations and interpretations of "the given", as philosophers have sometimes called it, which occur early in the perceptual process, are concerned primarily with such matters as the separation into figure-ground, the general shapes, the colours, textures, etc., leading to the categorizations of recognition. Later interpretations, besides correcting earlier misconceptions, probably involve such matters as the context and further meanings and implications. That is, the earlier and more primitive categorizations are combined, elaborated, and given added connotations from past experience through the action of the belief-system. That such elaborations may be enormously complex is evinced by the difficulty encountered when one attempts to recount the exact sequence of events of an aesthetic experience of the kind involved in the reading of a poem or the contemplation of a painting.

Often it is the categorization of the context in which the event is embedded that may greatly influence the selection of the final category utilized. For example, suppose a straight stick is placed in water such that half of its length is submerged. If we look at the stick from a certain angle we may very well categorize it as being bent – that is, if we have not yet observed that the stick is half submerged in water or, if we have, we are not aware of the effect that media of differing refractive powers have upon the path of light. Once, then, we are aware of the context, and have beliefs about the influence of the context upon the object, we may categorize the stick as being straight, even though we might continue to say that it "looks bent".

There are therefore times at which we must distinguish between the way a particular object or event is *sensed*, and what the object or event is *believed* to be. In terms of the present model, the earlier *sensing* of the object would correspond to the interpretations of the earlier provisional categorizations, while the final *believing* of what the object or event is would correspond to the final categorization. The stick standing in water may be *sensed* as looking bent, but it will be *believed* to be a straight stick half submerged in water.

Both sensing and believing involve the action of beliefs and the selection of a categorizing response, etc., so that these two processes are really not different in kind, but are simply a matter of the position *in a series* of interpretations. We shall see, in the next section, that the distinction made here between *sensing* and *believing* has not always been made clear by psychologists in their discussions of

A Theory Language for Cognition

perceptual problems, and this has led to much acrimonious debate over exactly what is perceived.

There are, of course, many other perceptual illustrations of the bent-stick type in which the provisional categorizations are not always in agreement with the final categorization. For example, looked at from the top of the Empire State Building, cars in the street below may be said to "look like" (be *sensed* as) toy cars, but they will be *believed* to be normal-sized cars observed from a great height. Or, standing on the sleepers of a railway, the rails themselves may "look as if" (be *sensed* as if) they converge at the horizon, but they are *believed* to be parallel. In these rather special cases, what we have learned on previous occasions to categorize in one particular way simply does not correspond with the actual case in the present instance. That is, our previously learned perceptual beliefs leading to a particular categorizing response do not have perfect "ecological validity". Indeed, an important part of one's perceptual maturation is in the learning of those contexts wherein it is the better part of wisdom to disregard previously valid perceptual beliefs. On the other hand, most perceptual situations are such that the perceptual beliefs we hold do have generalizability, insofar as they have an "ecological validity" which is trans-situational, and in which the provisional categorizations do correlate highly with the final one. In this sense, then, despite their popularity in psychological theorizing, the examples cited above are not "representative" of the "natural" perceptual situations.

Memory

We have spent some considerable time illustrating the development of a perceptual theory and, as a result, cannot go into so much detail over the other cognitive processes; but we shall treat each, briefly, in turn. This is, it will be remembered, an outline, and as such it will need to be made more specific at many other levels of description. This matter is taken up again more fully in Chapter 15.

The memory of a human being should be thought of as a storage system; this is how it will be viewed in the next chapter when compared with a computer storage.

The contents of the storage are, clearly, what we have chosen to call "beliefs"; these may vary between perceptual and general beliefs, and they may also differ in their degree of generality. This, it must be admitted, is little more than a possible description; but the real problem now is to explain how the storage works and, later on, how we are to interpret these results in neurophysiological terms.

The most obvious analogy to adopt is that of a filing system. Information is stored, and utilized as needed, with the restriction that every file cannot be found at a moment's notice, if at all. This is because all the information that occurs to an individual in a whole lifetime could not possibly be stored.

Items of information in the form of beliefs are stored, and their availability is a function of their frequency of occurrence and recency. This is merely saying that the last notes put into the file are liable to be the best remembered, and those that are frequently put in are well remembered. But more important than these two factors is the factor of value. Those items which have the highest value are going to be retained, even when and if it is necessary to throw out some of the older information to conserve space.

As to recognition, although we have tended to think of it as almost the same as perception, yet clearly it is dependent on the value and the context of the occurrence. It is the context which makes one event more likely to be perceived than another, and this has sometimes been referred to as the "set" of the person.

Ability to recall information is subject to those conditions already mentioned, and this leads to another related problem. To what extent should we distinguish between different sorts of memory stores? Is there, for example, a short term and a long term store? The answer is probably in the affirmative, and we might distinguish between their uses as between *learning* something and *having learned* something. How much language and signs generally enter into this aspect of behaviour it is difficult to say; as always, we can lay down detailed blueprints and see how they fit the experimental facts, and this is what is now being done.

We shall not pursue memory as such any further here, but it is of course implicit in all that is being said about cognition, and it would be wrong to think of memory as something different from the cognitive process acting-as-a-whole. This is a danger we must continually guard against, the danger of over simplifying the facts.

Thinking

The word "thinking" is used in many different ways, one of which denotes the process of making inferences and solving problems, without necessarily trying out each hypothesis (belief) in practice – something of which we know humans are capable. The same sort of argument must be applied here as to memory, for thinking is a process of the brain which is not separable from memory and perception. We shall use the word to apply to more than those things of which we are consciously aware, and we shall regard thinking as a process in the memory store which involves the logical, or approximately logical, re-sorting of the beliefs held at any particular time. This entails working out inductive and deductive inferences showing consistency, and so on.

The thinking process is a stimulus-response process, or a sequence of states which involve the derivation of logical or quasi-logical consequences, as well as the process of scanning and selecting alternatives, which was alluded to earlier in this chapter.

It is well to remember here that we should be careful to avoid multiplying any of our entities needlessly; from the molar point of view it is enough to show a specified set of outputs for a specified set of inputs, making only the minimum number of internal assumptions. Later on it will be appropriate to worry about making it fit with neurological facts and other details, but in the meantime our aim throughout such theorizing should be to look for the simplest system that will do the job.

In line with what has already been said, it seems unnecessary to make any separate category for problem solving; it is another manifestation of the ability to reason both deductively and inductively, and it overlaps the problems of thinking and learning. This can be dealt with better when we have discussed the cybernetic approach to learning, but at least it may be said here that, in the terminology of this chapter, learning is the acquisition and strengthening of beliefs.

It is natural that the problem of consciousness, or rather, self-consciousness, should come up at this point. For Hull and Tolman and most of the theorists of learning – and of perception, too – the problem of self-consciousness is a long-term one, one that could not be solved from a behaviouristic point of view until a much firmer foundation had been derived for the well-documented processes we have called "cognition". Not that we are going to claim that self-consciousness is yet understood, although it is fairly clear that the time is coming when some account of it should be possible. Indeed, the question will now be considered tentatively.

It seems possible that self-consciousness – by which we mean awareness that our feelings are something that we ourselves have – is brought about as a result of the development of language. No doubt feelings of pain and pleasure, and even possibly more complex states of doubt and frustration, may be attributed to all organisms; but when the situation becomes symbolized, the use of the word "I" makes it clear that I realize that I am myself a separate entity, and my feelings are my own and not other people's, although other people may have similar feelings to mine, and even at the same time. This is not to say that the words come first and the awareness of self after – indeed it seems to be the other way around – but the idea of self seems to be near to the point where language will be used, and where the possibility of symbolization exists, whether or not these symbols become manifest in language.

That a system which can symbolize other things, and other people, should be able to identify and symbolize itself should not seem very surprising. What may seem most important is the fact of having feelings, but this is inevitably bound up with the development of a nervous system that is capable of recording feelings, which is surely an attribute that occurs very early in organic development. In this respect there is perhaps no special mystery about the whole question. Difficulties that have arisen have been in two major fields: (1) The use of words to refer to our own feelings in a language we think of as private because, although the meanings are public, only we ourselves can confirm the truth of the assertions. (2) The failure to realize that ideas and feelings can be the direct and immediate activity of the nervous system. Our ideas are surely operations of the nervous system, and although we can, as it were, describe their content in words (other nervous activities), this does not in any sense mean that ideas are completely different from words. The confusion here is largely to be laid at the door of certain philosophers who will insist on searching for a certainty that cannot be achieved – or so it appears from the vantage point of the behaviourist.

Ideas and Imagination

If it is to be assumed that ideas and imagination are operations of the nervous system, and that we may truly be directly aware of them, then such a theory demands a little more discussion. If our assumption is correct, then there must be some means by which we can reproduce some part of the same effects on our sensory systems as we can by the presence of an external object of which we become

A Theory Language for Cognition

aware. There is indeed some evidence that when we have "ideas", or are thinking about certain things, changes occur in our musculature and our general internal state which mirror some part of that state as it is when the things are actually occurring, rather than just being thought of.

Imagination might be said to be more than this, since we shall want to say that the organism has the possibility of conceiving of events that may not have occurred, or may not ever occur, and this is easy enough to anticipate. The input system must have the possibility of classifying properties and, given sets of properties to classify, it will obviously be capable of throwing up sets of properties that bear no actual resemblance to any existing set. It is in these terms that we shall think of the process of imagination. The having of ideas represents the response to a symbol which would occur if the item that was symbolized were actually there. We might, for example, have the idea of an aeroplane, and since the word is associated with the item aeroplane in a particular way, some sort of image of an aeroplane may actually occur. But we must postpone this question until we have a clearer idea of what is intended here, that is, until after we have had some discussion on the cybernetic development.

Meaning

One of the big problems for philosophers and logicians is to say what the word "meaning" means. This is a logical problem insofar as other words have to be found that satisfy certain standards of appropriateness. But for the psychologist the problem is different, and perhaps easier; we have merely to see the way in which language is actually used. The problem of meaning tends to arise only when the organism is divorced from the words he uses, so that instead of being able to refer to organismic behaviour, he is seeking to explain words and sentences in isolation, which is extremely difficult. The workings of language are not, of course, wholly understood by psychologists, but it is possible to carry out experiments on language to find out as nearly as possible what people refer to, whether these be thoughts, ideas, or whatever.

In this book no serious attempt will be made to utilize our psychological and physiological knowledge to shed light on philosophical problems, but it is firmly believed that this would be possible; and furthermore, that philosophers have created many of their own problems in a vain chase after certainty, insistence on arguing in linguistic terms alone, and their failure to use experiment and the scientific method in general.

An Example of the Theory Language in Action

The analysis of the first section of this chapter has some immediate applications with respect to the controversy between those who contend that experience has little or no influence upon what is perceived (the nativists), and those who contend that experience is a major determiner in what is perceived (the empiricists). This controversy, which involves the transactionalists and their critics, can now be revealed for what it primarily is: a problem of language. It is created by the use of certain terms in various different and ambiguous ways. Both empiricism and nativism reflect some aspects of the truth, and their differences have hinged on two different interpretations of the same set of terms. These different interpretations have led to the examination of highly selected data, and within this selection, confirmation has been found for some aspects of the respective theories. The arguments have thus taken on a certain circularity, and the result has been an increasing terminological confusion.

We have already stated the essentials of perception in the theory language, and the vitally important fact that arises is that the processes which have been variously and vaguely labelled "sensing", "seeing" (or "hearing", "touching", etc.), "perceiving", "believing", and so on, refer to the complex stages of the operation which starts (say) with the impinging of a visual stimulus on the retina, and might conventionally be said to be completed by some action leading to confirmation, or falsification, on the part of the organism. In our terms, it begins with activating stimuli, and ends with either an overt or covert response. The confusion that has arisen in the past is over just how these processes should be described in detail. Indeed, this is our problem: to construct a suitable terminology, or linguistic framework, for the proper discussion of these perceptual problems. This is obviously not the whole answer to the problem of perception, but it will help to avoid confusion over the description of perception, and this is virtually the whole answer to most nativist-empiricist disputes.

We should now consider further some examples that were discussed in an earlier section, taking first the stick half immersed in water. If the observer is asked how the stick is *perceived*, he may be at a loss as to how to answer correctly. This is, of course, because the word "perceive" is vague, and may be taken to mean any subset of the set of Partial Categorizing Responses (PCR's), even including the final one. If the observer says he perceives the object as a bent stick, it implies that the *cues* have been adequately categorized, but not all the *clues*, and the word "perceive" is taken to apply to some subset of PCR's that have not sufficiently fulfilled their full clue function, in that they have failed to tell the observer that, since the stick is immersed in water, it is probably straight in reality. By "in reality", we mean in the ordinary sense of being seen under some standard conditions, and with respect to, say, tactual clues. If, however, the observer took a slightly broader interpretation of "perceive", he might have included such a clue about the immersion in water, and would then have said that he perceived a straight stick partially immersed in water. Of course the answer to the original question is a terminological matter, and depends on the manner on which the word "perceive" is interpreted. Exactly the same difficulties apply to other cognitive words, such as "sensing", "seeing" and "believing".

Many writers on perception have taken the term "perception" to be synonymous with "sensing", and yet surely "sensing" is usually intended, in natural language, to refer to a smaller subset of PCR's than does "perceiving", for if not, it would be difficult to see any use at all for the two different terms. Indeed, in terms of such subsets we surely mean them to be ordered thus:

$$\text{sensing} \subset \text{perceiving} \subset \text{believing}$$

at least in one interpretation, or perhaps thus:

$$\text{sensing} \subset \text{seeing} \subset \text{believing}$$

(by "$\subset$" we mean "contained in") with respect to the visual modality, where "perception" is left vague, sometimes tending, particularly by nativists, to be nearer to "sensing", and by empiricists nearer to "seeing" or "believing"; indeed, the more extreme empirical theories of perception, such as transactionalism, seem to place it as even more general than "believing". It is therefore difficult to avoid the conclusion that nativists and empiricists have disagreed mainly over how the word "perception" should be used, and have accordingly carried out experiments which support their own particular usage. The Gestaltists, as an example, have tended to choose abstract stimulus complexes which are almost wholly devoid of experimental factors, and have thus limited the number of clues to the minimum, while the empiricists have generally done the opposite.

Let us now consider some further examples. First, the distorted rooms of the Ames demonstrations. If, under the specified conditions, an observer looks at a distorted room and reports it as being normal, he may be making this statement with respect to the full range of PCR's (right up to and including the FCR), i.e. he really *believes* it is normal; he has, in the words of C. S. Peirce, "no reason to doubt" that the room is normal. It may be argued that this is because he lacks the cues and clues that tell him of the distortion, but this, of course, is not an analogous case to the stick immersed in water, where his *beliefs* may more obviously be different from his *sensings*, i.e. the clues *are* observable in the stick-in-water problem, but not in the case of the distorted room; furthermore, it is quite apparent to any rational observer that a specially distorted room (distorted, that is, with the object of deceiving) could look normal if viewed from a particular angle. The reason, then, that his interpretation (or belief) is that the room is normal, is that normal-appearing rooms, in experience, *are* normal. He therefore believes this both as a result of his sensings and as a result of the rest of his relevant experience. If any doubt is felt about the experiential factor, it will quickly be cleared by a consideration of the situation of an observer reared in a *space* which is non-rectilinear; for instance, the life and development up to manhood of a child who wore contact lenses that "bent" all the lines we normally call straight. We should also bear in mind the two different ways in which *experience* might then work. It would modify the actual sensory apparatus, and it would also modify the central factors which in turn modify our sensory evidence. We might compare these cases with that of the Necker cube which presents a single activating stimulus, but allows at least two three-dimensional interpretations – in this case, symmetrical.

Now we are faced with a more difficult question. Does the observer actually *see* events differently, as a result of the experience, or does he merely *believe* these events to be different? Once again we are in terminological difficulties over how broadly, or how narrowly, words such as "see" should be interpreted in terms of PCR's. In natural language the word is vague, and there is no reason to suppose that any observer can wholly divorce what he *sees* from what he *believes*. Indeed, such evidence as we have – for example from trained artists – strongly suggests that this is a relationship which can be greatly changed with careful training.

It seems, then, that we are forced to the conclusion that there is

A Theory Language for Cognition

no sensible test that can be applied to the situation where the experimenter says "report only what you see". This is the case both because of the vagueness which clouds words like "see", and because of the non-verbal difficulties observers have in separating one subset of the PCR's from the total set. The most obvious answer to this psychological dilemma is to concentrate on an investigation of the sensory systems from a strictly physiological point of view. This, indeed, is the culminating point of this analysis; it points up the near-impossibility of progressing further in perceptual experiments without recourse to physiological hypotheses, and it also points out the serious difficulties attendant upon the verbal instructions in any perceptual experiment.

A further consideration of "parallel railway-lines" cases, and "cars viewed from the top of the Empire State Building", brings out the difficulties well. In each case, a process of sensing (primitive recognition) takes place, and two converging lines, and some tiny cars, may be said to be *seen*. With respect to the parallel lines, there is a clear distinction – as with the stick in the water – between what is *seen* and what is *believed*. Nobody would expect (in the ordinary sense of the word) to see railway lines as parallel, viewed from the back of a train, if the phrase "see railway lines as parallel" is to be taken to mean, "see two lines that appear to stay equidistant from each other throughout their length". One of the *meanings* of "parallel lines" (i.e. one of the strong beliefs that exist about parallel lines) is that they should appear to converge, from certain viewpoints. Similarly with cars: one expects them to look tiny from the top of the Empire State Building. The philosopher's popular example is also analogous: you expect a circular coin to look roughly elliptical from certain angles.

We are well aware, then, that these problems cause linguistic and logical difficulties for the philosophical theories of perception; but what problem do they offer to psychology? There is no problem. No one claims that we should see the railway lines as parallel, i.e. appearing equidistant from each other (though, incidentally, viewed from perpendicularly above, the section of lines immediately below would appear parallel); nor, indeed, has anyone argued (to the best of the writer's knowledge) that experience would make you *see* (in this sense) such things. The whole argument is over the word "see". You may *see* (in one literal usage of the word, obviously near the sensing end of the continuum) the lines as converging, and yet you may also *see* (in another sense, near the believing end of the continuum) the lines as parallel. Here it is absolutely clear that the word "see" is being taken in two different senses. For this verbal confusion both nativists and empiricists must accept some blame.

The processes we are concerned with are the seried processes, or set of interpretations, which may start, say, with *sensing* and run through to *believing* (the successive PCR's). It is certainly clear that in all the examples quoted, the beliefs depend, as it were, on the making of the correct inductions with respect to sufficient cues and clues to interpret the object, and the context of the object viewed. It cannot, however, be said, even in *apparently* purely visual problems, that such beliefs necessarily depend on either visual or non-visual clues exclusively; nor is it always possible to separate out the *sensing* from the *believing*. For example, under artificial circumstances, such as in the use of some abstract designs in the laboratory, or by the use of reduction-screens in the case of the constancies, our clues are seriously curtailed, and we are forced to believe what we literally *sense*. Under natural circumstances, where we view cars from the top of the Empire State Building, railway lines from the back of trains, sticks partially immersed in water, and so on, we have clues in abundance which allow us to interpret in a manner which is obviously a function of experience. The point here is, of course, that by "interpretation", we mean finally, "with respect to a belief", and beliefs are built up in experience; so that in our model the function of experience with respect to clues is axiomatic. However, this should not be taken to obscure the fact that experiential modifications may also be built into the sensory processes themselves; we should also remember that certain perceptual beliefs may be innate.

The best that can be suggested at the moment is that such terms as "sensing", "seeing", "perceiving", and "believing", be used with constant awareness of their great vagueness.

We believe, then, that the psychological problem of perception is largely divisible into two parts: (1) That of finding a proper terminology (linguistic framework) for the processes involved – this book is attempting, at least, to initiate this procedure – and (2) The physiological studies of these sensory processes.

There is one more important point that must be made clear with respect to the nativist-empiricist controversy. In distinguishing "seeing" from "sensing", to take one example, we recognize that we *can* define these words as *meaning* anything we please, but in trying to explicate them we have assumed a difference which sometimes appears to exist in ordinary usage, and then we have suggested how such a difference could be given a sensible explication. The nativists and empiricists in their quarrel may ascribe any *meanings* they choose to their cognitive terms, but they *must* formulate their disagreements over empirical facts in the *same linguistic framework*. This, we claim, they have not done, nor even recognized that they have not done so. If they could have agreed on, or even recognized, external questions (about their framework), they would have found that there were no internal questions of the kind that have appeared in their discussions.

Chapter 13

CYBERNETICS AND COGNITION

Before we discuss the relation between cybernetics and cognition (George, 1961) we must first say something about the methods and purposes which collectively we call "Cybernetics", and here we shall emphasize only those aspects of cybernetics which are concerned with cognitive behaviour and, perhaps, biology. Cybernetics is, of course, also closely concerned with physics, engineering, and much else besides.

Cybernetics is a new science, or rather, it is a new discipline that overlaps many accepted sciences, and proposes a new attitude towards those sciences.

In certain respects Cybernetics represents an old point of view dressed in a new garb, since its philosophical ancestors are the Mechanistic Materialists of the eighteenth century: Helvetius, Diderot and La Mettrie. It should, however, be emphasized that it is no more than the bare thread of materialism that links the two, and it should be quite possible for those who are radically opposed to Mechanistic Materialism to accept at any rate some part of modern cybernetics, if only for its scientific utility and its methodology, at least with respect to problems of cognition. We will now consider, in outline, the main ideas of cybernetics.

Cybernetics might be briefly described as the science of control and communication systems. It is concerned primarily with the construction of theories and models, both in symbols and in hardware. It insists on a further special condition that distinguishes it from ordinary scientific model-making and theorizing, in that it demands a certain standard of *effectiveness*. In this respect it has acquired some of the same motive power that has encouraged research in modern logic; this is especially true in the construction of artificial languages and the use of operational definitions. Always the search is for precision and effectiveness.

The concept of an effective procedure is therefore central to cybernetics, and it springs primarily from mathematics. In mathematics, the question as to whether certain parts, or even the whole, of mathematics is effectively derivable has always been important. It was Hilbert (1922) who asked whether it was possible to derive all the theorems of classical mathematics in a purely machinelike manner. The theorems of Gödel (1932) and Church (1936), and the classical work of Turing (1937) on what is known as the Turing machine, gave answers to these questions as far as mathematics was concerned. It was possible to show that all of classical mathematics could *not* be produced in this manner, although most of it could. These results have actually led to misinterpretation outside mathematics, in that they were thought to imply that there were some mathematical operations that could not be performed by a *machine*; but this certainly does not follow from the work on decision procedures. What does follow is that a machine, to deal with these operations, would need to be able to compute probabilities and to make inductions, and it must necessarily be agreed that such a machine, being probabilistic, may make some mistakes in its computations, exactly as, under the same sort of conditions, a human being performing the same operations would be liable to error.

We must view a decision procedure as a mechanical method of a purely deductive kind for deciding what follows from a particular set of axioms. Let us illustrate the point.

If the problem to be solved is one of finding two from a finite set of numbers that have a certain property A, say, then we can enumerate all the numbers to which the property might apply until we either find or do not find two numbers with the said property. This procedure is sometimes described as one which could be carried out by a completely unintelligent helpmate following only the simplest routine procedures. These are many such decision procedures in mathematics, and *very nearly all* classical mathematics can be shown to follow such a pattern; but this leaves untouched the problem of how mathematical theories were constructed in the first place.

By "effective", then, we shall mean the construction of a theory that can be translated into a particular blue-print form, from which an actual model could, if necessary, be constructed. It has much the same properties as we associate with the operational definitions suggested by P. W. Bridgman (1927, 1936). To avoid ambiguity over the terms of our scientific description we insist that they be clear and precise enough for us to draw up a hardware system from them. We have already seen how necessary this is in cognitive problems.

The principal aims of cybernetics may be stated as follows:

(1) To construct an effective theory, with or without actual hardware models, such that the principal behavioural functions of the human organism can be realized, and in this book we are interested especially in cognitive functions.

(2) To produce the model and theory in a manner that realizes the functions of human behaviour by the same logical means as in human beings, again, for us, this means especially cognitive functions.

(3) To produce models which are constructed from the same colloidal-chemical materials as are used in human beings. This we shall not discuss, except in so far as some reference has already been made to nervous activity.

The methods by which these three aims are realized can be summarized under the following headings: (1) Information theory, (2) Finite Automata, (3) Infinite Automata, including, especially, Turing Machines, (4) Finite Automata, including especially logical nets, (5) The programming of general purpose digital computers, (6) The construction of all the models, in any fabric, which might collectively be called "special purpose computers" – these may be both digital and analogue.

Let us briefly enlarge on these methods. Information theory, for example, is a precise language, and a part of theory of probability; it is capable of giving a precise definition of the flow of information in any sort of system or model whatever, and has been used already to describe various behavioural and biological models, especially those of the special senses, and this means particularly the eyes and ears. Descriptions in information theory are, broadly speaking, always translatable into descriptions that are couched in logical net terms. Sometimes one is the more convenient, and sometimes the other, and sometimes both may be used together.

The concept of a *finite automaton* requires careful consideration. This is an effective method of defining any system that is constructed from a finite number of parts, which we may call elements, each of which may be capable of being in only one of a finite number of different states at any given time. The elements of the system or model (these words are synonymous here) are connected according to certain rules, and the system as-a-whole has an input and an output, and we are concerned with the structure of the automaton which is defined by a specified set of rules, and having a specified output for a particular input.

If we allow the number of states or elements to be infinite, then we would be describing an infinite automaton, of which a well-known example is a Turing Machine. This is made up of a potentially infinite tape which is ruled off into squares, a scanner, and a control. The scanner scans one square at a time in turn according to the instructions which make up the programme. It can move either one square to the left on the tape or one square to the right, and it can write a symbol on the square or erase an existing symbol which is already on the square. It was with such a theoretical machine that Turing was able to show that all of what we *normally* mean by mathematics is computable in an automatic manner.

Logical nets, which are of special interest for cognition, are paper and pencil blueprints or models which are known to be effectively reproducible in hardware, and we will use them as illustrative of the class of finite automata.

The general purpose digital computer is a hardware machine made up of an input and output system, a storage which includes a control system, and an arithmetical unit. It can be described in logical net terms as a finite automaton, and is equivalent to a Turing machine in its capacity, provided that it always has access to all the information from its previous computations. We shall be discussing its cognitive significance in the next chapter.

The special purpose computers are hardware examples of automata which are intended to mimic some aspect of the world, or to perform certain special operations. The best known examples of these, from the biologist's point of view, are perhaps those of Uttley (1954, 1955, 1959b), Grey Walter (1953), Ross Ashby (1952, 1956), Claude Shannon (1950) and Gordon Pask (1958, 1959a), but there are many more, such as those built at Bristol by the author (1958, 1960, 1961) and B. L. M. Chapman (1959).

The Behavioural Problem

In this section I would like to describe some of the general principles that have been adduced as a result of regarding certain behavioural systems from the viewpoint of cybernetics.

It was Hayek (1952), in America, who first suggested that the method of human perception was dependent upon a classification system. This suggestion was followed up by Uttley, who built a model of a classification system wherein he assumed a certain set of primitive properties, $a, b, \ldots n$ which could then be partitioned into subsets of these properties $1, 2, \ldots n$ at a time. This is the same essential principle on which the input of the digital computer operates, and it seems to be essential to the human visual system (as well as the other special senses) in one form or another.

Such a classifying system is consistent with our knowledge of the empirical world, which we divide up into classes and properties, and which is a reversal of the process which seems to be essentially the function of the special senses. In the next section we shall give some account of the human visual system, in which we shall rely from the start on the concept of classification.

Looking back at what was said about perception in earlier chapters, we can see that the principle of classification is consistent with what we know about the process of perception. By this we mean that recognition can be understood in general terms as that of classifying (or categorizing) subjects into sets, whereby we simply have the problem of saying what the probability is that a particular subset "belongs to" a particular set. This is the basic manner in which all the special senses might work, although many complicating factors connected with the particular structure of the special senses may be expected to obscure the simple notion of classification.

Behavioural Nets

Let us illustrate more carefully the organization, or structure, of a classification system. It can be briefly summarized. There is a classification system with respect to all the input elements, say, $a_1, \ldots, a_s$, and a set of counter elements operate to count the number of times that any particular subset of these inputs occur together, that is to say, the number of occasions on which they are counted as occurring at the same time. For example, $a_7 a_8 a_9 a_{10}$ may be a small pattern that makes up a simple event which fires the appropriate input. Then the B_{ij} is the name we give to the counter that occurs in connexion with such a subset and its relation to the whole set of which it may be a part, either in the sense of being a part of some larger object, or being related to some other object or event. The use of the letter B is closely associated by intent with the term "belief" which we used in the previous chapter.

Now there will be a certain probability associated with each subset at each time t_i, with respect to its completion as a set, or its probability, at any instant, of belonging to some complete set, while still incomplete. This count will be in terms of previous experience as represented by the simple counters associated with each combination. This process is best thought of as mirroring much of human perception wherein we recognize an object by some small part of it, or by some of the relations it contains, always with a chance of being wrong.

Supposing a subset $a_2a_6a_8a_9$ is recorded at instant t_r where the record is made by B_{2689}, that element which is the conjunction counter for $a_2a_6a_8a_9$. The past count is such that $a_2a_6a_8a_9$ has occurred as a subset of some set – which we will call A for the sake of brevity – more than with any other such set including itself alone. A is associated with another such set B where, given A, the probability of B following, within some finite set of instants of time, is given by a proper fraction m/n and designated p. This process, taken over a finite period of time, is called a stochastic process, or a Markoff chain, where each event is conditionally related to the next by some probability which changes with experience as the number of occurrences of these events increases.

The above brief characterization of the central aspect of recognition does not preclude a whole range of different peripheral sensory systems such as the one previously outlined, which contribute the information handled by the central classification system just described.

We shall use $A, B, \ldots, N$ to designate lengthy subsets of event names $a, b, \ldots, n$ that lead to the B's which now, on the same basis of counting their occurrence, are seen as *learned* associations with respect to different inputs. In other words, the molar events are $A, B, \ldots, N$, and the B's are any associations between two events from the set $A, B, \ldots, N$, and we can extend the definition to any number of events whatever occurring as far apart from each other in time as we like.

Many different temporal relations may occur, according to whether one event leads to another *irrespective of a response* by the net, or whether there is a *necessary* or *contingent* dependence on some appropriate response being forthcoming. The model, then, is a stochastic one wherein there will be a contingent probability associated with the next event in terms of those events (or the single event) that have already occurred. What will thus be stored by the model will be a record of patterns of events, and their temporal sequence, and their associated probabilities that may, of course, change their tendency with time. This rightly suggests that for recognition purposes we shall count the occurrence of simultaneous sets and subsets, and at least pairs of the sets over two successive instants of time; and it follows from this that the cognitive system in organisms is to be represented by a contingent probability table which is subject to continual revision.

Although we shall not discuss it here in detail, the model must have a *motivational system* that will actively select or reject certain combinations of events as "to be encouraged" or "to be avoided", and these two classes *could*, of course, be measured by the use of a continuum of values instead of a two-valued system. Without this selective process, the organism will not show "purposive" behaviour which is essential to *learning*. Our motivational system, in the simplest case, involves the mapping of all stimulus-response relations on to one of two sets of elements; these "encourage" or "discourage" the association. This also implies that, as well as a probability, each pair of event-names (B's or "beliefs") stored must also have an associated *value number*, and this may be taken to range over negative as well as positive numbers, indicating the avoidance as well as the reward aspects of certain associations. These numbers, too, must be able to change as a result of experience.

If a particular *B-value* (the value associated with a belief) increases, then it represents a further successful occurrence of some combination of events; if it decreases, then it shows that combination to be actively unsuccessful; if it remains stationary, then there is no change with respect to that particular *belief*. We mean to imply here that the association is between an event (stimulus) and an event (response). A belief about an association may be increased as its value decreases where a consequent event is highly "undesirable" – another indication of the need for a belief to be characterized by two numbers. All the steps, from the firing of inputs in sequence up to the change of belief values, can be shown to be enacted by a simple machine made up of two-state switches and capable of performing the basic discriminations of the environment and counting the number of their occurrences. We shall not add the obvious possibility of a permanent store to the model at this moment, although all the information on the counters (regarded now as a *temporary* store) could clearly be pushed into a permanent store at any time; we mean, here, a simple permanent store like that of a general purpose digital computer, or its equivalent in logical nets.

In terms of the previous chapter, the dual purpose system mentioned above suggests a distinction between perceptual and cognitive beliefs, where "belief" is still a theoretical term, and "perceptual beliefs" differ from what we have arbitrarily called cognitive (exclusive of perceptual) beliefs by virtue of whether they are derived directly from the perceptual process, or indirectly, via the storage system and the logical operations that can be enacted upon it. A third essential aspect of the net, already mentioned, is in the selective capacity of the motivational system.

The most obvious factor which any human nervous system must include in some form is a storage system; this, of course, has already been discussed, and it is indeed abundantly clear that without the ability to record previous experience, no human being could behave in an intelligent manner. This question has been analysed by Culbertson (1956), who showed that automata without memory could, in fact, exhibit what seems to be intelligent behaviour, but this does not in any way invalidate our main point, which is, of course, supported by the introspective evidence of events we can consciously remember.

Many different methods of storage have been constructed in hardware, including chemical storage systems. These different systems can be utilized to produce certain sorts of results in conjunction with certain types of input, and on these lines a direct investigation can be made of the central nervous system with the idea of discovering which methods are most plausible, neurophysiologically. There is some evidence on this point that suggests the use of at least two different sorts of storage, perhaps in a primarily chemical form, and operating in a manner similar to the registers of a computer.

The brain itself is an *inductive system*, capable of making hypotheses and testing them, able to assess probabilities, form hypotheses about hypotheses (beliefs about beliefs), and so on. Various theories and models have been built to show that this property of induction can be achieved by the methods that include classifying, counting and generalizing. This is one of the important contributions of cybernetics to cognition.

Uttley (1954, 1955) has built a conditional probability machine with some of the required inductive capacities, and two small computers have been built at Bristol capable of exhibiting the same properties. Here, we shall illustrate the operation by reference to work we have done in the programming of general purpose computers (more fully developed in the next chapter).

Our model, it will be remembered, has molar input letters $A, B, \ldots, N$, representing events in the environment; the output letters we can call $R, S, \ldots, Z$. Now the environment, as we have seen, is to be thought of as made up of some sequence of the input letters $A, B, \ldots, N$, and the order and frequency in which they occur is something that has to be known (or learned) by the machine, if it is to behave intelligently – to predict, etc. – in such an environment.

The model has the input tape fed into it, and it counts the occurrence of the letters and the number of times one particular letter is followed by another, and the number of times a letter follows two other letters, and so on. The machine can now scan the tables and discover the rules of the environment in the manner we have described. It "realizes", for example, that A is always followed by B, and – as one further possible hypothetical environment – B is followed by G if and only if the machine itself responds to B by R.

In this way the model builds up a symbolic picture of its environment and the relations between the events that occur. These relations include the well-known logical relations of contingency, necessity, implication, etc. Since, however, the environment is not necessarily fixed, the tables will, in general, themselves be changing as the events change. To put it very simply, the counters feed their information directly into the tables which occupy registers in the computer.

It is clear that the instructions given to the model, and placed in its store, may be wholly independent of the environment that is punched on to its input tape. If the environment is punched on to the tape by one programmer and the instructions by another, neither will be in any position to say what the computer may be expected to do by way of making responses. Even if one programmer performed both programming operations, in which the environment was lengthy and complicated, it would still be quite impossible in practice for the programmer to decide what the model's behaviour was going to be at any instant. Finally, it should be noted that it is perfectly possible for a man to sit down and punch out a series of letters at random, place the tape in the computer, and discover the relations that exist between those letters, and the logical implications of their arrangement, by studying the storage of the computer.

In practice this technique has been used with a general purpose digital computer, but because of the slowness of the punch and of the reader, it was found easier to divide the computer into two parts, one playing the part of the environment and the other playing the part of the organism. Many particular environments have been investigated, some of which will be discussed in the next chapter.

Work on motivation, self-consciousness, emotions, and a machine theory of genetics, are further examples that are of direct relevance to cognition, and well merit our attention, but they cannot be pursued further here.

Applications to Molecular Theories

Having dealt with some relevant matters concerning the background of our subject, we can now proceed to get to grips with more molecular matters.

Approaches have been made from many different aspects; the nervous system is certainly the primary one, but there are also genetics, endocrinology and other biochemical features, cell membrane formation, an analysis of the nervous impulse, and a good deal more besides. From all these, as an example of the application of cybernetics, we shall select the visual system as a suitable illustration (George, 1960).

In discussing vision we must also make some mention of the other special senses, and language, memory and other properties generally attributed to the central nervous system. Obviously we need a model, using a logical net to illustrate the various principles, whereby the visual system may be studied. Such a model is in fact being built at Bristol, and comparisons have been made with actual visual systems.

We must consider the layout of the retina, the firing of the retinal elements through the restriction of the optic nerve, the method of classifying such information, and the storage of that information in such a manner as to make recognition possible.

We must now outline the conventions of the logical net notation, so that the subsequent precise descriptions will be clear.

The basic concept is that of a cell or element which has a threshold represented by a fixed real integer which we will call h. The elements are all precisely alike except for their thresholds and their mode of connexion with each other. They are each assumed to take one instant of time to fire, thus delaying any impulse travelling through a network of elements by one instant.

The elements are connected to each other by fibres of which there are two kinds, or rather, they have two different types of endings on the cells, one of which is excitatory and the other inhibitory. The excitatory endings will be represented by a filled-in triangle (see Figure 21), and the inhibitory endings by an open circle.

A network or collection of elements which are partially connected has three types of element – in this sense we distinguish the elements purely in terms of their connexions.

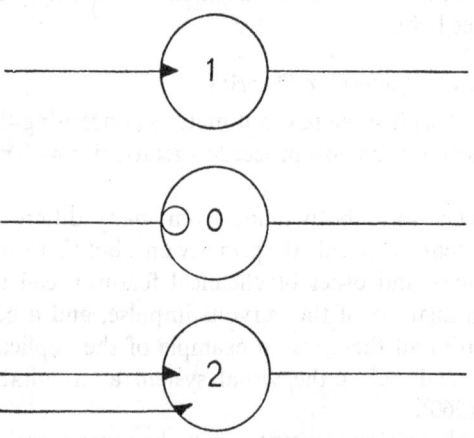

FIG. 21. SOME LOGICAL NET ELEMENTS
The top element is a simple delay-element, the second fires all the time unless it is inhibited by its input firing, and the third is a "conjunction" element which fires if and only if both its inputs fire together.

An input element has unconnected input fibres. These are always drawn on the left of the element which is represented by a large circle. Output elements have unconnected output fibres, and these are drawn on the right of the elements. The inner elements have no unconnected fibres whatever.

The following rules apply to the construction of these networks:
(1) There can be any finite number of inputs for any element, but only one output, although this output may bifurcate to any number of elements. The point of this rule is that, whereas the various inputs may be firing or not-firing, the output is either firing for all bifurcations or not-firing for all of them. (2) No element in the system may be totally unconnected. (3) The output of an element may also be

its input; such elements are said to be elements with loops, or more briefly, "looped elements". These are fundamental to the storage of information. (4) The conditions for the firing of an element are as follows: The preponderance of live excitatory fibres ("live" means carrying an impulse at that instant) over live inhibitory impulses must at least equal the threshold number for the element, so that it then carries a pulse on its input; the output becomes live in the next instant. (5) The system is quantified with respect to time, so that the firing of particular elements is said to be at particular instants of time.

The logical nets can, of course, be drawn like electrical circuits, but they can also be represented by logical formulae. Thus the algebra of classes (or Boolean algebra), suffixed for time, is a sufficient description for almost all practical purposes, although for looped elements it is usual to use the lower functional calculus. The calculus of relations can be used to describe the functioning of the system. This distinguishes the physiology of the system, as it were, from its anatomy.

It need hardly be added that the very fact that our model can be precisely described, and uses a mathematical notation, is a cause of some optimism for the future precision of behaviour theories. This could be the thin edge of the wedge, opening the way to make all behaviour theory mathematical.

Figures 22 and 23 show logical nets for the purposes of classification and storage referred to in earlier parts of this chapter.

Rather than deal very generally with the bits and pieces of the human anatomy, physiology and behaviour that can be modelled, it will pehaps be more useful to show how one particular application can be carried through in some detail, using the particular method of logical nets. It should be understood that we have chosen the visual system because our knowledge of this indicates its especial suitability for this sort of treatment; it is by no means the only one so treated.

Let us first consider the retinae. This will obviously be mirrored by an array of elements in duplicate, both mapped on to the inside of a roughly spherical shell. For practical purposes we can think of it initially as a single array that may be set out in any manner whatever. The particular shape, and its duplication, we shall initially regard as incidental to the major properties we shall be interested in mirroring, although we are aware that this will involve the temporary exclusion of matters dependent upon binocular vision.

In this single array we may number the elements, and make some

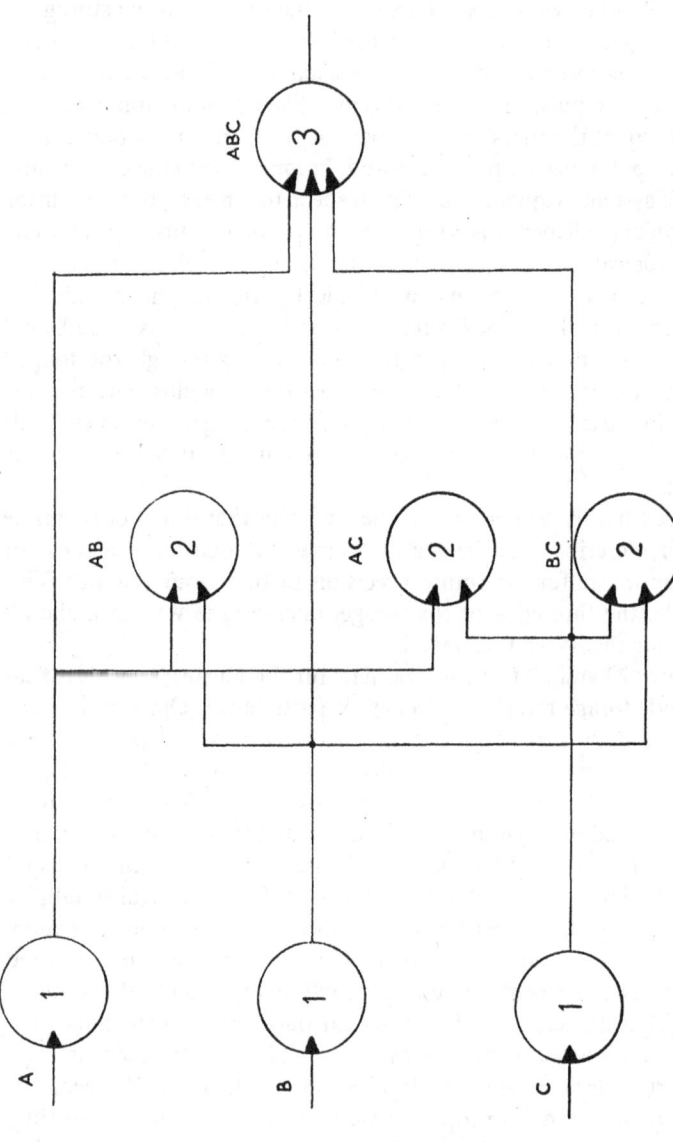

Fig. 22. A Classification Net

This net classifies inputs A, B and C into the conjunctions AB, AC, BC and ABC.

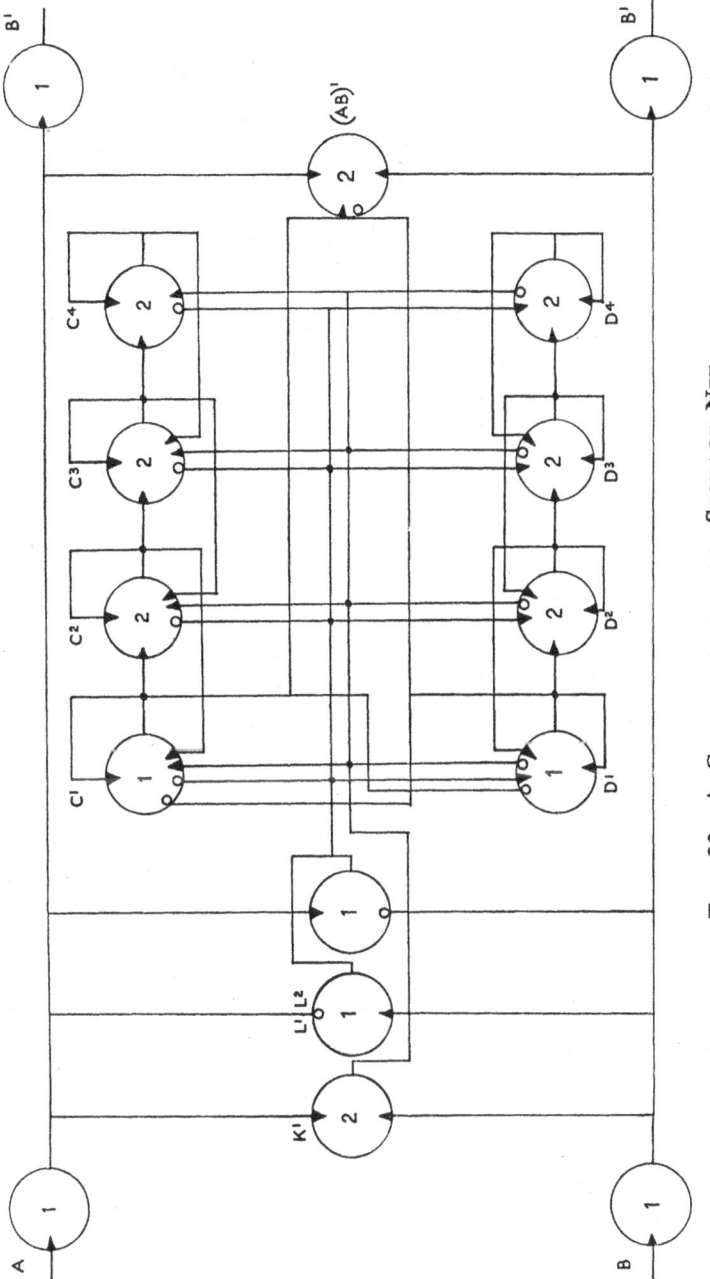

FIG. 23. A CLASSIFICATION AND STORAGE NET

An illustration of one of many types of conditional probability nets. This one classified with respect to two inputs and has eight storage elements.

tentative suggestions as to what properties such an array must have, to be able to carry out such functions as shape recognition, colour vision, and various other visual functions that are at least partly determined by the retina.

Figures 21 and 24 show a sample of some of the elements that the retina might contain. Figure 24 shows an on-off element that fires

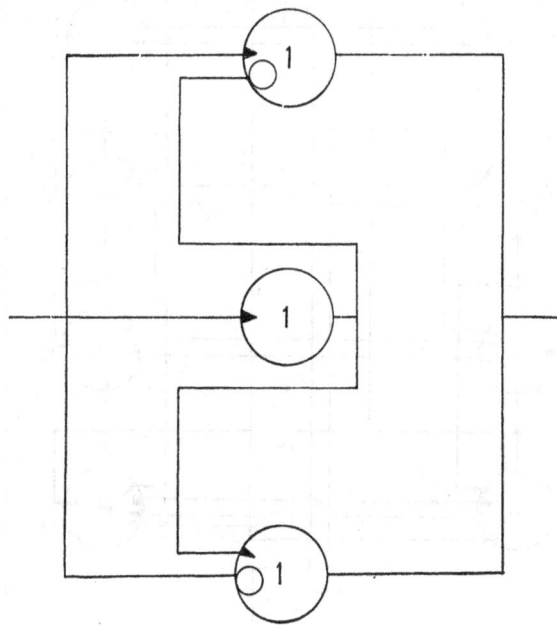

FIG. 24. RETINAL ELEMENTS
This figure can be interpreted as an "on-off" element, while the first two figures of Fig. 21 could be thought of as on-elements and off-elements respectively.

with a change of stimulation, as firing either stops or starts. Figure 21 represents elements which fire when stimulated or when not being stimulated, and these together possibly make up the bulk of the retina. Elements which fire only at the outset or cessation of stimulation may be said to be a special case of the on-off element; they will be called "on" and "off" elements (Figure 24). The first type represented in Figure 21 will also be called "on" elements. Let us assume initially that these elements are randomly and densely packed all over the array. The outputs from these elements will be assumed to run across the surface of the array and funnel through one point called the "blind spot", by analogy with the human eye. The on-off and other elements may be capable of being mirrored in many different ways, and we are not committed as yet to biological accuracy.

Let us now suppose that the fibres that are led away through the blind spot are connected to a classification system of the kind illustrated in Figures 22 and 23 (which, of course, shows only enough elements to indicate the nature of the organization). We will suppose, further, that every fibre from every retinal element is connected to the storage system directly, and called by its retinal name. A *retinal name* is used here merely for our own naming purposes, and for retinal names we shall use the same letters $A, B, \ldots, N$ as before.

If we now place a figure, such as a solid square, against the retina so that its projected shape fires those cells that lie inside its boundaries and not those that lie outside, then a certain set of retinal on-elements will be fired and its complementary set will remain unfired. The off-elements will not fire (will be inhibited) inside the square, but the on-off will, of course, have fired along the boundary, allowing the store to recognize a characteristic set of inputs.

The set fired is recorded in a storage system that is attached to the classification system. Here each output from the classification system has a storage set so that it is fired and stores the information each time a set of pulses is received, as well as giving off responses. The particular set fired we shall call the "square" set. If it is fired again it may be said to produce a response identical with the one originally elicited; but it will be seen, by the nature of the connexions in the storage system, that there will be no need for the whole of the square set to fire on subsequent occasions in order to elicit a response similar to the one originally produced.

At this point we can change our description of the operation to a simple set theory description, since this is what is implicit in our classification and storage system. This means that any subset of the total square set may be liable to elicit the square response. What will in fact decide this matter will be the extent to which subsets in the past, assumed to be a sample of the square set, may have been responded to in a manner "satisfying" to the organism.

This last point requires some elucidation. If our recognition system is to be *effective* in the manner described, it must be able to tell us, with some degree of probability, whether a subset is a sample of a certain larger set or not. Confirmation of this (necessarily modifying the probability) can be achieved through the sampling of the sets in the visual field, or by acting on the assumption of correct identification, and then discovering any discrepancy in the subsequent outcome of the whole context of some piece of behaviour.

The first and most obvious limitation restricting our model is the fact that if we project on to the retina another square which is slightly larger, or smaller, than the one already "learned", it may fire no element in common with the first set; we must therefore ask why there should be any similarity between the first set and the second. There are two possible answers to this; the first is through a scanning operation.

To make the new square elicit many of the same responses at the level of the subsets, we must arrange that it can scan the contours of the figure which is presented to the retina; and to do this we must effect a gradient across the face of the retina such that the retinal centre (or central area) will move along the contour lines. Before discussing how this might be achieved, we should mention that, to fit with the facts of eye-movements, we must have a certain oscillation of the eye around whatever line is being fixated. This is in keeping with experiments on the *fixated* eye, which is known not to remain still, and it has the effect of keeping the on-off elements on the contour lines firing steadily to transfer a total outline of the figure to the classification system, although, of course, this is insufficient to elicit the same subset of responses from the classification system. It is here that the condition of scanning comes into play; indeed, we shall say that the fact of eye movements is a direct result of the scanning operation of the eyes. Even in the fixated eye we shall take it that scanning cannot be wholly suppressed.

At any instant that the retina is stimulated by the presentation of a figure, there will be a centering response that moves the figure towards the point of maximum excitation. Should it happen at any instant that a number of maxima are equi-distant from the centre of the retina, then those eye movements (which occur even in the resting state) will immediately bring one point into the maximum place and thus cause movements along the contour lines to this local maximum. As the maximum is reached, so the feedback effect is diminished to a minimum, causing the next point to become a maximum. This is simply because the feedback, causing the movement, increases with distance from the retinal centre, as well as with intensity of stimulation. This means that the scanning of a figure will proceed indefinitely, unless or until the tendency to scan can be removed by the storage which suppresses the scanning operation – although the suppression is never so complete as to entirely overcome incipient scanning movements, which continue to be observable in the form of eye movements. However, we must leave this question of storage control for the time, but with the comment that the argument here comes near to that used by Hebb (1949) in his theory of the manner in which perceiving is learned.

The effect of centering and scanning could be achieved in many ways other than exactly as we have described it; for example our model could scan a field with differing potentials such that a point of maximum may become diminished as it travels across a graded scanner, setting up new maxima and thus perpetuating further movement. What is important is that we can see how to construct a system in electronic form that would have this sort of ability.

Two significant points should be noted about this model. In the first place the gradient across the retina may divide into two parts, that part that brings the figure on to the central area of the retina – where in fact the sense of movement gives way to sense of detail – and the movement that still remains on that retinal area sensitive to detail, but which now is necessary to the actual scanning operation. It is not being suggested that two separate mechanisms are necessary for this, although there is some biological evidence that this is so. The evidence is, crudely, that peripheral photo-receptors have many more many-one connexions (perhaps a measure of feedback strength for centering) with their bi-polar cells in the retina, than have the more central photo-receptors, yet eye movements will still occur when the whole figure is within the virtually rod-free area. This is clearly a matter that can only be decided by further experiment.

Our second point is that the classification and storage diagrams of Figures 22 and 23 are not necessarily effected at a single stage. Indeed, it seems likely that classification proceeds by stages in a hierarchical fashion, with the first stages being retinal and the final stages cortical.

This last point is closely concerned with another important supposition. It has been suggested that the visual (and other sensory systems) are primarily set-theoretic in their mode of operation. This implies that a particular *concept*, such as a line or a point or a figure like a *triangle*, must involve the sequential firing of closely related subsets of elements. If this also, then the nature of the classification system

– in however many stages it may occur – will be astronomically numerous in its use of elements, since it must take account of every possible figure as well as every actual figure. This suggests that we should also be able to show a method for self-classification.

A vast number of questions now arise as to the capabilities of our model. For instance, we would expect it to be able to produce other effects, either already observed or now capable of being observed, in the human eye; but before we consider this point, necessarily briefly, it is important to remember the nature of the storage organization and the nature of motivation. This seems essential because it is difficult to see how one can account for all the visual effects already mentioned, without some discussion of these vital factors.

We are not concerned here with this general problem, but it is of interest that we cannot wholly account for purely visual effects without a consideration of it. It arises because, in the process of recognition, our mode of discovering whether our methods are correct or not is dependent on the result of our subsequent actions. If these actions are in keeping with our anticipations, then the implication is that our recognitions were correct. Without such a test we simply would not know whether or not they were correct.

It is not proposed to draw logical nets here to indicate the motivational influence, although it would be easy to do so, for it is clear that if in our classification and storage system we designate two of the inputs as negative and positive, then obviously other variables, as they become associated with them, will take on the same characteristics. All of this is vital to the reproduction of organismic behaviour, and no doubt it is connected with what has become known as its "purposiveness". It is essential at this point to realize that an inductive and purposive system of the kind we have in mind is capable of effective self-programming, or creating new "goals" for its activities to the same extent that human beings do so. No new technical problem is involved.

Within the compass of the motivational system we must now consider the storage arrangements, or rather, various possible storage arrangements.

Here the complexity becomes too great to discuss adequately in anything less than a whole book; too great even to illustrate in terms of logical nets. However, since it is clear that our storage system must have certain special properties, we will consider for a moment what are probably the most obvious ones, which are, that the system should store information on the basis of frequency, recency, and value (or urgency) of occurrence, where the *value* is, of course, derived from its association with the positive and negative variables of the motivational system.

The arrangement of storage raises problems which bear on the economy of the system. Suppose the optic nerve contains about one million fibres, and they act in the binary fashion we have assumed, then a complete classification system of the form shown in Figure 3 would call for 21,000,000 elements, which is clearly ridiculous. Reliable estimates have suggested 10^{12} as something like an upper bound for the whole of the central nervous system, from which we can immediately see the inevitability of incomplete classification, whether or not that classification is self-selecting.

Our present problem about the nature of the storage system is simply as to whether we should postulate many different types of store or not. On the whole, as we shall see in the next chapter, it seems easiest simply to *order* the items stored in a hierarchical fashion.

Since we are not primarily interested here in discussing storage systems in logical net models, but only in mentioning them insofar as they are clearly bound up with vision, we shall cut the present discussion short; but before we leave the matter altogether, we must mention the problem of language. This is only just beginning to be studied, and it will obviously prove to be extremely complicated, since it should go some way to focus on the overlapping interests of logicians, semanticists, philosophers and psychologists, as well as biologists.

It can be said, here, that a system of labelling can be associated by the model itself with objects perceived and actions made, and relations between the two. This association can be achieved by a model in exactly the same way as we have already described. The problem is largely bound up with the gradual reconstruction of human language with respect to human environment such that a new syntax can eventually be constructed. For our purposes here it is important to note two very crucial facts. Language, while apparently involving an astronomically high number of elements, will also have the effect of allowing the model to use linguistic generalizations as a succinct store of information. This itself implies that there must be the possibility in the human brain of operating by an overriding control of ordinary associations as a result of language.

Language is almost certainly directly connected with vision in the human being, since the words (concepts) such as "line", "point", "curvature", and so on, will all arise as a result of associating words with particular sensory experiences. It can be seen from this that certain familiar figures will immediately produce the response of naming, and certain words such as "line", "point", etc., will be aroused in the storage, so that a small sample may be enough for the response "triangle" or "square" on an almost instantaneous sample of the environment. This is in accordance with suggestions about the perception and recognition of shapes, and of the learning of this perceptual process, which go back to the work of Hebb (1949).

Retroactive Inhibition

We now turn to other fairly well-documented aspects of learning that seem to be accountable in our present model.

Consider the following three lists of stimulus-response connexions:

LIST 1	LIST 2	LIST 3
A–B	A–D	M–N
C–D	C–L	O–P
E–F	E–B	Q–R
G–H	G–J	S–T
I–J	I–H	U–V
K–L	K–F	W–X

and then consider the change in the B-counters (the beliefs as counters) when List 1 is successfully learnt. Let us suppose, for simplicity, that the only B's affected are in the first row of the following table. If there is an increment of 1 for each occurrence, then, after n trials, assuming the value number remains constant and that we can consider only the association number, the table will read:

$$\begin{pmatrix} nn \ldots n \\ oo \ldots o \\ \ldots \\ oo \ldots o \end{pmatrix}$$

Here, n can be thought of as being simply the number of rewarded occurrences, so that the probabilities associating different combinations can be computed as needed.

Now it is clear that there will be a great difference in the nature of the subsequent matrices according to whether List 2 or List 3 is next used. Let us suppose that they are represented by the second and third rows respectively of the B-table, then they will appear exactly the same in that after r trials they will have the form of the table above, with either the second or third row filled with r's, but whereas in the case of List 2 the presence of the r's will be completely ineffective in producing response until $r > n$, in the case of List 3 it will be effective as soon as $r > 0$.

The reasons for the above are quite simple. The probability of a particular response being made to a particular stimulus is given wholly by the previous experience of the system as reflected in the counting devices attached to the classification system. Thus, for associations like A–B, given A there will be a response B and not D, whereas M will be responded to immediately by N, since it has no other association.

The above argument says that our conditional probability net will show the characteristic that learning theorists have called *retroactive inhibition*. This can be given two different interpretations in practice, according to whether it refers to the use of conditional probability in recognition (or perception) itself. The tied nature of associations giving the probabilities could be said merely to cause confusion as to the identity of the object perceived, since, to put it simply, there would be many different physical objects having many of the same properties. On the other hand, we could consider whether – and if one has to choose, this seems the more likely – it is the relation of consecutive perceived events (already composed of many subproperties) that become confused simply because they are similar, in that some part of an association is already tied to another event.

As a simple example of the last interpretation, consider the following. The event A ($a_1 a_2 a_3$) leads to B, and event C ($a_1 a_2 a_4$) leads to D. Where only $a_1 a_2$ occur, there will naturally be a confusion as to whether B or D is to follow.

The work on transfer of training and stimulus generalization referred to in Chapter 4 now becomes immediately relevant and the reader will see how the description given there is immediately relevant here also. Indeed the simplest possible translation can be made into machine terms.

To recapitulate what was further said in Chapter 4, let

$$A \to B$$

and

$$C \to D$$

be relations wherein $\to$ means "is followed by". And suppose

$A \to B$ is *always* followed by $C \to D$; this means that at the next instant $B \to C$ is a *necessary* relation (i.e. B and C are necessarily related), necessary, that is, for the organism. It still remains a matter for public verification to say that $C \to D$ is a necessary relation. $A \to B \to C \to D$, as we should now write it, is a "slice of behaviour" that involves one necessary relation with or without the other two relations being necessary, and this means that the conditional probability for $B \to C$ must be 1. This necessity, and indeed the probability for the other purely contingent relations, may be said to be dependent upon, or independent of, some response on the part of the organism. We can have the same contingent and necessary temporal relations where the necessary response does not immediately follow, and under these circumstances we write our relation:

$A \to \ldots \to X \to \ldots \to B$, or more briefly, $A \Rightarrow X \Rightarrow B$.

The necessary and contingent relations can now be written:

$$A \Rightarrow X' \Rightarrow B \Rightarrow Y' \Rightarrow C \Rightarrow Z' \Rightarrow D \qquad (6)$$

and (for all responses N) $A \Rightarrow N' \Rightarrow B \Rightarrow N' \Rightarrow D \qquad (7)$

where N ranges over all possible responses in the organism.

The simplest sort of example would be (to translate into everyday terms) a description of my actions on leaving the house. I shall take a raincoat if it looks as if it is going to rain. If I forget it, then I shall necessarily get wet if it rains. If I take my hat it will not make any difference to whether it rains or not, since my actions are irrelevant to the possibility of rain, although they are directly relevant to whether I get wet or not. All events are related to each other (for me) by contingency, necessity or independence.

The above interpretation is simply that of a typical stochastic process, where the sequential conditional probabilities are stored with stimulus and response letters – directly reminiscent of the systems of Hull and Tolman.

The process of generalization arises whenever two subsets in the input system have common letters. For example, *abcdefg* and *abcdefh* are common members of the set *abcde*, and if we write A for this set we can see clearly that if f and g are properties which, while possibly recognized, are independent of the outcome of the response, they may thus lead to generalization. Indeed, such set-theoretic inferences can be drawn on any of the relations existing in the store.

We have suggested before that it seems reasonable to add a permanent store to the simple counting device with its temporary storage

Cybernetics and Cognition

systems; in fact a logical net can be drawn in pencil and paper – or built in hardware as a general purpose computer – wherein information in temporary storage will, at some time and according to certain conditions, be transferred to a permanent store. One might guess two sorts of interacting conditions in which the transfer would take place; firstly, where the degree of confirmation is high, and secondly, where the association is at the habit level. The phrase "habit level" is, of course, a possible point for discussion, but what is intended here is that there are certain relations that involve no interference, and the association is actually known. The problem is to provide the appropriate response for some specified outcome, and apparently the system cannot provide it unerringly until a number of trials have taken place; this may reflect the presence of random elements in our connexions. This serves to draw our attention to the difference between the *learning* process – which is perhaps dependent upon the temporary store – and the *learned* process, which is dependent on the permanent store. This is at any rate one way of thinking of the problem.

An alternative, and roughly equivalent, method would be to regard the particular connexion as fixed (or saturated) after some stage in learning. The distinction is usually drawn between temporary and permanent storage registers in digital computer design, and although it is not obviously necessary in uneconomical automata, it is precisely through economy of space and elements that this distribution comes about. Here it is suggested that all the counters are in permanent storage, and some small subsets of all the counters are used for all actual counting; when an association has passed a certain level of count (all of which are in agreement) then no further counting will occur, and the production of the stimulus elicits the response. The recurrence of a doubt (where an expected outcome with high probability of 1, or nearly 1, fails) about an association would then renew the counting process. Such a counting and transfer arrangement is very simple to reproduce in our model.

These examples will no doubt be found sufficient to show the generality of our cybernetic model, and its special relevance to cognition.

Chapter 14

COGNITION AND PROGRAMMING A COMPUTER

An alternative, although equivalent, means of approaching cognition by way of cybernetics is to consider the manner in which a general purpose digital computer should be programmed to learn. But before that we must say just a little more about computers.

Computers are usually thought of as being either digital or analogue; the distinction is, roughly speaking, between the representation of variables by discrete states, wherein, for example, a particular key, like a typewriter key, is pressed to represent a particular number; or by a continuous system wherein a physical state, such as a voltage or current, represents a variable. The very name analogue suggests the use of an analogy or model for a process, but increasingly it is the digital computer which is being used for analogue purposes.

Digital computers are large switching systems which represent numbers by electrical pulses, usually in a language called binary code, using just two symbols such as 0 and 1. They are able to store numbers and instructions, and compute the answers to mathematical and other problems; they are also used in the control of certain processes. The use of digital computers is being extended almost daily to new fields, and it is to one of these that we shall now draw attention.

One important aspect of digital computers is that they require precise instructions in the form of what is called a programme, and although some time and trouble may be expended in providing the programme, once provided, it can supply a vast array of results in a very short time – far shorter, in fact, than could be achieved by any human being, or even group of human beings.

The digital computer is incomplete until it is programmed (given its instructions). What is called a general purpose digital computer

Cognition and Programming a Computer

is simply a computer that can be suitably programmed to perform any computation, and indeed may become the analogue or model for any process.

Programming the Computer to Play a Simple Game

Proceeding from our outline for the basic idea of programming, our next problem is to deal with the inductive programming of the digital computer. We shall consider this in roughly the same historical order as it has occurred, starting with simple, special cases.

Oettinger (1952), Shannon (1950), George (1960), and others besides, have previously discussed the possibility of teaching computers, that is to say, of getting them to learn things, such as how to play games like chess. In every case, however, the feeling was that a process of *insight* was necessary in order to play such games, and this the computer has not got. The position is that what has been called "insight" seems to depend upon taking over information from one situation, and using this information in another situation. Or – and this is, in essence, the same thing – building general principles which can be seen to apply to more than a single, isolated case. This much is surely obvious from a consideration of our earlier discussion of insight-learning and the work of Köhler, Ruger and others.

The result of these considerations is to make it seem very artificial to programme the computer to play one particular game such as chess, or noughts-and-crosses; nevertheless, such an example is necessary to illustrate the method used.

The first point is that, unlike the teaching of a child, we can assume no prior knowledge whatever in the computer. It has never had any experience, it has no knowledge at all, and it starts, therefore, with empty registers. For its first game, then, it must be explicitly told what it has to do. By analogy with the computer, that which is innate in the human being is already built in.

We shall consider noughts-and-crosses, since it is a simple and well-known game. The first thing we must do is to number the squares of what we may call the noughts-and-crosses board, using the numbers 1 to 9 inclusive, naturally in binary form. The numbering of the board itself seems to raise a problem, for the actual choice of the numbering directly affects the statement of a winning position, or rather, a won game. There are many convenient ways of carrying out the numbering, and the most obvious is to number simply in rotation from 0 to 8 or 1 to 9 (see page 237), or even at random. The nine numbers representing the nine squares of the noughts-and-crosses board; a rather special numbering is shown on page 235 which is convenient for the use of the programmer.

The need then arises for a number for a won game, a lost game and a drawn game. These will be, say, 9, 10 and 11 in binary code.

The storage system must be considered next. Clearly, the registers of the computer must be used in such a way that the order in which the moves are made is recorded, as in our logical model. Against each order, e.g. set of moves, there must be a number, which we shall call the "value number", which increases or decreases according to the success or otherwise of the particular play. We can, say, add 1 for a win, subtract 1 for a loss, and leave unchanged for a draw. We do not need to take the whole nine moves of a game together and give an evaluation to that; rather, we can break down the total sequence into subsequences of, say, three successive moves, starting with the opponent's move followed by the computer's own move and followed, in turn, by the opponent's move.

A number of further points arise, of course, since it is necessary to keep a record of the complete set of moves making up a game before it is possible to decide whether the moves are good or bad. In other words as in our cognitive model of Chapter 12, we may have delays before confirmation takes place. Here this merely represents the fact that we cannot tell whether a hypothesis is good or bad (true or false) until we have tested it and seen the outcome.

The problem, then, is to tell the machine the rules and then get it to learn the tactics. There is, of course, a somewhat arbitrary division between rules and tactics, and it is worth mentioning that the rules can themselves be learned, provided that the computer is able to watch the game being played, i.e. provided a sample of games is fed into it for analysis into component values. This implies the use of the computer as a sequential analyser, and since this is so, it is convenient to regard a tactic such as the following to count as a rule for our example purposes. When a single computer analyses all the moves, without actually playing a game, we have the analogue of a "thinking" process as opposed to a learning through performance.

The rule we will illustrate is well known in noughts-and-crosses, but to make it, and our subsequent discussion, clearer we will select a numbering scheme for our board, and start to play some games.

Cognition and Programming a Computer

The board will be numbered in the following rather special way for purposes of illustration:

$$8\ 3\ 4$$
$$1\ 5\ 9$$
$$6\ 7\ 2$$

This has the added convenience for the programmer of being able to state in simple terms the winning or losing of a game. A game won is a game in which three numbers adding up to 15 are selected by one player before the other. Indeed, from the computer point of view, noughts-and-crosses can be redescribed as a game of playing in turn and seeing which is the first player to select three numbers that add up to 15.

In terms of the above numbering then, our rule is to check the board state to see whether two numbers have already been selected such that a third number, not yet selected, collectively adds up to 15. If so, then this number should be selected, either to win the game or to stop the opponent winning.

In practice there is a further problem, which is that if you wish the computer to learn about its environment, or learn to play a simple game (which is the same thing), its speed will be greatly affected by the slowness of its input and output, to say nothing of the comparatively enormous delay created by its human opponent's thought. It was therefore found convenient to divide the computer into two parts, say, A and B, and programme A with all the rules *and* the tactics, and B with the rules only, and then let B learn the tactics by playing the game.

The following chart shows the flow in general terms for the complete operation. We next see a series of games played, the original, randomly chosen set of values having been attached to the registers. These can be stated as follows. The selected Value Tables have the last number representing the value, in each case.

FLOW CHART FOR NOUGHTS-AND-CROSSES PROGRAMME
PLAYED BETWEEN TWO COMPUTERS A AND B

In practice A and B can be two different sets of registers of the same computer.

```
Place instructions containing
both rules and tactics in A.
```

```
Place the random numbers in the storage elements of B.
These represent the "values" of the combinations of moves
made by B.
```

```
Place instructions containing
the rules only in B.
```

```
When the board state is presented to A it fills in a letter
previously vacant according to its explicit instructions. Then
transfers record of board state to B.
```

```
When the board state is presented to B, it first checks
whether there are any two numbers among the winning
sets of triads, which have both been filled by the same
computer, and if the third number making up the winning
triad is so far unused it must fill it in. Otherwise it proceeds
to the next step.
```

```
B now searches through the appropriate registers to find the
maximum value number and makes the move accordingly.
"Appropriate" here means for games started by A and
reading 5/8/3, that all the registers starting thus and with
next move 1, 2, 4, 6 and 7 must be checked. There will be a
convention for cases of equal value numbers. It then trans-
fers record of board state to A, provided the code letter for
win draw or loss does not appear. If they do then proceed
to next step.
```

```
W, L or D having appeared, B puts 1, -1 or 0 on to every
move made in the game and then destroys the copy of each
move that he has made and proceeds to next game, thus
returning an empty board state to A.
```

```
5/1/0   5/7/6/1/1   5/6/3/1/1
5/2/0   5/7/6/2/2   5/6/3/2/0
5/3/0   5/7/6/3/1   5/6/3/4/1
5/4/0   5/7/6/4/3   5/6/3/7/2
5/6/1   5/7/6/8/2   5/6/3/8/1
5/7/2   5/7/6/9/1   5/6/3/9/0
5/8/0
5/9/0
```

The game will then be as follows:

```
5/7/6/4/2/8/1/9/D
5/7/6/4/8/1/2/L
5/6/3/7/2/8/1/9/4/D
5/6/3/7/2/8/1/9/4/D
```

after which they will remain constant until the computer changes its second move, which is at the moment 3. This sample is short and rather artificial, but it is sufficient to illustrate the method. At this point it only remains to add that the computer can easily perform the operations described, and it very quickly learns the important tactical steps, after which it never loses. One other point should be noted: the computer B *never* has exactly the same statement of the tactics as A, since A plays on a purely deductive basis, following a rule which is verbal, whereas B carries through the steps of checking the maximum values from the matrices; in practice, of course, this will lead to exactly the same result.

This point is connected with the statement that we would not want to claim "insight" on the part of either A or B, since there is no possibility here of taking over a result and using it in another situation. To grant the circumstances for this to be a possibility, the computer must be taught at least one other game, sufficiently similar to noughts-and-crosses, and with the record of the noughts-and-crosses experience still available to it. For these results to be utilizable we should need the computer to generalize its results.

A simple explanation of how such a generalization may come from noughts-and-crosses alone is suggested by considering an alternative numbering scheme for the board, say,

```
1 2 3
8 0 4
7 6 5
```

and then examine the following games:

$$0/1/2/3/L$$
$$0/1/2/4/L$$
$$0/1/2/5/L$$
$$0/1/2/6/-$$

It is clear from this short sample that all sequences of moves which follow the starting move of 0 will have the general form

$$0 \; m \; n(n+4) \qquad (1)$$

if they are not to be losing.

The principle which can now be directly extended to all the moves of the game is completely general, and eventually states in the form of (1) a decision procedure sequence. It should be noticed that the statement of (1) implies the cyclic nature of the number; thus 11 is the number 3.

The ability to make the above generalization depends upon the ability to recognize numerical differences and to state general mathematical forms, and this is something which it must separately learn, unless it is simply told. It can also be added that for any board state some general principle can always be discovered, although it may be more unwieldy than (1) above.

Auto-Coding

A very interesting problem, from our point of view, is that of Auto-coding. The reason that auto-coding has been introduced into the computer field is to avoid some of the complications of programming, and so making expert demands on an unduly wide range of people. The problem can be put this way: If we know a suitable – that is to say, a simple and sufficiently precise – language, we will wish to instruct the computer in that language, and to do so we shall need an interpreter. For this, the dictionary suffices, so we build the dictionary into the storage system, and the computer translates our language into the form of its usual programme. This raises some important points.

In the first place, language has been seen all along to be closely bound up with control operations, both deductive and inductive. We can, indeed, illustrate the difference we intend between deduction and induction precisely in terms of language translation. In the auto-coding problem, where the translation takes place between

Cognition and Programming a Computer

two known languages, the operation of translation is a *deductive* one; but when one language is not known, the operation is *inductive*.

Inductive translation is by no means uncommon. In wartime, the breaking of enemy codes was inductive; archaeologists have the inductive problem of discovering previously unknown languages; and of course, above all, the scientist is continuously trying to find the appropriate generalizations about the world he observes. He could be said to be translating the language of nature. In the same terms, this book is trying to break the code of cognitive systems.

The situation is exactly mirrored, in a trivial way perhaps, by the computer learning to play noughts-and-crosses, or any other game. The problem is to construct a dictionary from which language translation takes place, or to construct a model in axiomatic form from which deductive inferences can be made. The interesting point is now being brought out that models or dictionaries or axiomatic systems are all much the same in their use. Indeed we are saying, in effect, that models are often verbal, even usually verbal.

Inductive Programming

To make our discussion clear we will use the following notation. Let $A, B, \ldots, N$ represent input letters as before, and $Q, R, \ldots, Z$ represent output letters. These letters may be suffixed, if necessary, giving a potentially infinite stock of input and output letters. The mode of generation may be quite general, so that at any instant whatever, although the number of input and output letters used is finite, the number of letters can always be increased.

We can now state the problem as being one of setting up a dictionary which relates input to output letters, and according values, and also perhaps probabilities, to such relations by virtue of differential reinforcements.

This vital factor has been previously mentioned in learning. It entails, quite generally, that for every input letter M, say, there will be an output letter Y, and for every choice of M and Y there will be a probability of some further input letter N, and an assessment of the value of N for the computer. It has to be the case that the motives, or some motives, are built in. For human beings the main motive is undoubtedly that of survival.

The question of constructing new or modified goals must be left for the moment, but will be returned to after a further discussion of the general inductive programming procedure. This is most easily done in practice by dividing the computer into two parts and letting one part play the role of the environment and the other that of the organism, although, in describing the matter, it is easier to think of it as a tape that is punched with the details of the environment and passed into the computer. We shall talk of the work in terms of the latter model.

We shall have, then, a tape made up of input symbols representing the environment, and the problem of the computer will be to categorize the relationships between the letters on the input tape. For example, if A is followed by B if and only if the computer prints R after A, then we say that the occurrence of B is contingent on the occurrence of R on the output tape. This means, of course, that the input tape must be a function of the output tape; it is what logicians call a *contingent* relation (this is something we have already discussed), and it represents the fact that what people do may change the nature of the environment in which they live.

It may also be the case that the machine's response to a particular input letter will have no effect whatever on the next input letter, and in such a case the logician will say that the two letters on the input tape – say, C and D – are *necessarily* related.

Quite obviously these are two limiting cases, and in between we have relations of varying degrees of complexity. Thus E may follow F if and only if some combination of R, S and T is printed on the output tape. This could be regarded as the analogue of the machine solving a problem; indeed a scientific problem could be regarded in just this light as a particular set of relations existing between input and output letters. The idea of controlling the environment emerges when the computer is in the position of being able to "anticipate" every input letter by virtue of the previous input letter, and change the next input letter whenever that is desirable. This, of course, depends on the selective reinforcement of the system.

In this way a computer can ensure that a control is maintained, by storing information made up of the occurrence of successive combinations of symbols, and by ascribing probabilities to these combinations of symbols. This always assumes that the ability to control the succession of events is in fact possible.

Clearly, if the input letters are random, then the relations set up are likely to change quickly and make prediction difficult.

The storage registers are not fixed in their length, and this presents a difficulty. Obviously we shall want to store events of what is sometimes called length three (cf. Tolman's *expectancy* or Krechevsky's *hypothesis*), which means simply an input letter followed by an output followed by an input, e.g. $A/R/B$. But this may not be enough, since the probabilities associated with an event of say, length five, is not the same as the product of the probabilities associated with events of shorter length that make up the event of length five. Thus

$$p(A/R/B/S/C) \neq q(A/R/B).s(B/S/C) \qquad (2)$$

where p, q, and S are probabilities. In a particular case, of course, they may be equal. The organism can nevertheless often proceed with sufficient accuracy by assuming that (2) is in fact an equality. But problem solving behaviour calls for an extension of the length of events used when the problem is not soluble with events of too short a length. This indicates that there must be means for generating events of greater length as they are needed as a result of failure.

The storage systems described represent the well-known methods of statistical sequential analysis of the stochastic type. It is a matter of associating probabilities with successive elements of a sequence, where these probabilities are changing regularly as a result of each successive input. In fact it is probably undesirable that all the probabilities should change quickly, and there will almost certainly be some method available whereby, once a particular relationship is well established with probabilities approaching 0 or 1, the relation is not made subject to this Markov Chain procedure unless at some later time it is realized that predictive operations, made in assumption of the truth of the relationship, turn out to be false.

The above argument means that in a more complete inductive programme – certainly if one were mirroring the behaviour of a human being – we should have two sorts of storage, one for relations that are *being learned* and another for those that are *already learned*. This links up with work that has been done recently on *Heuristics*, which are intermediate solutions in the solving of a lengthy problem. It also links up with what we have said about cognition in the human being.

A tactic in noughts-and-crosses can be learned by the differential reinforcement of moves in a game, where all moves in a game lost were scored –1, and all moves in a game won were scored +1, even though some of the same moves may occur in either game. This does not matter in noughts-and-crosses, where the range of possible moves is small, and discrepancies in move-calculation are soon worked out; but in a long game like chess, it would take an astronomical time to evaluate every move in a game, and an equally long time to learn a decision procedure by such a method. We must therefore look for intermediate or simplifying principles.

Obviously just these sorts of *heuristics*, or simplifying principles, enter into chess as played by ordinary humans. They have rules of thumb that guide the strategy or tactics of the game. It is not easy to say which tactical generalizations are used by chess experts, and whether they are conscious or unconscious. They could certainly be formulated in an inductive programme in the same way as in the generalizations which have been discussed earlier, but we shall try and show that language leads to an alternative formulation.

Language for the Computer

We now wish to add words $X_1, X_2, \ldots, X_n$ to our system, and we wish the computer to have a potentially infinite number of words at its disposal; that is to say, it must have a means of constructing an indefinite number of words. The method, which is learned by example in humans, may also be learned by the computer, but for all practical purposes it will be built in. Indeed the learning process for computer becomes simply one trial, or it need be no more.

The principle of association, by which words come to be associated with "things", is exactly the same as the manner in which "things" have already been shown to become associated with each other. Indeed, it is clear that our input tape may contain words as well as event symbols; furthermore, there is really no need to distinguish these outside the machine, since the word will associate and precipitate an action in the same way as an event.

This raises many interesting problems for the programmer. It can be shown that computers can learn simple languages this way, and indeed the natural languages for them so to use are those languages which we call "logical". They are the logic of classes and relations, although here they are better called the logics of empirical classes and empirical relations, since they are descriptive and probabilistic. It is from this that ordinary language can be derived.

In practice we can see a clear link between this sort of programming and auto-coding, although at present most auto-coding is deductive, since the language is wholly "taught" to the computer in advance.

An exception to this statement, is the case of Generating Routines, so-called, which might be regarded as the equivalent of our learning programmes in auto-code form. This is a matter which we shall discuss later in connexion with an inductively programmed computer changing its own goal.

The general argument concerning inductive programming seems to suggest that no distinction, except one for purely linguistic convenience, need be drawn between words and concepts. The word "concept" might be used to apply to the development of a state, represented by a Markov Chain in the register in the computer, up to the stage at which it reaches verbal reformulation as a result of the computer now having a language with which to describe everything and anything that occurs to it. This includes relations between output events, between input events, and between output and input events. These inputs and outputs must also include words themselves, for it is now well understood that we shall want to distinguish between words about "things" and words about words.

A computer that has gone this far can, in principle, surely deal with the problem of transferring findings from one situation to another, and thus satisfy a condition that seems to be much the same as is needed in human "insight".

The whole problem of language goes a great deal deeper than we have so far discussed it, but much of this complication takes us outside the field of cognition to a consideration of the origins and development of language (Diamond, 1959). This matter is indeed too complicated to be discussed further in the present text, at least from a purely linguistic point of view. Suffice it that an automaton can be expected to build up the concepts appropriate to naming things and actions, and the distinction between things and actions leads to a distinction between nouns and verbs.

We shall now simply add a brief note about the probable effect on the automaton of linguistic inputs with respect to the stochastic storage system. It should be emphasized though that this is only one simple way of regarding the matter.

It will be supposed, as we have said, that words are learned by finite automata in the same manner as other learning takes place, which is essentially by the process of selectively reinforced association.

A brief description of a simple finite automaton that is capable of "learning" is one with inputs a_1, a_2, . . ., a_n, outputs r_1,

$r_2, \ldots, r_m$, and an internal storage system in the form of a Markov Matrix:

$$p = \begin{pmatrix} p_{00} \, p_{01} \cdots \cdots \\ p_{10} \cdots \cdots \cdots \\ \cdots \cdots \cdots \, p_{nm} \end{pmatrix}$$

Where $\sum_{v=0}^{\infty} p_{ij} = 1$ and $P_{ij} \geqslant 0$ for all i and j, since the P_{ij} are probabilities. They prepresent the probability of and input a_k occurring, given that an input a_i has occurred, and that an output r_j has occurred. In other words the probabilities are over two successive input events, but contingent upon an interpolated output event.

The set of total possible events depicted in this simple system is the set $a_i r_j a_k$ for $i = 1, 2, \ldots n$; $j = 1, 2, \ldots, m$; $k = 1, 2, \ldots, l$; with permutations on the indices i, j, k.

Now this sort of system must be selectively reinforced so that the "goals" or future events are evaluated in terms of some specified yardstick. Associated with each and every event is a valence number

$$v_1 \geqslant v_2 \geqslant \ldots \geqslant v_m$$

Thus given an input a_i the automaton scans the triplets $a_i r_j a_k$ where $i = x$, say, and $j = 1, 2, \ldots, m$, $k = 1, 2, \ldots, l$, and selects the triplet with the highest valence; for equal valences it takes that valence with the maximum probability. Ultimately, we shall need to specify more sophisticated optimization conditions, but this is sufficient to exhibit the general effect of language.

In terms of the stochastic learning system, let us suggest the effects of language in very general terms.

Some subset of the inputs $a_1, a_2, \ldots, a_s$, are "auditory" inputs and we shall call these $b_1, b_2, \ldots, b_r$, and some subset of these are linguistic inputs and we shall call these $\alpha_1, \alpha_2, \ldots, \alpha_t$. Naturally the distinction between $\sum_{j=1}^{r} b_i$ and $\sum_{i=1}^{t} \alpha_j$ is one that will be learned by the organism, but for our purpose we may take this distinction as already having been learned, in other words an appropriate auto-code is presumed supplied.

Now the effect of a "linguistic" input will be to modify the behaviour of the automaton and one way in which it can do this is by modifying the elements of the Markov matrices for probabilities

Cognition and Programming a Computer

and values. Language acts as a weighting function l_i say such that any subset of probabilities p_j may be re-stated in form,

$$l_1 p_1, l_2 p_2, \ldots, l_i p_j, \ldots$$

and similarly for the valences, giving

$$l_1 v_1, l_2 v_2, \ldots, l_i v_m, \ldots$$

In practice this means that probabilities or valences, or both, may be modified to take any values in the closed interval (0, 1).

The new value will be a function of the *confidence* shown in the source of information. This can be stated as a variable factor $\sum_{j=1}^{m} k_j$ and then $\sum_{i=1}^{m} l_1 = f\left(\sum_{j=1}^{n} k_j\right)$.

We shall not investigate the form $\sum k_j$ should take in this brief account, but some part of what is entailed is obvious enough and can be simply stated:

(1) The expected "goal" of the source system at that moment or in that range of moments, and
(2) An invariant basic loading with respect to overall confidence in the source.

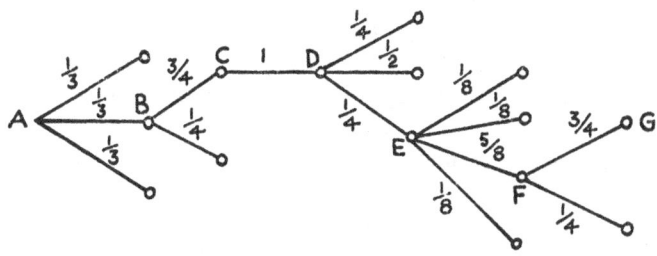

Fig. 25. A Stochastic Route
The graph shows a possible routing from A to G.

Now very simply, in diagram form, the automaton has the problem of selecting a route through a lattice, say, and takes the route shown in Figure 25. The route is through the transition probabilities listed in the diagram from *A* to *G*. Now Figure 26 shows a modification which results from changing the probabilities at the fifth step.

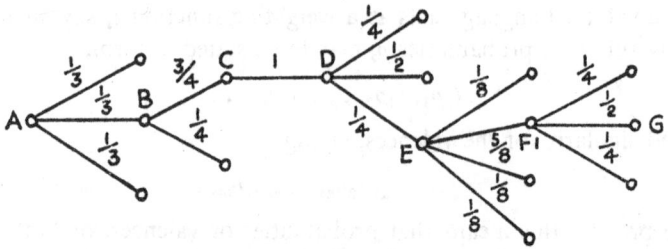

Fig. 26. A Modified Route
This graph shows the stochastic route of Fig. 25 with the fifth conditional probability modified.

The change is the one that we shall say has been brought about by a linguistic stimulus. No such *sudden* change could be otherwise achieved, except in terms of a sudden change in reinforcement.

The implication is that the linguistic input will, when fed into the automaton, according to its confidence level directly affect the probabilities. Its effect is that of the weighted probabilities which exist in the source system.

The only point of this brief example is to illustrate the possible linguistic effects from the point of view of an automaton (or computer) and we shall develop the point no further.

At this stage we must underline the two methods of approach. We can get a computer to behave inductively with respect to events which are not named, or through the language developed to name events. The former approach is almost certainly the first to be considered for practical purposes, so we shall now say something about this.*

Non-Linguistic Induction

At an earlier stage we represented the material on which a computer works as a set of numbers. This means that all the operations of a general purpose computer are mathematical operations. From this point of view, games like noughts-and-crosses are problems of set theory. The same argument exactly applies to other games like draughts, chess, and even card games, although there may be

* This whole question of language in finite automata is at present under investigation. It seems perfectly possible to accept a certain duplication of "words" in the automata. Some words being in the machine language (storage organization comparable to nervous activity in the human) and the other words being in an auto-code and representing language in human use.

Cognition and Programming a Computer

additional conditions to be satisfied. The significance of all this is that we want the most complete basis for all possible arithmetical operations, and this we find under the name of Primitive Recursive functions.

Primitive Recursive functions are the general class of functions that include everything that normally occurs in classical mathematics; the operations of addition, subtraction, and all other mathematical operations, can, of course, be exemplified in this way. This means that if the computer has the power – by virtue of being programmed – to carry out any primitive recursive operation it can do, it seems, as much as anyone could hope to do in learning.

This still leaves open the problem of transmitting information about shape and order which seem to represent a vital factor in the human being's approach to O's and X's.

Changing Goals

There has been some argument among cyberneticians as to whether a computer can or cannot change its own goals. There may be something of a semantic problem involved here, but in particular terms, which will be explained, it most certainly can change its goals. This is, of course, necessary if the model is to be useful to psychologists interested in cognition.

If the computer is differentially reinforced, then with respect to a certain subset of variables, it will perform optimalization operations. This is like putting survival above all else in a human being. But these are by no means the only goals, since in the inductive associative process we can evaluate every association with respect to its contribution to the optimalization of the basic variables. A simple example of this is to say that when an event is associated directly with something obviously good for survival, it becomes thought of as itself good for survival. We may call these other goals secondary goals, and these, of course, will change according to the changing circumstances upon which the computer is making its inductive inferences. Similarly, there is no reason why we should not ascribe specified values to the basic goals, and these may become non-basic if and when a secondary goal exceeds the basic goal in value; such things seem to happen with humans when they are prepared to sacrifice their lives for some cause. But rather than pursue the philosophical implications of this, we will consider its cognitive importance. It perhaps should be said that techniques such as "bluffing" which normally enter into games and is very difficult to actually reproduce in a computer programme can in principle be learned in the same way as any other principle, whether general or particular.

Cybernetics and Cognition

A good deal of our space has been devoted to summarizing some of the results of cybernetic research, and in the previous chapter we made a specific attempt to forge a link between cognition and cybernetics. The time has now come to say something more explicit on this matter.

In the first place we should ask about the relation between the learning theories, such as those of Hull and Tolman, and cybernetics research. If we consider Hull's theory, it will be remembered that he dealt with S-R units which are strung together into a stochastic process of the same kind as the one analysed by the computer and the logical nets. In fact, the resemblance is much deeper than that, since the concept of differential reinforcement that we have used is very similar to that of Hull.

In our computer programme, and also in our logical nets, we have assumed some such concept as a primary drive, and further, that initially neutral stimuli take on this drive, or motivated characteristic, by virtue of their association with the primary drives.

Tolman's theory is essentially the same in its interpretation of needs and cathexes, where the secondary cathexis that becomes associated with an original neutral stimulus is simply an alternative rendering of what the computer may said to be doing.

In Tolman's theory, we have seen (page 114) that there is a less direct use of reinforcement, and here the distinction between Tolman and Hull is largely a matter of emphasis; many of Hull's learning activities spring *from* needs, whereas for Tolman they often accompany and participate, but may not initiate, learning.

Tolman's basic association unit is S-R-S rather than S-R and, as with motivation, we might say that the emphasis has gone away from the habit type of learning towards the more sophisticated type, where emphasis is on the *next* state, rather than a mere response to a stimulus.

In our computer learning, as we shall collectively call it, the same stochastic methods are used, but we shall not lay heavy emphasis on S-R or S-R-S as a "basic unit," since learning can be seen clearly to depend upon very complex associations, of which S-R and S-R-S

seem rather simple special cases regardless of the interpretation we place on the stimulus (*S*) and the response (*R*).

Our computer experiments seem to point to the fact that our methods of describing learning must be *effective*. This means that we must pay attention to the sort of advice that has been given us by theory-constructors such as Woodger (1937, 1939, 1952, 1954). We must consider what our assumptions (he calls them zero-level statements) are, and make them explicit, and give them an operational definition. The use of the computer lends further emphasis to the point.

To return to the essentially Markovian (Markov Chain) nature of learning, it seems clear that the length over which our conditional probabilities must spread is a function of the complexity of the problem to be solved (or the operation to be learned), and the extent to which the organism is motivated to learn it. When the problem of cognition is analysed in this way we tend increasingly to see it as being bound up with the physiological organization of the special sense receptors, and the structure of the memory store.

The principles of the input and the output depend, no doubt, upon a classification principle, whereas the central problem is that of organizing the information for storage.

The details of the storage organization are still rather far from having been completely worked out, but good progress has been achieved towards the behaviouristic ends. Programmes have already been designed which order information such that the most valuable comes out in the first registers to be scanned; information with high probabilities comes next; which is to say that urgent matters are dealt with first and habits next. If the input does not demand an urgent response, but merely elicits a habit response, then it enters into the bulk of storage where matters are still more obviously being learned. There is, of course, an exception to this, in that the first set of this large set has been generalized into "beliefs", so that some arbitrariness may have been enacted on the facts. These will not matter if the degree of arbitrariness is not too great. In other words it will not matter if we treat Mr Smith exactly as we treat Mr Brown, provided that the difference between them is sufficiently small, i.e. so small that we shall get similar sorts of results, from our point of view.

Finally, we come to the situation where learning is still occurring. This will naturally lead to the longest delay in responding, subject to the facts suggested in Chapter 12. Of these, value and probability are the most important, but these variables also cloak the other factors of recency and frequency.

Motivation represents built-in stimuli, and the development of secondary motivation is brought about by association. The pattern of learning events is clearly beginning to emerge from studies of this sort, and it is perhaps not too much to claim that we understand how learning occurs; and although we do not understand either the biological or the social details sufficiently well to allow us to make predictions beyond a very limited range for individuals, we certainly can claim that cybernetics has contributed a great deal towards this emerging pattern.

Chapter 15

MEMORY

In a book on cognition it may seem unnecessary, at first sight, to devote a separate chapter to a study of memory, since it is in the nature of learning theories that they should imply something about the organization of memory, both in animals and humans. On the other hand, while there is a great deal of work in cognition that implies the organization of memory, there is much less that deals with it explicitly.

It seems worth while, therefore, spending some time on the study of how human beings remember, and we shall discuss not so much what we consciously remember as what we must, in fact, be able to remember in order to perform the actions we carry out. In a sense, the prototypes of behaviouristic memory experiments are those of the kind transacted by Hunter (1913). They involved a delay between the observation by a rat of a light flashing above the door of one of many possible entrances, and the releasing of the rat to see whether he could choose the appropriate door. The appropriateness of the door, of course, was the result of previous conditioning between the flashing light and some form of "reward".

Quite clearly, *we must be able to remember*, and our chapters on learning and on cybernetics, and our discussion of recognition, have all laid emphasis on the need for an appropriate storage system; indeed, a storage system must obviously exist where learning and intelligent behaviour exist, and our present questions, therefore, are concerned with how were remember. It would be easy – too easy, in fact – to say that we remember by drawing out of storage a record of what has been previously experienced.

Bartlett (1932) has shown fairly conclusively that remembering is not the mere reproduction of previous experience, but is rather a creative process which is directly linked to previous experience.

Before we discuss some of the experimental evidence, it is

important that we should make one or two distinctions. By the word "remembering" we imply two or three different processes. In the first place there is "recognition", which is nearly synonymous with "perception", though perception is slightly more general in that it includes the case where items are presented to the organism for the *first* time. Then there is "recall", which involves the active remembering of a name or a scene without that name or scene being presented to the organism. Thirdly, there is "retention", which is very similar to learning in that it is concerned with how information is retained in the storage system at all.

The implication of the word "retention" is that information may be actually forgotten, and so we have the definite problem as to how it can be forgotten; but before we can deal with that there must be a prior discussion of the manner in which the human storage system works.

In terms of Hull or Tolman, and indeed in terms of our own theory as suggested in this book, it seems that we store information in the form of simple associations. We have called these associations *GBU*'s, or "beliefs", and they are thought to be symbolized as implications of the form "if . . . then – ". It is further assumed that these associations are stored together according to their similarity in the sense of happening together, or being similar to each other in some other respect, or indeed according to more than one of these principles.

Certainly, also, we should want to argue that these beliefs differ in their degree of generality. If an event A occurs and is followed by another event B, then this may confirm not only the association between two particular occurrences, but also the relationship between classes of occurrences. Indeed much the same could be said for the "expectancies" of Tolman and the "habits" of Hull, but perhaps it has never been sufficiently clearly said.

Our discussion of cybernetics has suggested some further principles of memory, and these, in turn, were dependent on previous work on learning. It seems that the memory must have priorities of recency, frequency and value, where the last named takes precedence over the others. The idea that events of great value will be available in the unconscious, and that these memories must be released by careful treatment, comes from psycho-analysis. This implies that events of great value may be remembered and made available, although they are neither recent nor frequent. This is something that seems to fit all the experimental facts of memory, but what remains less obvious is whether or not there is an active inhibiting of certain of these memories. This indeed raises the whole problem of how we forget.

Now it is quite clear that we could not reasonably be expected to remember everything that happens to us, yet there is much evidence that suggests that we have stored away much more information about our past than would previously have been thought possible. The answer to this problem seems to rest on two considerations. In the first place we have at least a two-stage memory system – in fact, it may be many more than two – and most of the items of the environment of which we are potentially aware at any instant never get past the first memory store. In terms of our earlier terminology, we have a myriad of potential stimuli at any instant, but only some of the subsets are actually effective stimuli, and it would seem that only those that pass the temporary store level are in fact filed away in our more permanent memory store.

But even beyond the first level, or temporary store, there may be gradations of permanence, and these in turn may represent simply the degree of value, etc., attributed to each event.

Our second point is that forgetting is made up of two different processes, first, the loss of information from consciousness – and this no doubt depends upon active inhibition – and secondly, the loss of information from the whole of the memory store, a process that one might expect simply on the basis of replacement of memories with the passing of time, where the information lost is expunged from the least permanent (least important) end of the continuum.

It will be obvious by now from the manner in which we are discussing memory that we are thinking about computer-like systems, or at any rate systems that store information by explicit physical changes of structure, and this necessarily represents events in a coded form.

Now if events can be represented in some coded form, this would be sufficient to account for some of those results in memory experiments which show that memory is never a mere reproductive process, but is rather a creative process. This necessarily follows, we shall argue, when it is remembered that in representing events by a set of symbols, we are abstracting from the characteristics of the events, and in trying to reverse the process we are bound to have lost (and, perhaps as a result, invented) a good deal of information.

The older behaviouristic view (Osgood, 1953) stated that "forgetting is a direct function of the degree to which substitute responses are associated with the original stimuli during the retention interval". This sort of retroactive interference is something we would accept as a large part of the present behaviouristic theory, but by itself it is certainly insufficient.

Bartlett (1932) has contributed, by means of a series of skilful experiments, to our knowledge of the memory as a constructive process. His emphasis is on meaningful material, as opposed to many earlier studies such as the classical ones of Ebbinghouse, in which nonsense syllables were used. However, from our point of view it seems possible that the distinction between the two methods is one of degree only.

One objection to Bartlett's experiments – and this applies also to the Gestalt experiments on memory – lies in the method of serial reproduction.

Hebb and Foord (1945) and George (1951) have shown that serial reproduction as a method tends to bring into focus an operation of selectively forgetting in terms of the last reproduction. The Gestalt psychologists' claim that the trend of memory traces is towards the symmetrical denotes, in fact, a mere loss of information.

Particular Aspects of Memory

There are many peculiarities of memory which, while being perhaps such as we might expect to find, are nevertheless important enough to record.

The first is sometimes called the Ward-Hovland Phenomenon, and is concerned with reminiscence. By "reminiscence", here, we mean the fact that human beings are capable of considering things, of "going over" past events in their heads. It is part of the problem of experimental psychology to explain exactly what this sort of "going over" operation is, but at least it is familiar in the intuitive sense. The particular effect of the Ward-Hovland Phenomenon refers to an improvement in performance within an interval of from two to five minutes after learning has ceased.

Another phenomenon connected with reminiscence is called the Ballard-Williams Phenomenon. This is also a reminiscence effect, but operating over a much longer period.

In the non-intuitive sense it can be seen to be possible that further transfers of information may take place after events have occurred and been stored. This indeed is essential, since there can be no doubt that stored events are the material from which generalization and

Memory

logical inferences, both deductive and inductive, can be made. This means that there is a stimulus-response activity going on inside the organism all the time, and it is essentially covert in character.

This sort of activity, which might perhaps be regarded as a chain of cognitive events operating on the basis of association, relative value, logical inference, etc., is of course the process we commonly call "thinking". We shall be discussing this thinking operation in the next chapter, and here we shall say no more than that it is very close to learning, in that it is made up of a series of *GBU*'s, or beliefs, operating in a chain (to use our earlier terminology), and that reminiscence is a part of what we should call "thinking". To avoid any misunderstanding about this let us say again that by "thinking" we do not mean only that which we are conscious of reminiscing over – to quote a particular case – but rather that it is the total set of transfers and operations that take place in the brain without immediate external stimulation.

There is, in fact, some doubt as to whether we should expect that the human being can think, or carry out these internal cognitive operations, at the same time as it can deal with input. The probability is that it cannot, and that it must switch at high speed from one sort of operation to the other; but there is no certainty about this. Clearly we cannot depend in any sense on introspection, and as far as the objective facts of the nervous system are concerned, we are in no position to say exactly how it works.

Another effect that must be mentioned is the Zeigarnik effect. It is clear from experiments performed by Zeigarnik (1927) that if subjects are asked to carry out a task, but have the task taken away from them before they have finished, they cannot forget the nature of the task. This, no doubt, is a link in the connexion between remembering and motivation, a matter to which we must shortly give further consideration.

An illustration of an experiment testing the Zeigarnik effect is provided by Bogolovsky (see Osgood, 1953), who asked himself the question as to whether the effect was due to interference with the task, or to interference (which had occurred) with another task, with resulting emotional effects.

Bogolovsky and Guthrie (1941) thought up twenty paper-and-pencil tasks, and these tasks were presented in a random order, so that each task was either (*a*) completed following a completed task, (*b*) completed after interruption of the previous task, (*c*) interrupted following a completed task, and (d) interrupted following an interrupted task.

The results of this controlled experiment showed that the frequency of recall under condition (a) was 108, under (b) 120, under (c) 94, and under (d) it was 116.

These results, of course, show no Zeigarnik effect, and it is thought that this adds further support to the general belief that the Zeigarnik effect only appears when motivation is very high, as it certainly was in her original experiments.

It will be quite obvious by now that we can never wholly separate motivation from learning, nor memory from either. We might have included in this chapter some further discussion of retroactive inhibition, transfer of training, and even such matters as massed and spaced learning, but since these have received some attention already in earlier parts of the book, at this point we shall merely summarize their effective connexion with memory. Indeed, all that need be said now is that the experimental data on transfer of training suggests strongly that the ability to perform a series of tasks with the minimum of difficulty depends upon the tasks being similar, and on their being without particular steps such as would actively interfere with the transfer. The very fact of similarity may imply the use of some general principle to facilitate the operation of learning some particular task. This merely confirms the sort of theory we have outlined, where there are sets of beliefs becoming activated, and where appropriate general beliefs will facilitate the responses to particular effective stimuli.

A concept like "set" is clearly included here as relevant to the functioning of the memory, and simply refers to the fact that a state of expectancy, in the more everyday sense of the word, will occur in various particular contexts. This has already been mentioned, but to remind ourselves of the point, we are arguing, of course, that the system is stochastic in operation. Events are stored in sets of length 2, 3, etc., and these events, or their symbolic representation in storage, are connected by probabilities that are themselves the result of previous experience. An event of length 4 or 5 is a context for its components, and many particular, lengthy patterns will become very familiar to us. Thus, when A occurs and B follows, we may immediately recognize the context $ABCDE$, and this leads to the expectancy of CDE. This state after AB is called the "set" towards CDE.

We have also seen that the work on learning sets suggests the two-stage memory system, two at the very least. In fact we shall now say that the two-stage system could be a many-stage system, but we shall refer to no more than two until it transpires that more than two are necessary. All this is true only in default of any further physiological information which might settle, or at least help to settle, the question.

We shall conclude this brief chapter with the reminder that the methods of learning and the degree of motivation involved affect the way information is remembered. It seems reasonable to hazard the guess that this is so because there are at least two stages of memory, and even within these stages there are definite priorities, and when information is lost or suppressed, it is an operation enacted on a particular subset of the ordered set of events stored.

Chapter 16

THINKING

As in the case of the previous chapter, it may be felt by some readers that so much of what has already been said in this book, especially about learning, automatically covers anything we might say about thinking, that the implication might be drawn that a special chapter is therefore unnecessary. Actually, it seems unlikely that many people would argue in this way, in view of the *conventional* distinction between studies on thinking and problem solving on the one hand, and learning and perception on the other.

It is quite obvious that as long as we are following the behaviouristic approach – which this book has so far followed – we shall be likely to minimize these distinctions. Certainly we mean by "thinking" something more than that of which we are immediately aware, by way of connected images, etc., in consciousness. It is not easy to define "thinking", but perhaps it will be of interest first to have a look at some of the definitions that have been proposed so far.

Bartlett (1958), writing on *thinking*, suggests the following definition which, he admits, may be rather limited.

> Thinking is the extension of evidence in accord with that evidence, so as to fill up gaps in the evidence; and this is done by moving through a succession of interconnected steps which may be stated at the time, or left until later to be stated.

This definition is, in a sense, a definition of a typically inductive operation. It is apparent that it does not cover the deductive inferences which organisms must also be able to perform, and it seems to be closely associated with what we are conscious of, since it is likely – one would hardly be justified in stating the case more strongly – that the deductive operations are unconscious, by and large, while those that are conscious will be mostly inductive.

Thinking, for Bartlett, is a high level form of skilled behaviour, and with this we shall readily agree, as we shall with his distinction

Thinking

between what might be called tied and adventurous thinking. In some situations where inductions are required there are many constraints and a good deal of evidence, while in other situations there is little of either.

Bruner, Goodnow and Austin (1956) have placed their emphasis on the categorizing behaviour shown by human beings. They regard the act of categorizing as having vitally important consequences for human behaviour. They are:

1. It reduces the complexity of the environment.
2. It is a means of identification.
3. It reduces the need for learning.
4. It is a means for action, and
5. It permits the ordering and relating of classes of events.

Now we can clearly see that categorizing behaviour is closely akin to the classification type of system mentioned in our discussion of cybernetics, and discussed more fully elsewhere (Uttley, 1954; George, 1961). It is also closely linked with logic which, of course, deals precisely with classes and relations and their ordering. We shall be returning to this relationship later on.

Recognition is based on categorizing, or perhaps more immediately on a classifying system, and the whole operation critically depends on the ability to *generalize*. We saw earlier that in trying to programme a computer to learn we needed to *generalize* in order to save space. Saving space had the effect of facilitating speedy response, which would be impossible if every event were separately stored, and the whole store searched through before a response was made. The question of urgency of response came up for consideration somewhat earlier, and it is obviously very relevant to human behaviour. It is the need for urgent responses, as well as the need for saving space, that encourages categorizing into classes; but the categorizing itself is helpful in (and of course arises from) pointing out similarities between events, while overlooking certain differences which, it is to be hoped, will not be crucial in some particular context.

The point about reducing the need for learning is well illustrated by the frequently used mathematical technique of reducing some problem to one that you have already solved. This is much the same as assuming that some one situation is like another situation, and that therefore we should try the same solution.

This form of approach by identification is a particular instance of what is called "insightful" behaviour. This becomes markedly obvious when the two situations are effectively the same and the solution works. The external observer would certainly tend to use the word "insight" in describing it.

Bruner, Goodnow and Austin also emphasize the importance of validation, which we, also, emphasized earlier. They talk of validating by a criterion, by consistency, by a consensus of opinion, and by what they call "effective congruence", by which they mean a consistency check coupled with the subjective feeling of certainty.

For Bruner and his associates, then, thinking is very much a categorizing process and an inference making procedure similar to the one we ourselves have already suggested. They define the general field of cognition as "the means whereby organisms achieve, retain, and transform information", and certainly the transforming is closely involved with the method of categorizing.

In talking of thinking and problem solving, the idea of a concept soon arises; indeed we might have said the concept of a concept (beliefs about beliefs are already familiar). In turn, a concept might be thought of as "the common element shared by an array of objects", or, "the relationship between the constituents or parts of a process". We might even say that concepts are *ideas*, and these may be expressed in words, although the exact relation of language to concepts is not clear.

We might think of language as a method of eliciting the concept or idea, the word being a sort of stimulus which conjures up some subset of attributes, sometimes including, of course, some accompanying images. But we must leave the discussion of the relation of language to thinking until the next chapter. It will be apparent that the previous chapter, on memory, and the next one, on language, are both closely integrated with this one, as all three are with the rest of the book.

Osgood (1953) gives a criterion for thought being present in animals. He says that clear evidence for thought will be obtained "in situations in which the relevant cues are not available in the external environment at the time the correct response is required, but must be supplied by the organism itself".

This criterion emphasizes the important role of memory in thinking, and indeed if we accept the fact that in the theory of learning we must make a distinction between *what is learned* and *what is performed*, as experiments such as those on latent learning seem to suggest, then thinking and learning are hardly distinguishable. It is for these

Thinking

reasons, of course, that Hull, Tolman, and the other learning theorists have devoted relatively little time to study directed specifically at thinking, as opposed to learning.

At this stage we can see that what we shall mean by "thinking" will be a process of classifying and categorizing, and the subsequent association of events stored, involving signs, and even language signs in humans, such that the logical operations of deduction and induction can be carried out.

Experimental Work on Thinking

Ruger's (1910) puzzle problems, in which pieces of wire had to be disentangled, are among the examples involving thinking that we shall briefly quote. These puzzles are often cited as examples of *insight* because there is a sudden drop in the performance curve. We shall of course argue that this sort of sudden drop represents a thinking operation, assuming always that the sequence of operations that lead to a solution of the puzzle problem are, on the average, equally difficult.

The problem solving situations that meet Osgood's criterion are many, and some of Kohler's (1925) early experiments are illustrative of the point. He found that chickens and other organisms could learn, when separated by a fence from their goal object, to go quite a long way back from the fence in order to circumvent it. Another example is the famous stick problem which was solved by *Sultan*, and mentioned earlier in the book. These experiments led Kohler to talk about insight learning, and here we are coming very close indeed to thinking.

Hunter's (1924) delayed reaction experiments could also be cited here as illustrating exactly the same point.

We shall next say something about experiments that purport to be on the subject of concept formation.

Hull's experiments have already been mentioned; he concluded that concept formation was in no way different from ordinary discrimination learning. It will be remembered, however, that Hull's subjects had to look for common features in a set of events, and give those common features a name. This has been criticized as ordinary learning when it has been applied to the process of naming, though it may not be quite a fair criticism, for it is not clear that concept formation is essentially different from naming, at least in the early stages.

The principal objection to Hull's ideas on concept formation – a typical criticism of all behaviourism – is that understanding when to use a label or name appropriately is not necessarily the same as *understanding* the abstract concept. This is really a philosophical matter, and we shall refer to it again shortly.

Many experiments, such as those of Smoke (1932) and Kohler (1925), have dwelt on discriminating relations rather than common elements, but in fact the difference is hardly likely to be crucial; indeed, common or identical elements are, in a sense, just a special case of discriminated relations.

Going back to the Bruner idea of categorization, we see that relations are as capable of being categorized as sets of objects or events of any other kind; one only has to consider the close relation between the calculus of classes and the calculus of relations in logic to realize how trivial the distinction is. On the other hand it is clear that there are many different bases for categorization, such as colour, shape, relation to other things, use, the fact that they were seen at the same instant, and so on.

Piaget (1928, 1930) has made a number of observations in the field of the development of concepts in the child, which show fairly clearly that many stages of discrimination are necessary in experience before adult conceptualization occurs. For example, the idea of an independent objective world (a world which is independent of the observer) is something that rarely, if ever, occurs in the very young. The idea that things move and have a consciousness of their own is very difficult to throw off; for the child, the world is egocentric; he is essentially the centre of the universe around which, and in terms of which, everything else is judged.

It is interesting to notice how the history of human thought mirrors, to some extent, this gradual throwing off of the cloak of subjectivity; and how at the same time the subjective comes back in a sophisticated way, in philosophy with Phenomenalism, and in physics with the Principle of Indeterminacy. This does not really persuade us that science can never be objective, but we do see that it cannot be completely dissociated from observations; indeed, one of our best sources of ready-made data on human thinking is in science itself. Scientific theories and the solving of scientific problems illustrate well the capabilities of human beings. This in itself is a good reason for psychologists, who are interested in thinking, to study science generally, and the logic and philosophy of science in particular.

There has, in fact, been a wealth of experiments on human beings in problem solving behaviour and thinking, and we would emphasize this because attention has tended to have been focused more on experiments of the same sort of animals. We do not, of course, aim to reproduce all the vast body of experimental evidence here; Osgood (1953) and many other textbooks of experimental psychology give the necessary references for those particularly interested in this aspect of cognition.

Philosophers and Thinking

Price (1953) has written a great deal on the subject of thinking. His approach is that of a logician who is making logical or verbal distinctions in trying to describe his own thinking operations, and one of the first problems he discusses in his book is the well-known philosophical problem of Universals. He emphasizes the important point that the world is made up of events that are repeated again and again, not only in properties such as colours, but in sets of properties like those we call "objects".

In contrasting the Theory of Universals with the Theory of Resemblances, Price dwells mainly on his own intuitive knowledge of the physical process we have called thinking. For the behaviourists – and let us make no mistake about it – it is very much to be thought of as a physical process, probably involving the human brain. But Price's aim is slightly different from our own; his aim is to make distinctions which can be adequately mirrored by our language.

It is, of course, appropriate to mention Ryle (1949) in this same context, since he has pursued an aim that is essentially philosophical and logical, and has yet dwelt on some of the characteristics of the manner in which humans seem to think.

Indeed, a great deal of epistemology is of relevance here, for the reason that there are clues to be learnt from our logic and language that mirror to some extent our manner of thinking. The danger is that we should substitute informal and anecdotal techniques for experimental ones, and no experimental psychologist would wish to do this. On the other hand, there are certain linguistic problems that cannot be altogether separated from empirical facts, and these can be greatly clarified by a consideration of a logical or philosophical kind. In other words, in a discussion we are concerned with examining the meaning of the words we use, and at the same time we are trying to examine and describe facts.

The main objection that psychologists may have against the philosophical mode of approach is that philosophers do not pay sufficient attention to the experimental and objective facts; they believe that these can ultimately be reduced to the private and immediate experience of all of us; whereas the scientist, while keeping a careful lookout for linguistic traps, is convinced that the philosopher tears his logical problems from their proper behavioural context. Nevertheless, the fact remains that, from the purely scientific point of view, the psychologist can learn a lot from philosophical rumination.

Korner (1959), in writing of conceptual thinking, has discussed a subject even closer to, and more intimately concerned with, the psychologist's interests. He laid great emphasis on Ostensive rules and their application; Ostensive concepts, as he calls them, being defined in terms of ostensive bases. But, as he says,

> The fact that non-ostensive concepts are never applicable to an ostensive basis still does not settle whether or not they actually have bases.

This raises the whole question of how non-ostensive, or apparently non-ostensive, concepts can be used, such as in the relation of mathematical truths to actual experience. The answer lies almost certainly in the fact that ultimately these apparently non-ostensive concepts are either ostensive themselves or are so closely related to ostensive concepts that they should be treated in an identical manner.

Now while it is no part of our intention here to consider logical and philosophical matters in detail, it is nevertheless a matter of psychological importance to discover how concepts arise and how they are defined. We also need to know how they are logically analysed, as this sheds a great deal of light on the subject.

Conceptual Analysis

We shall, of course, argue that what we call concepts are represented by states of the nervous system. We store suitably coded information which refers to particular events, and from these events we form generalizations or concepts by categorizing, which means, by overlooking differences and noting resemblances. These operations are all surely represented by what may be described as changes in the nervous system, though it is difficult here to choose a phrase which is not slightly misleading. However, in this book we are not primarily interested in the molecular changes, but rather in the molar changes; hence it is sufficient for us to think of the setting up of what we have called beliefs.

We shall think of the word "belief" as being virtually synonymous with the word "concept", and we shall now look a little further into the experimental evidence.

Reed's experiments (1946a, 1946b, 1946c) deserve some mention in this context, and we shall take them as illustrative. He worked with cards on which were written such terms as "coffee", "clay", "carrot", "green", and so on, and these words were capable of being sorted into sets, of which each set contained a nonsense syllable as its name; for example, "carrot", "turnip", etc., were, of course, in the vegetable group, and were given the name "BEP"; "green", "red" and "blue" came in the colour group and were called "DAX", and so on.

Each card has written upon it several of the words, chosen at random, and in the experiment the subject is asked to sort out the word on the card which is relevant to a particular concept. Thus, a card having, say, "answer", "highest", "airplane" and "red" written on it would have "red" as the DAX word.

Clearly, the idea that red is a colour word, and has common properties with "green" and "blue" is already known, and indeed the idea is necessary in order to be able to classify under the concept name DAX.

This experiment demonstrates the formation of a new concept name based on distinctions that are already understood.

Reed measured the degree of learning and retention by the number of promptings needed, and carried through the experiment in a number of different conditions. His general findings suggested that concepts are easily learned where motivation is high, where retroactive inhibition is at a minimum, and where logical relations help to point out a relationship; and all these things are taken together in the complex learning situation.

Heidbreder (1946, 1947) has done another set of experiments rather similar to those of Reed. She showed to her subjects a series of 16 drawings which could be classified into 9 concepts, with nonsense names for each set.

We shall not further discuss the experiments here, but it is of interest that Heidbreder defined a concept as being a logical construct which, through signs or symbols or both, is transferable from situation to situation, and communicable from person to person.

This sort of definition distinguishes words from concepts, and indeed this is almost certainly the best way to consider concepts themselves, since at the molar level it seems quite valid and appropriate, and even necessary, to call a concept a logical construct, or perhaps, better, a theoretical term.

We have recommended exactly this sort of procedure ourselves, and in this respect it might now be valuable to turn for a moment to a consideration of the picture we might expect to get of *everyday behaviour* in our own particular terms.

An Application of the Language Theory

We shall now describe some snippets of everyday life, using the language developed earlier in the book. In the choice of actual situations for our demonstration purposes we shall try and give some samples of the principal types of recognition, linguistic usage, etc., that occur in actuality.

This shall be our first piece: "A man is sitting in a chair, in a state of drowsiness, when he hears his name uttered by a voice which he recognizes as that of a close relative whom he has not seen for a long time. She repeats his name, and he gets up quickly, looking around to try to locate the voice."

Initially, beliefs are being transformed into expectancies along a certain chain of associations, and situations are being constructed around the past, i.e. new (composite) beliefs are emerging which are themselves constructed from single successful situations, and made into an imaginary stream of successful situations. We shall call beliefs about the non-actual "imaginary", and this is a type of belief formation, like dreaming. We simply mean to imply here the systematic formation of GBU's or beliefs, where these might be called conceptual in that they are certainly not tied to any immediate perceptual situation.

The effective stimulus state is brought about by an auditory stimulus, which leads to a state of alertness. On hearing his own name uttered, a whole new set of beliefs $B_1, B_2, \ldots, B_n$, which already existed, are now aroused. "That's a voice I haven't heard recently ... That's a female voice ... It's a fairly young female voice ... A kindly person ... Aunt Agatha was kindly, but she's not young ... It could be Mabel ... No. Her voice was slightly flatter ... She lived in a flat ... No, in a house ... Long time ago ... It's like my wife's voice ... etc." Finally a belief occurs, "It's Angela," and there is an accompanying feeling of confidence.

A series of further beliefs is now aroused, involving memories of the past, of Angela and her various associations, and a response activity is evoked, to get up and see where she is, to look around in the direction that the auditory stimulus suggests. The question, "Where is the voice coming from?" represents the belief that the voice is coming from somewhere in the direction being looked at. It is not, of course, suggested that all these statements, or others of a similar sort, would be actually uttered; some may be uttered without being heard externally, and some might have emerged as an ejaculation. Saying the name "Angela", for example, would have quickly evoked the confirmation needed.

The voice speaks his name again, and by this time all the associations for Angela, all the beliefs in the form of memories of the past, the length of time that has elapsed since the last meeting, and the possible reasons for this meeting, are flooding into consciousness. At the same time a far greater range of beliefs is being evoked outside consciousness.

Motivation was aroused initially by the pleasant associations of the female voice; it was familiar, and demanded recognition. The drive of curiosity, at least, was operating, and this sudden motivation caused the flood of beliefs to be transformed into expectancies; but clearly only a very few of them were connected with action. Although the hearer turned around and rose to his feet when his name was spoken, this in no way keeps pace with the complex thoughts that are taking place.

We may assume that the beliefs aroused are not all on the same level. We shall expect beliefs about his own memory to occur, as well as about his ability to recall voices, etc., being strengthened as a result of this successful recognition.

Let us now consider a more visually oriented case, such as the following: "A man is walking along a road on which he expects to meet a particular friend. He sees someone he recognizes, but cannot place him at all, partly because he was not expecting to see him, partly because he did not associate him with that particular town. but mainly because he was not the expected person."

The same initial state described in the previous example now occurs. A set of beliefs is operating, mainly now at the habit level, and affecting the motor response of the human musculature so that complex muscle patterns are taking effect. He may also be thinking in the conscious sense, and since he is actively expecting to see a particular person, we may expect him to have beliefs which amount to recalling experiences of the past at previous meetings. Some details about the face and build and manner of the expected person are aroused in the form of beliefs; there may also be more general beliefs about the nature of reunions of this kind, to the effect that they are a good thing, or a bad thing.

At the moment of the meeting there is a perceptual belief aroused about the familiarity of a face. The name of the expected person is on the tip of the tongue, but it is stifled as an inappropriate response when recognition leads to the belief, "No, that's not him." Having already alerted a whole set of beliefs about someone else, it is difficult to get away from that *set* of beliefs and think in terms of a wholly new set. The only immediate association is one of familiarity, but there is a distinct feeling of bewilderment because, somehow, expecting one person and seeing another suggests an association between the two people that makes no logical or causal sense.

There is no point in dwelling further on this sort of example, but it will be of interest now to see exactly what it is that we have done.

We could of course map out a formal sketch of all the probable beliefs included at any instant, and the whole network of their association (this would probably involve us in cybernetics); but we notice in passing that whereas we hoped in some sense to capture the meaning of what is commonly meant by "belief" in our choice of terms, we have in fact captured a great deal more. Every doubt and question is catered for by the word "belief", and this suggests that we should discuss different types of beliefs. In this case weak and strong beliefs have already been catered for, and the weak belief is reasonably called a "doubt". We may call another type of belief "interrogative", and so on.

More important than the appropriateness of terminology is the point that we, as external observers, are in no position to know what beliefs are likely to be aroused by an effective stimulus; indeed, we do not even know what constitutes an effective stimulus in the *a priori* sense. This is inevitable until we are in a position to measure some aspect of the history of the individual, and have some measures of the internal state of the person. These measures must also be closely correlated with particular experiences. The EEG, for example, might indicate that certain types of belief are being aroused. The trouble is that, in order to understand what each person was doing, we should have to be able to apply the necessary instruments at the actual time predictions are made, and that is clearly difficult, if not impossible.

In other words, as far as the human situation is concerned, all we have achieved is a slightly clearer conceptual picture of what is likely to be going on. We have a descriptive language which, in principle, is capable of being translated into precise terms at any level of description. This may allow us to describe rat experiments accurately, under well-controlled conditions, or even human experiments in special cases such as at the psychiatrist's interview, but it provides little of the precision necessary for our everyday understanding of people. We are not much further on than the novelist who is familiar with no more than certain traits of different types of individuals, and what they signify in terms of the beliefs that are being activated at any time by a particular set of circumstances.

It seems clear at this point that no purely molar theory of cognition is likely to be able to answer all our questions, and this is why we branch out into animal studies, cybernetics and physiological experiments; and indeed more and more we bring all these studies together. On the other hand, there is nothing that these disciplines do that really affect the everyday situation, except to provide some of the signs for the correlations that we are seeking, and which ultimately may allow us to predict in the everyday context.

It can of course be sensibly objected at this point that although everyday behaviour must not be inconsistent with our theories of behaviour, it is not the job of a scientific theory to predict every practical occurrence as it occurs. It would be difficult for a physicist to predict exactly what will happen to his boulder as he pushes it down the slope from the top of the hill; so also we find the same difficulty in psychology. What we are searching for, rather, is a systematic language that does the minimum of violence to the facts, and allows the maximum amount of reinterpretation at other levels of description.

With this clearly in mind we may return to the specific problem of thinking.

Motor Aspects of Thinking

There is one other aspect of thinking that demands our attention, and this is exemplified by the experimental research of Jacobson (1929, 1932) and Max (1935, 1937).

By placing electrodes near the motor end-plates of efferent fibres they picked up minute changes in potential that could be amplified and photographed, and they found a correlation between the motor activity and "mental" activity. Jacobson made the further discovery that, through progressive relaxation of the musculature, all conscious mental activity could be eliminated. He did this experiment by getting various subjects, who had been trained in relaxation, to perform various tasks involving thinking. These subjects were then asked to "imagine" movement of limbs and eyes, and the resultant motor patterns were similar to those produced by actual movements.

Max (1935, 1937) used deaf mutes for the reason that they thought, as it were, with their fingers, and he discovered that a certain special pattern of muscular potential was in fact associated closely with their thought processes.

In Max's experiments dreams were also relevant; it has been known also from other work that dreams are closely connected with actual physical stimulation. What is not known is, of course, the actual relationship between changes of the musculature and thought, whether in the waking or the dreaming person.

It is of interest that muscle potentials can be recorded even when the subject claims that he is unaware of any images. This may be taken to suggest that it is the feedback from the musculature that is recorded by the central nervous system which makes the individual conscious of internal changes of state.

Naturally one would like to think that images could be explained in these terms, and there is some reason to believe that they can be so explained. But it is also probable that another source of images, while still the result of central stimulation, comes from the storage registers of the brain itself. It seems unlikely (though not impossible) that the *only* source of images is through muscular feedback.

In view of the recent neurophysiological evidence relating to the reticular formation, it seems possible that it is the stimulation of this part of the nervous system, which seems to be so closely bound up with consciousness, that is important to the effects of muscular feed-back.

There still remains a great deal of work to be done at this increasingly molecular level of cognition, and we must leave the subject here.

In Summary

What we can say about thinking is that it is closely connected with learning, and that if we use the word "thinking" in the behaviouristic sense, we shall no longer wish to maintain the distinction between thinking and learning.

At the same time there is a distinction to be made between problem solving, conceptual thinking, and learning, although perhaps learning itself might be said to include the other two.

Thinking at least must include the logical operations of deduction and induction – if we care to think of induction as a logical operation. Certainly induction itself includes the process of categorizing that is central to the activity of thinking. There remain, then, the methods for solving problems, for confirming or falsifying concepts, and indeed the formation of those concepts themselves.

It seems certain that in human behaviour this whole matter is closely bound up with the use of language. We shall therefore be carrying on this chapter in the next one, where we shall deal with linguistic behaviour.

Chapter 17

LANGUAGE

We have so far avoided talking explicitly of linguistic behaviour, and indeed linguistic behaviour is that aspect of cognitive behaviour which is least often tackled by experimental psychologists. This is not to say, however, that there is not a good deal of experimental evidence in this field, but it is a small amount relative to that existing in the other fields of cognition.

The reason for this comparative lack of attention is that, with the development of behaviourism, animals have been increasingly the subject of experiments, whereas the study of language is virtually confined to human beings.

We have already said something about language in our chapter on cybernetics, but this was necessarily brief, and was clearly inadequate. We shall now try to fill in some of the details.

In the first place, language plays a vital role in human behaviour. It is clear that sentences or utterances elicit responses in the form of further utterances, physical actions or both. The words used elicit behaviour by virtue of some such rather vague criterion as "making one think of something". It is a problem to which logicians, philosophers and semanticists have addressed themselves; they have tried to give a clearcut definition of what it is that a *sign* does that makes it so important for human behaviour.

Charles Morris (1946) is one of those who, influenced by C. S. Peirce, has tried to describe sign behaviour in psychological or organismic terms, but he has been criticized considerably, especially by philosophers, for just this sort of approach to the problem. We shall discuss this matter a little later.

It is important now to mention that signs – by which we mean meaningful utterances – must fulfil one of two roles; they must arouse concepts or they may arouse further signs, or indeed both, but they cannot arouse signs or concepts *only* all the time. This raises the

Language

question as to whether we *think in words* or not, and I believe we should give this matter a little more attention before we discuss some of the developmental evidence.

If we think intuitively about the problem of language, we come to realize that we are aware of images, and perhaps also feelings, that are closely associated with words, but are clearly *not* themselves words. Equally obvious is the fact that words are not the same as the "things" they refer to, the referents of words. This being agreed, we might ask whether it is the word that acts as a sign to elicit the associations which occur for each word, or whether it simply precipitates a stream of further words.

In the previous chapter we discussed some aspects of concept formation, and noticed that it hinges on seeing similarities among differences, and vice versa. This leads in turn to generalizations which, we might guess, are quite vital to the learning operation. Now it is difficult to believe that thinking is only the manipulation of words (or symbols and signs); one may admit that this is sometimes the case, but it seems equally clear that there are also other things involved.

Let us look at the matter another way. If language is necessary to thinking, then animals without language cannot think. As behaviourists, we do not want or expect this result; we say therefore that animals either have language, or that they are able to think without it. Most animals have such a limited set of signs at their disposal that it is difficult to believe that it qualifies for the term language at all, and so we seem to be in a position to say that there is something else that makes thinking possible. We immediately move on to the word "concepts", and we can perhaps agree that it is synonymous with words like "beliefs", words that we have used ourselves in describing behaviour.

We have come to assume, then, that stochastic stores are not only used in learning from description, but they are also used in learning by acquaintance. This raises the question – one that really comes outside our present compass – of how the nervous system is able to code information which is presented, for example, in visual imagery, into a form that is easy to store. The answer is that the nervous system codes words and "things" in much the same way and, from the point of view of the nervous system, the word and the referent are very closely connected. Indeed, should we not guess that, in the interests of economy, words are more usually stored than events? This, it is true, still leaves a nagging doubt on the subject, but it is surely also true to say that words are going to be generally remembered more easily than the detail of actual events.

But let us leave this matter for the moment with the idea in our "mind" that we are capable of storing words and concepts, and that they are closely related.

The Development of Language Behaviour

There have been a number of different theories of the development of language in the child (Piaget, 1928, 1930, 1955), and most of them emphasize the imitative nature of the process.

There is perhaps a sense in which the development of language in the human race could be said to parallel the development of language in the child; but here the process is rather one of imitation of nature itself than an imitation of a brother or sister or parent.

Physically, the process of speaking, and even hearing, is quite complex, but it is describable in physical terms. There seems little doubt that man himself started language from simple grunts that became associated with different states. This is perhaps a sign process initially, in which the words are largely onomatopoeic, but later these sounds will be used to refer to things when those things are not actually present, and here we are moving from the sign to the symbol situation.

Early studies of children show that, in most languages, most of the phonemes used in adult speech are reproducible by the child within the first few months of his separate existence.

It is now suggested that in the case of the individual, selective reinforcement and generalization operate to lead increasingly to specific sets of sound that eventually become the familiar language of the society.

In other words, language is learned by essentially the same process of association whereby anything else is learned by an organism.

But obviously, having said this we have not said enough, because, as we have seen, there are many different views as to the nature of general learning, and all these views have been directly applied to the learning of language. This means that we have a substitution theory of learning, an effect theory, an expectancy theory, and possibly other theories too.

The use of effect and expectancy ideas are embodied in Morris' semiotic theory, and we must now say something about this.

Morris' basic problem is to define a *sign*, and it is clear from the start that he wishes to give a behaviouristic definition. His definition is what we have called a Glossary definition, and reads as follows:

> A *sign*, roughly, is something that directs behaviour with respect to something that is not at the moment a stimulus. More accurately, if A is a preparatory stimulus that, in the absence of stimulus-objects initiating response-sequences of a certain behaviour-family, causes in some organisms a disposition to respond by response-sequences of this behaviour-family, then A is a sign. Anything that meets this condition is a sign; it is left undecided whether there are signs that do not meet these conditions.

Now this definition must be supported by some further definitions. A *preparatory-stimulus* is a stimulus that influences a response to some other stimulus. A preparatory-stimulus necessarily causes, at the time of stimulation, a reaction in the organism for which it is a stimulus, but this reaction need not be a response; it may, for example, be the action of a gland.

A *behaviour-family* is any set of response-sequences that are initiated by similar stimulus-objects and that terminate in these objects as similar goal objects for similar needs.

This definition of sign has been criticized by many writers (e.g. Black, 1953). The concept of *disposing to respond* is not perhaps clearcut, and it is even more difficult, on this sort of definition, to separate language signs from other signs. Morris actually defines language signs (lansigns) as signs in a language system, and there is no further distinction made.

The easiest way to regard this matter, perhaps, is to accept the fact that language signs do not, in any fundamental sense, differ from other signs. This may indeed be inconvenient for some philosophers, but it may nevertheless be a fact. Language is not essentially different from other sign activity merely because it modifies the state of the organism. It is clear that words and concepts are associated in a complex way in which any one of them may give rise to a whole mixed set of the others.

Signs, by this reasoning, are grounded in behaviour, and cannot be wholly understood outside the behavioural contest. This is one objection to a purely logical analysis of real-life situations; it is certainly a well-known fact that the use of words is not the only way to convey meaning; a gesture or a glance can equally clearly convey a meaning, either with or without the use of words.

It looks as if words should be regarded as emerging from the general complex as a relatively precise sort of sign activity. Languages are extensions of behaviour, and this is something that has become increasingly apparent to the experimental psychologist.

Osgood has approached the problem of signs somewhat differently, in that he has tried to associate the sign and the "object" through the disposition itself and the behaviour elicited by the object. Words are thus thought to represent things because they reproduce a replica of the behaviour towards those things.

To quote Osgood's own words:

> A pattern of stimulation which is not the object is a sign of the object if it evokes in an organism a mediating reaction, this (a) being some fractional part of the total behaviour elicited by the object, and (b) producing distinctive self-stimulation that mediates a response which would not occur without the previous association of non-object and object patterns of stimulation.

This probably comes nearer to the sort of behaviouristic definition of sign for which we are searching. One might say, however, and more simply, that a stimulus or activating stimulus acts as a sign if it makes you *think* of something other than itself. This may seem clumsy, but if in fact we interpret the word "think" in a behaviouristic manner we have more or less what we want. The previous association of sign with reference is not a necessity, except in the special case of formal or public designations where the sign is supposed to make you think about the reference of the word if the word has a public reference, or a private reference if it only has that. Alternatively, words can be said to refer to concepts, and the formal word-concept relationship is the definition. This may be, in practice, one of the many associations elicited by a stimulus. The point, here, is that these are merely formal subsets including, particularly, lansigns.

A Further Analysis of Signs

Let us now look further into the subject of defining signs, and lead on to another term, "meaning", and see how far the form of analysis can be maintained from a behavioural point of view.

We will define a *sign* as a property of a stimulus, or the subset of the set of all possible stimuli that has *cognitive effect* on some organism x.

By "cognitive effect" we shall mean an organic response, not necessarily overt, to some aspect of the organism's environment other than the immediately given stimulus. It may, as a particular case, be said to *dispose the organism to respond to*, or *make the organism think about*, something other than the stimulus itself. This, as it stands, makes it indistinguishable from other stimuli, simply because signs and stimuli are not capable in general of a completely clearcut distinction. The exact nature and phrasing of the distinction is a matter for further empirical investigation. Empirical investigation, of course, includes thought about the words used, and also observations of the things that the words refer to.

Now *meaning* appears in this system as that property which, when possessed by a stimulus, for some person X, makes that stimulus or sign, sign carrying. This process, close as it is to the process of association, has long been connected with psychology, and it is sufficient to outline, broadly, the notion of meaning. It has been pointed out that the meaning that is so characterized is too broad for logical, and perhaps philosophical, purposes, since it seems to imply that any word may signify any proposition whatever to any particular person, and so indeed it may, for it does seem to be tied to personal experience. As an instance, "manx" may mean Charlie's dog to me, because I think about Charlie's dog when the word "manx" is used. This is perfectly satisfactory up to a point, and in fact it characterizes the cruder meanings of unsophisticated private experience. Professor C. I. Lewis (1946), for example, has said:

> To ascribe an objective quality to a thing means implicitly the prediction that if I act in certain ways, specifiable experiences will eventuate. If I bite this, it will taste sweet. These, and a hundred other such hypothetical propositions, constitute my knowledge of the apple in my hand; these are *the meanings which this presentation has to me now.*

We need to go further when we are considering the careful use of language; when, in short, we are considering problems that philosophers (and logicians?) are usually worried about. Let us now consider how the behaviouristic semiotician deals with what is manifestly a sign-activity, the use of language.

Any analysis of signs – and this includes language signs – must, as Morris has pointed out, be undertaken in terms of unanalysed signs. Thus, we *assume the meaning* of certain terms that we feel are sufficiently well-known, and carry out an analysis in terms of them, and eventually use the construction for analysing these terms themselves. Hence we would try to start from terms that are behaviourally acceptable, and then derive a description of language in use and *meaning* from the behavioural situation. We may now, without loss of generality, consider the case of a conversation between two people, X and Y. Our analysis may start when X makes a noise which we can call an utterance. This utterance is a stimulus to Y (and indeed to X himself), and may of course refer, in primitive sign-using activity, to some sort of here-and-now events, and it may be accompanied by what we would call gestures, in particular, the gesture of pointing. Y may learn, given time, that when certain gestures or sounds are made, X needs something, or expects some action on the part of Y. If X says "wolf", and Y sees a wolf approaching, Y soon learns that there is an appropriate response to the word, which acts as a sign for the referent: The word "wolf" for a wolf, and so on.

If we extend this simple stimulus-response activity a little, it does not take us long to understand that words are sorts of signs that can refer to things other than those here-and-now. Indeed, whole phrases can be used to describe certain states of affairs, various tenses of verbs being introduced to give, in abbreviated form, a description of things that have already taken place, and so on.

Now in human communication we have gone a very long way in systematically developing our sign-activities and, partly for the sake of teaching our offspring, we have categorized the terms used in utterances. We shall return to this matter anon, and in the meantime let us analyse further the relation that exists between a more sophisticated X and Y. X utters a statement S, and Y acts – in the broadest sense – in terms of S. He responds to the stimulus S in a complex manner which pays attention to what is called the *meaning* of S. This meaning reflects X's intention in uttering the words, and was itself a complex behavioural event. Y has to place an interpretation on S which is in accord with the general *context* of the words used, and with the circumstances in which they were used, such as the gestures, expressions, etc., used by X. There can be no absolute guarantee that X's intended meaning will be the same as Y's interpreted meaning, although there is some reason to suppose that a good approximation can be obtained. There are, of course, dictionaries, rules of syntax, conventions, etc., which help to eliminate ambiguity, but the final test must be in the responses elicited.

There can be little reasonable doubt as to the success of communication in relatively primitive circumstances, where the degree of approximation to the intended meaning may need to be only slight. Thus, if X says, "Bring up the bricks", Y may not be in any reasonable doubt as to what is intended, and his manner of achieving this end may not matter much. A failure to understand may be followed by a simple demonstration on the part of X. Operational definitions are well known as more sophisticated equivalents of this same technique.

If, however, X and Y talk over matters of a more abstract and precise nature, then, notoriously, difficulties start to occur. Our methods of communications are now being strained beyond their normal use. At this point it will be rewarding to go back again to study the historical progress of language.

Historically, X and Y found that they could make marks on paper that represented the sounds they made. This was probably not a very difficult step forward, for if they could learn spoken words it would be fairly easy for them to learn, by using a method of marks, to associate sounds with the marks. The next step was to make the language economical, and we have in fact learnt to use (we are now temporarily transferring to the written word) a few elements (letters) combined in various ways to give families of words, such that similar words can be used to refer to similar "ideas". It should be noted, parenthetically, that words or whole utterances do indeed represent *states of mind* of the utterers; these have sometimes been called propositional attitudes. We categorize the types of words we use, first syntactically into verb, noun, etc., and then along similar lines into object words, relational words, logical words, syncategorematic words, and so on. Here we are reminded of the sort of distinctions we made when discussing language in the context of the computer.

The above history, admittedly over-simplified, leads the analysers to use their language to describe their language. This, of course, involves the well-known *mention* and *use* distinction. We must also bear in mind that they are also using their language to describe external events, internal (or private) events (including a description of how language derives from behaviour and, of course, that behaviour itself). We are now in some difficulty through the complexity of the interrelations involved, for at this stage, as a matter of unfortunate fact, the problems have been sorted out into many *different* problems, and these different problems have occupied the attention of different people who have sometimes lost sight of the essential unity of the situation. The linguistic specialist has become involved in the construction, and the analysis of the structure, of different languages, and this has led to various special notations, such as those used for music, shorthand, and other practical needs, while the important development has been toward the complete formalized systems of language.

We can see, in the light of these ruminations from an armchair about empirical facts, that our conception of primitive meaning was in line with the development of linguistic usage. We have to remember that when we have formalized a part of a language, or perhaps by the use of dictionaries and the like, have stipulated a meaning for a word, we must include this rule in what the sign makes the person think about, for example, "Manx makes me think of Charley's dog"; and also, among other things, a rule – if indeed we know what we call the correct meaning of the word – which tells us what we *should* think about, and what our interlocutor Y will expect us to think about when he uses the word, or perhaps what we expect that Y will expect us to think about, and so on.

We can for many purposes neglect the fact that it is X, in particular, or for that matter, Y in particular, who is using the particular signs, and this is precisely because of the fact of public stipulation, which is subject to exactly the same rule as all other signs. The rules of correct use are explicitly sign used by X and Y. If we develop an alternative construction or reconstruction, we can do it from this point of view.

Thus it is a necessary and sufficient condition that a sign, to be a sign, will depend upon making someone *think about* all the associations of the term, including that one that has been publicly stipulated (by lexicographers, etc.) as the public signification.

By "think about" we mean, of course, something empirical, a behavioural response; something that is an act on the part of some organism. We do not mean – and it would cease to be behavioural if we did – what we take to be the introspective use of "to think about". If we take "think" in the introspective sense as an approximation to this behavioural usage, we have all the problems crowding back. A sign, indeed, is definable not as a syntactic unit, but as a behavioural one. This, no doubt, will be a barrier to many, and it reminds us again that we are assuming, by inductive inference, certain facts which amount to a solution (or at any rate a hypothesis) of the mind-body relation. We are *not* making introspective terms like "mind" or "think" our starting point, but hoping to *give an account* of their introspective significance *within* the framework of our behavioural semiotic.

The development of formalized languages is vital to the whole question of meaning. We can start with a set of marks on paper which can be made to generate other marks according to certain rules. These sets of marks are quite *formal* in that they represent anything whatsoever that can be represented by the sets of marks and their mode of generation. In fact, only those sets of marks have been set up which are known in advance to allow an interpretation which has some practical end. Thus we may use marks that satisfy certain simple rules, in which the marks themselves may represent our notions of one, two, three, . . ., in our language. The marks we use can be 1, 2, 3, . . ., and we can construct a system of formal marks that seem to be capable of interpretation as our arithmetic, which is basic to our whole language of mathematics.

Now from this formal set of marks we can go beyond the laying down of syntactic rules; we can take up a semantic view and say that the marks are to become signs or symbols which are to be mapped on to another set of marks or objects, and this may be done in any one of a number of ways, such that there can be many interpretations of the same calculus. In Braithwaite's terms this means that the calculus, or calculi, can serve as a sort of model for some theory, which is essentially an interpretation of the calculus.

The linguistic expert who has made the above sort of progress will now be tempted to deny that linguistic problems are in any way connected with the historically given languages and the users of the language. We might, with Carnap (1942), try and formalize the meanings of the formal marks by including rules of designation in the system, and it may be possible to reconstruct languages and their *meaning* from the foundation of formal marks on paper. Ultimately, however, what is being reconstructed is the behavioural situation in which X and Y are speaking to each other. The process of formalizing a system of marks can only take place within the structure of a previously given non-formalized language, and it is therefore clearly impossible to avoid the same sort of dilemma as that which caused the accusations of *psychologism* against the pragmaticist. How can a formal system be used to interpret a language when the formal system was itself constructed out of that language? This in fact reminds us again that there is a sort of self-reflexive property involved in all investigations with respect to the foundation of those investigations. It can be seen from this that logic, too, is ultimately rooted in organism, and that psychology, or explanation of organism, is rooted in logic and language. And all of these, the philosopher will add, are rooted in philosophy. However, even if this is conceded, the point is not really as to where the application of the word "philosophy" begins and ends, but that all forms of explanatory system must be based on assumption, whether explicit or implicit. One might therefore claim that philosophy is the introspective (and retrospective), and therefore private, acceptance or rejection of these assumptions. The reasons given for acceptance or rejection are public statements, and part of a science, and they are dependent upon a process of decision which reduces the utterances to a set of assumptions upon which they are based; this issue cannot be dodged by their concealment in concepts "inside a person's mind".

Thus, rather lengthily, we would argue in claiming that the problem of language is a major problem, still to be solved by *experimental psychologists*. Let us now illustrate some of the experimental beginnings, rather slight though they may be, that psychologists have made.

Some Linguistic Experiments

Since we are advocating the experimental method, and have already spent some time clarifying the background of the language problem, some examples of linguistic experiment would seem to be in order.

We should perhaps mention at this point that many of the field experiments done by anthropologists are extremely relevant, in particular, those of Benjamin Lee Whorf (1941); but we are in fact now thinking of experiments in the very much narrow sense of the laboratory experiment.

Foley and Cofer (1943) used a transfer method to try to discover something about the learning of words. They used six lists of words, of which one was a control list, one a test list, and the other two pairs of lists were of synonyms and homonyms.

The procedure was, in essence, to give the subject either the control list, or the homonym or synonym lists, and after any one of these five, the test list. The best performances were after the homonym lists, and one should mention at this point that the homonym lists were homonymous with the test list, just as one of the synonym lists was synonymous with the test list. Not too surprisingly, the synonym list that was synonymous with the test list came out better than that which was not synonymous with the test list.

The main point, however, is that the sound association was rather more effective than the meaning association. Other experiments have shown different results, and we may suppose that there is a lot more

Language

to be done on this sort of thing, and the results given are quoted as illustrative of a method of approaching language problems experimentally.

Osgood (1948) carried out some experiments on language behaviour by using nonsense letters as stimuli, and meaningful adjectives as responses. The subjects learned five items in each of three meaningful relations. They all learned that some letters stood for a word – such as "elated" – and they were then given some interpolated learning in which the same letters as stood for "elated" now stood for "high" or "low", and so on. Then they relearned the original association with "elated". The upshot of this was to show that words learned tend to elicit words of similar meaning, but resist especially words with opposite meanings.

This experiment, like the previous one, is not of vast importance but it is noted as illustrating the possibilities inherent in verbal, situations.

Other experiments have been done on word association, with results which lend further support to the idea that the ordinary associative principle is operating, although here apparent opposites will often occur which make the above experiment seem a rather special case of the ordinary verbal memory associations.

In the context of experiments with language we can classify all the work on the statistical analysis of language (Shannon, 1949; Zipf, 1935, 1949). The work done in analysing the statistical structure of English and other Indo-European languages is now well known, and it remains a matter of psychological significance that most Indo-European languages seem to have a very similar measure of redundancy.

We shall not discuss here the theory of information (Shannon & Weaver, 1949); some of the important results have been already considered in the earlier chapters on Cybernetics, and a number of experiments have been done in this field. Their significance is noteworthy in that many interesting results can be shown to occur, such as those giving the approximate rule that the number of meanings that a word has is proportional to its frequency of occurrence. But more important than this is the fact that we are discovering methods for measuring the flow of information, and this is clearly of great value in assessing the effectiveness of learning, and very helpful in understanding something of the structure of languages.

Carnap and Bar Hillel (1952) have tried to develop a semantic theory of information in the belief that the traditional theory deals only with what are syntactical issues. Of course there is a sense in which cybernetics is trying to deal with the pragmatic theory of information, but it is doubtful whether the Shannon theory as it stands is convenient for behaviour analysis, or even the analysis of linguistic behaviour.

The importance of this sort of statistical analysis has already been sufficiently emphasized, but it is necessary to bear in mind that there is still a gap of some dimensions between these various approaches to learning in general and the learning of language in particular, as well as the use of language.

One last example of an experimental approach to language is to be found in the work of Arne Naess (1952). He tried to work out a theory of interpretation and preciseness by carrying out empirical investigations to discover what words and phrases were synonymous and equivalent in meaning, though differing in preciseness, and so on. The method was that of the questionnaire, and though the difficulties are obvious enough, at least there is a breaking away from the analysis of language in terms of what one individual *thinks* other people mean by words. Here we are actively trying to discover, in an operational manner, what other people mean by words.

The complications of language are indeed very great, and a lot of work remains to be done on all these matters.

Phonetics

Another approach to language is, of course, through the actual processes of speaking and hearing, and here we have a firm link between language and the special senses. This, again, is an important field for psychological analysis which has not been much investigated; however, linguists (Brown, 1956) and semanticists have done a great deal of work in the analysis of the structure of languages from a phonetic point of view.

If a phone is defined as the smallest distinguishable speech sound, then the phoneme is the smallest unit in speech that makes a difference to the possible meaning of a statement; and a morphene is defined as the smallest semantic unit. On this basis we can build a multitude of categories which represent the well-formedness of phonemes, and the various variables in spoken words that themselves convey meaning to a listener. These include juncture, stress, tone, intonation, and possibly more besides. Certainly such speech is part of the wider context of behavioural communication which includes gesture and movement, and which makes any purely logical or linguistic analysis of language very difficult.

Space forbids that we carry our cognitive problems into the field of descriptive semantics or linguistics; in any case this is a highly specialized field which must eventually be linked up with the psychological and philosophical approaches to linguistic problems.

In Summary

The subject of linguistic behaviour is vast. It is also largely untapped by psychologists, and although it is a complicated field in which to work precisely because of the many different possible approaches, there seems little reason to doubt that our understanding of human cognitive processes can never be complete without such an analysis. The very fact that we can learn by description as well as acquaintance is a reminder of just this.

Chapter 18

IN SUMMARY

In the outlines of the problems of cognition with which this book has been concerned, the main object has been to supply a straightforward account of the field of cognition and its principal problems in a tolerably rigorous form.

Our intent has been to present the evidence, not as a textbook, but rather as from a fairly definite standpoint. Among the main features of this standpoint is the feeling that, in the past, psychology has tended to concentrate too much on isolated problems – such as rats running mazes – and not enough on the integrated nature of the cognitive problem. Furthermore, psychologists have often neglected allied sciences and methods, and actively disregarded the help that was made available by the philosopher even though, and partly because, the philosopher's help turned out to be different from what philosophers themselves imagined it to be.

The rigour comes into cognitive theory in the attempt to be linguistically precise, and to use mathematical and axiomatic methods of description whenever possible, and this manifests itself most excitingly and most urgently in the field of cybernetics. Not that cybernetics represents the only approach to the problem of cognition; cognition stands in its own right, as something to be tackled from a large variety of different viewpoints.

Learning theory in recent years has worn just a shade thin, and the reason for this is that it is, clearly, not easy to distinguish various different attitudes to problems of learning. There are many different theories which cannot obviously be reconciled, and yet are not obviously different, or at least not obviously demonstrably different. It is this that has led so many people to say that the learning theorists are "ahead of the game", and should wait on more experimental evidence. The answer to this is that theory and experiment go hand in hand, and the troubles in learning theory have been due, as much as anything else, to a failure to bring the same experimental attitude to theory constructions as has been brought to the business of the collection of data itself.

In the particular chapters that are devoted to learning theory we have dwelt primarily on the theories of Hull and Tolman, though something has been said about the modern versions of these theories, and also about the theorists who have carried on the work started by Hull and Tolman. In particular, we have mentioned Spence as an advocate of Hull's theory, and Olds as one who has carried on a viewpoint similar in many ways to that of Tolman.

There are, of course, other particular and general contributions, and in this regard we would remind the reader that Seward, Wolpe, Glanzer, Uttley, Deutsch, Broadbent, Wyckoff, and many others, have also made their contributions to the subject.

Not only have we so far failed to discuss some of the special theories that have been suggested, we have also done less than justice to certain aspects of the present cognitive situation.

We shall go some way to repairing these omissions in this chapter, in order to give some idea of the flavour of the current situation in this field, and we shall start with the categories that have so far only been touched upon.

Perceptual Learning

As Drever (1960) has put it:

> In psychology our subject-matter keeps confounding our distinctions and what we have set apart we must always bring together again. So it is with perception and learning.

In this book we have consistently recognized the inseparability of perception and learning. Indeed it is clear that we perceive in terms of what we have learned, and learn in terms of what we have perceived. Hebb underlined the evidence for learning to perceive, and while the evidence, though clear, was not strong, there are not many people now who will doubt that much of the perceptual process has to be learned.

But it is more than this. Perception is an active process which does not easily fit into the framework of learning theories. It is, as some people have put it, a response process. Also, it is a transaction in the manner we have discussed in Chapter 10, and it is a sign process, as we have recognized in our discussion of language, and this means that it is natural to treat it in connexion with information theory (Shannon and Weaver, 1949; George, 1961).

All of this is clear enough without explicitly calling for a special branch of learning called "perceptual". Perceiving is plainly closely related to both learning and thinking; it may perhaps be more dependent on the anatomical structure of the organism, and as a result, may seem more stereotyped, but this does not mark it off especially. It does, however, go some way to account for the arguments about nativism and empicism, arguments that have not sprung up in the same way in learning and thinking.

It is natural that in following philosophical phenomenalism we should find similar studies in psychology. For example, Gibson (1950) and Gibson and Gibson (1955a, 1955b) have been strongly interested in the nature of the stimulus. Their emphasis is on the fact that sufficient information is perceptually available to make learning possible, and indeed to encapsulate learning within the confines of perception. In this, at any rate, they are treading a similar path to that of the Gestalt theorists.

While in our own theory language we have discussed perceptual beliefs, we have meant only to distinguish them from ordinary beliefs, by virtue of *their degree* of association with external stimulation. The distinction is, in other words, a distinction at the level of the metalanguage, as it were, and not of the system itself. At the same time it is clear that there is a sort of difference between a belief about the relation between two cues, or items, of the immediate environment, and a belief about information that has long been available in storage.

In fact, of course, this sort of distinction is just that which, when emphasized, leads on to the use of the term "perceptual learning". Our only immediate point is to remember that the use of such terminology should not obscure the actual relationship between learning and perception, or perhaps better, it should not obscure the fact that the two terms are both abstractions from a total process.

While making these statements about perceptual learning, one must also add that learning is at least as much a matter of stimulus association as stimulus-response association, and this again points to the appropriateness of such a term as "perceptual learning".

Discrimination Learning

We have already said something about discrimination and generalization, and thought of them broadly as two aspects of the same essential process.

It is quite clear that unless an organism is capable of generalizing, it will not be able to learn a great deal. We have assumed that general beliefs occur, beliefs which are strengthened by the reinforcement of the particular beliefs of which these are particular cases. The philosophical problem of Universals we have cited as coming precisely from this background of the ability to generalize.

Now granted the ability to generalize, there follows immediately the ability to discriminate. It is merely the fact that if similarities between events can be observed, then so can differences, otherwise the whole thing becomes nonsense.

We have sufficiently emphasized the need for making generalizations, and this need depends upon the urgent response and saving of storage space. It is for these reasons that the most important single problem in cognition at the moment is that of storing and organizing the information which the organism receives in the brain itself.

Enough has also been said about the possible mechanisms of generalization in the chapters on cybernetics. The main point to re-emphasize is that the operations of discrimination and generalization are wholly bound up with each other; one simply implies the other.

There are Two Kinds of Learning

We have agreed that learning may take a perceptual form, and this is the general nature of sign learning; it involves stimulus substitution. Equally well, learning may depend upon response substitution, where the search is for the appropriate response to a stimulus. Mowrer (1950, 1960a, 1960b) has continually laid stress on this particular point, and we may accept it as being the background of Pavlov's and Thorndike's views. If we think in terms of states, we can still think of learning as the association of states, but it is true that this draws attention away from the important details of the possible associations.

Avoidance training, in which the organisms has to learn the appropriate avoidance behaviour, seems to be learning which contains both the above types; the learning to avoid is a sign process, while the learning how to avoid is a stimulus-response process. In other words, the problem solving type of activity often involves finding the appropriate response to a given stimulus, while the perceptual type of learning tends to lay emphasis on the relations between stimulus items in the environment.

From the point of view of Cybernetics, it is clear that both, or all, types of learning can take place easily enough, and it remains only to map out in some detail the kind of thing that is happening in the human organism in the various circumstances met. Perhaps it would be better to say: which sort of emphasis is occurring in different human learning situations, since whatever method is adopted, it is still easy to regard it as a special case of the general method of association.

Mowrer's new Two-factor Theory

Fear can be conditioned in an organism by pairing a shock with a buzzer so that ultimately only the buzzer is necessary to bring about the fear response.

The fear response is a secondary motivator which acts as a drive to learn how to remove the fear by turning off the buzzer and thus removing the source of shock.

This view is, in essence, exactly the one expressed above, and we would readily accept Mowrer's statement.

Mowrer claims that this new version of his theory supplies a more satisfactory theory of punishment than that which we have had previously. The main point about punishment, for Mowrer, is that it now caters for conflict, the conflict arising because of the ambivalence involved in having to deal with noxious stimuli in order to remove them.

This sort of account reminds one of the ambivalence one might expect to find in a bomb-disposal unit. Similarly, Mowrer discusses *hope* as secondary reinforcement. Clearly, the sense of expectancy will be associated with signs – secondary reinforcers – and this may take the form of apprehension or hope. Generally, the hope will be associated when the secondary reinforcers are signs to the primary reinforcers, or at any rate have some similar relation to the primary reinforcers.

One of the most attractive features of Mowrer's work is the gradual interlinking of emotional and personality factors with cognitive ones, and the gradual broadening of the study of the individual to the study of society. It seems likely that this must be the next step. We know enough about learning now to investigate the broader social patterns,

In Summary

its emotional contamination and its biological foundations. Such large scale integrations lie just around the corner.

It is fairly clear how fear and hope enter directly into learning. It is perhaps equally obvious how other emotions, such as love, hate, surprise, and humour, also enter into social situations, but the details still remain to be worked out.

It is perhaps worth reminding ourselves at this point that Freud himself worked out theories derived from his main concepts, which were intended to explain humour and wit, as well as other social behaviour more broadly based than that which is normally attributed to cognition alone. Yet, on looking back, it seems that the study of cognition has been trying to supply a more precise foundation for our understanding of human behaviour – the same understanding which Freud himself sought. As the theory of cognition broadens out into the complex delta of emotional and so-called abnormal behaviour, in the broader social context, then the wheel has nearly come full circle.

For the writer, the problems of human behaviour started with the first readings of Psycho-analysis; then there was the sudden jump to experimental psychology and physiology, and the full range of biological methods; but at the same time there was the feeling that the human being had been lost in the range of the rigorous, or more rigorous, scientific method. It seems now that he is beginning to emerge again, the better for his disappearance into the laboratory for the best part of a quarter of a century. Not that this is the end of the matter; the wheel's full circle is only one of a whole set of circles, as it were, hierarchically organized, and still needing years, at least, of work at both neurological and sociological levels. This is not to say that the problems of cognition, or more general behaviour, at the purely molar level, are finally solved, but it does seem that they are now within hitting distance of solutions. This is suggested by the general trend towards agreement over the descriptive language that will be appropriate, and the general agreement over motivation, memory, learning and perception, and the mechanisms needed for cognition. The detail still provides matter for dispute, but this is now subordinate to the general agreement.

Cybernetics and Learning Theory

In a previous book (George, 1961) the relationship of cognition to cybernetics has been analysed in some detail *from the cybernetic point of view*. The present book has inverted the procedure, and discussed cybernetics within the framework of cognition. The point is, of course, that cybernetics offers new methods for solving cognitive problems, and its offers a framework for a clearer understanding of cognitive problems. The concepts of feedback, selective reinforcement, and memory stores, can be shown to be capable of exhibiting what we might call "cognitive behaviour". The concept of selective reinforcement effects the link with the work of Hull, Tolman, and the other learning theorists, and enables us to see their problems in a new relief.

Strangely enough, this does not, in and of itself, solve our problems, because cybernetic techniques are themselves held up for the want of a sufficiently compact notation, and a cheap and simple means of building very large-scale models; or perhaps an *effective method* for constructing growing and self-regulating systems. All this could probably be overcome if – or perhaps, when – a much larger computer becomes available, one with a great deal more flexibility than any yet existing. A possible alternative lies in the construction of special autocoding procedures, but this, too, tends to become an excessively complicated and time-consuming task. Nevertheless, one or more of these jobs must be undertaken before any real progress can be made in the realm of cybernetics, and also, as a result, in the necessary detailed study of cognitive processes.

Information theory offers possibilities, and indeed we are now suffering from a rash of work on information theory, although it can no more solve the general problems of cognition than any other method. What it does is to supply a compact and convenient notation for certain aspects of cognition; for the rest, it faces exactly the same problems as the remainder of cybernetics.

These difficulties do not in any way mean that there is not a great mass of detail which can be clarified in the immediate future. What one is concerned about is the fact that neither method can give us a really detailed cognitive theory as of now, and this, of course, applies to any other method, because we simply lack a means for supplying the necessary intimate detail.

Cognitive and Stimulus-response Theories of Learning

On the whole it seems "Old Hat" to argue about the relative merits of Hull's and Tolman's theories any longer. Each has made his contribution, and a considerable one at that. We see that, in broad terms, Hull's contribution has been to a great extent methodological, and

In Summary

Tolman's is more realistic in using theoretical terms that were more immediately applicable to human behaviour.

There is, however, no further need to discuss these two theories as they stand, since between them – and thanks to their associates – something like a theory of learning has emerged which is appropriate for embedding in a cybernetic mould, and to be linked to the other levels of the behaviour problem. But a few words may be added about language and notation as this, even for Hull and Tolman, was a central problem.

Hull and Tolman were seeking bases for the discussion of behaviour but, with very limited exceptions such as in the Mathematico-deductive theory of rote learning, they hardly attacked the serious problem of describing actual behaviour, nor was there any consideration of particular individuals in particular social situations. This could not, in fact, be expected of them, partly because they had a prior problem to handle; but the significant point is that in any case they could not have handled, with their notation, the complexities of human behaviour. Hull's notation is especially ugly, and Tolman's appears inadequate; even when formalized by McCorquodale and Meehl it still seems far from rigorous or even clear at times. Tolman's theory also suffers to some extent where testability is concerned.

Skinner, Guthrie and Thorndike, as well as Mowrer, and others besides, have still many major contributions to make to our understanding of learning, but it must be said that nothing more should be done at the moment to encourage further schools of psychology. We seek to emphasize the common and agreed ground, in search for larger integrations with ethology physiology, and mathematical and physical methods.

It was with the idea of the need for integration that the language outlined in Chapter 12 was proposed. Now this language is similar in many ways to Tolman's, and is not by any means ideal; but it can be made so. Other works could modify it, further refine it and formalize it. Some attempts have already been made in this direction, and have mostly come under the heading of Cybernetics (George, 1961). The other point is that the language used, and the empirical facts which the language is used to describe, are intermingled to some extent. We discover some new facts and we modify the language of our description, even to the extent of dropping a theoretical term, or acquiring a new one. It could be that an even larger scale reorganization may occur as a result of further experimental discoveries.

The important thing about all this is that language and science are bound up with each other, and one's dissociation from linguistic problems tends to be more apparent than real (Crawshay Williams, 1957). Obviously this sort of argument applies far less to some fields than to others, and it is perhaps for this reason that some experimental psychologists shun theory and concentrate on experimental fields where problems of language are least likely to occur. What, then, they cannot reasonably do is to argue that language presents no problems for psychologists, for they themselves have simply avoided the necessary fields where precisely these difficulties occur. Of the necessary fields, none is more obvious and more central than the whole field of cognition. This, as we know, means theories of learning theories of perception, theories of thinking and theories of linguistic behaviour, and more besides. Attempts to construct theories of cognition are attempts to grapple with problems of language and other forms of symbolic description.

Finally, let it be said that this book has tried to present some of the fairly well established facts of cognition, ranging from learning to language, and to suggest ways and means of handling this data. It is being assumed that general theories are still desirable, both for integration purposes and also for a direct understanding of human behaviour, especially in the broader context of social behaviour.

This is not to deny the usefulness of the experimental psychologist, working on a narrow front with intentionally limited *ad hoc* theories. What he in turn must not do is to pretend that his particular narrow experimental approach is the *only* approach. Both approaches are necessary, and the development of our understanding of human behaviour will come from many different people working at many different levels on many different sorts of problems. These different approaches must have an integrating framework, and this the theoretically minded psychologist must be encouraged to supply.

Learning then is a system of association and storage of a stochastic type. The principles of input depend both on specialized analysing mechanisms and classification, and all the terminology of perception and learning can be reinterpreted on such a simple base. It will be remembered of course that principles of reinforcement and generalization are necessary as is the use of signs.

From such a start a study of memory is a study of the storage system, methods of access and the ordering in terms of priorities of the information. Thinking is learning, on the inside as it were, and this means the formulation and use of concepts. Signs lead to symbols as a concept forming procedure, and all of these things can be rigorously formulated in cybernetic or other formal terms.

Now eventually our cognitive models, or theories – and Hull, Tolman, and Gestalt theory can be increasingly seen as representing special cases of the general procedure – must be tested on biological grounds. We need neurological evidence and ethological evidence. This means that the principal problems of cognition at the molar level are the increased precision of model constructing, and of course the search for new empirical evidence, where the second *at the molar level* is probably the less important.

Where we especially do need more empirical evidence is in the development of cognition beyond its present bounds, to include individual differences and social behaviour. Cognitive theory is a basis – or jumping-off point – for a study of precise theories, probably needing a computer, neurological theories of behaviour, and indeed chemical too, and the broadening of the field of the black box to something more like a social human being. It is in this background that we feel that it is primarily in the method of presenting and checking models and theories, and secondarily in acquiring information, that cognition will proceed in the next few years.

REFERENCES

AMES, A., Jr. (1951) Visual perception and the rotating trapezoidal window. *Psychol. Monogr.*, 65, No. 7.
ASHBY, W. R. (1952) *Design for a brain.* Chapman and Hall.
—— (1956) *An introduction to cybernetics.* Chapman and Hall.
AYER, A. J. (1936) *Language, truth and logic.* Victor Gollancz.
BAERENDS, G. P. (1941) Fortpflanzungsrershalten und Orrentierung der Grabwespe. *Ammophila campestris Jur. Tijd. voor. Entom.*, 84, 71–275.
BARTLETT, F. C. (1932) *Remembering.* Cambridge University Press.
—— (1958) *Thinking.* George Allen and Unwin.
BEACH, F. A. (1948) *Hormones and behaviour*, Hoeber.
BLACK, M. (1949) *Language and philosophy.* Cornell University Press.
BLODGETT, H. C. (1929) The effect of the introduction of rewards upon the maze performance of rats. *Univ. Calif. Publ. Psychol.* 4, 113–34.
BOGOSLAVSKY, G. W., and GUTHRIE, E. R. (1941) The recall of completed and interrupted activities: an investigation of Zeigarnik's experiment. *Psychol. Bull.*, 38, 575–6.
BORING, E. G. (1942) *Sensation and perception in the history of experimental psychology.* Appleton-Century-Crofts.
BRIDGMAN, P. W. (1927) *The logic of modern physics.* Macmillan.
—— (1936) *The nature of physical theory.* Princeton University Press.
BROAD, C. D. (1947) Phenomenalism. *Mind.*, 56, 120–1.
BROWN, R. W. (1956) Language and categories. In BRUNER, J. S., GOODNOW, J. J., and AUSTIN, G. A. *A Study of Thinking.* Wiley.
BRUNER, J. S., GOODNOW, J. J., and AUSTIN, G. A. (1956) *A study of thinking.* John Wiley.
CANTRIL, H., AMES, A., HASTORF, A. H., and ITTELSON, W. H. (1949*a*) Psychology and scientific research—I: The nature of scientific inquiry. *Science*, 110, 461–4.
—— (1949*b*) Psychology and scientific research – II – Scientific inquiry and scientific method. *Science*, 110, 491–7.
—— (1949*c*) Psychology and scientific research – III – Transactional view in psychological research. *Science*, 110, 517–22.

CARNAP, R. (1942) *Introduction to semantics*. Cambridge University Press, Mass.
—— (1952) Empiricism, semantics and ontology. In Leonard Linsky (Editor). *Semantics and the philosophy of language*. Univ. of Illinois Press.
CARNAP, R., and BAR HILLEL, Y. (1953) Semantic information. *B.J. Philos. Sci.*, 147–57.
CARR, H. A., and WATSON, J. B. (1908) Orientation in the white rat. *J. comp. Neur. and Psychol.*, **18**, 27–44.
CHAPMAN, B. L. M. (1959) A self organizing classification system. *Cybernetica*. Vol. II, **3**, 152–61.
CHILD, C. M. (1921) *The origin and development of the nervous system*. University of Chicago Press.
CHURCH, A. (1936) An unsolvable problem of elementary number theory, *Amer. Journ. Math.*, **58**, 345–63.
COGHILL, G. E. (1929) *Anatomy and the problem of behaviour*. Macmillan.
CRAWSHAY-WILLIAMS, R. (1957) *Methods and criteria of reasoning*. Kegan Paul.
CULBERTSON, J. T. (1956) Some uneconomical robots. In C. E. Shannon and J. McCarthy (Editors). *Automata studies*. Princeton University Press.
DEWEY, J., and BENTLEY, A. (1949) *Knowing and the known*. Beacon Press.
DREVER, J. (1952) *A dictionary of psychology*. Penguin Books.
—— (1960) Perceptual learning. *Ann. Rev. Psychol.*, **11**, 131–60.
EINSTEIN, A., and INFIELD, L. (1930) *The evolution of physics*, Simon and Schuster.
FEIGL, H. (1950) Existential hypotheses. *Phil. Sci.*, **17**, 2, 35–62.
FITCH, F. B. (1953) Review. *J. Symb. Logic.*, **19**, 229.
FITCH, F. B., and BARRY, G. (1950) Towards a formalization of Hull's behaviour theory. *Philos. Sci.*, **17**, 260–5.
FOLEY, J. P., and COFER, C. N. (1943) Mediated generalization and the interpretation of verbal behavior. II. Experimental study of certain homophone and synonym gradients. *J. exp. Psychol.*, **32**, 169–75.
GALLI, A., and HOCHEIMER, W. (1934) On perception. *Z. Psychology*, **132**, 304–34.
GEORGE, F. H. (1951) Errors of visual recognition. *J. exp. Psychol.*, **43**, 202–6.
—— (1953a) Logical constructs and psychological theory. *Psychol. Rev.*, **60**, 1–6.

GEORGE, F. H. (1953*b*) Formalization of language systems for behaviour theory. *Psychol. Rev.*, **60**, 232-40.
—— (1956) Pragmatics. *J. Philos. and Phen. Res.* 226-35.
—— (1957) Epistemology and the problem of perception. *Mind*, LXVI, 491-506.
—— (1958) Probabilistic machines. *Automation Progress*, **3**, 19-21.
—— (1960) *Models in Cybernetics*. Soc. Exp. Biologists. Symp. 169-91.
—— (1961) *The brain as a computer*. Pergamon Press.
GEORGE, F. H., and HANDLON, J. H. (1955) Toward a general theory of behaviour. *Methods*, **7**, 25-44.
GEORGE, F. H., and HANDLON, J. H. (1957) A language for perceptual analysis. *Psychol. Rev.*, **64**, 14-25.
GIBSON, J. J. (1950) *The perception of the visual world*. Houghton Mifflin.
GIBSON, J. J., and GIBSON, E. J. (1955*a*) Perceptual learning: Differentiation or enrichment? *Psychol. Rev.*, **62**, 32-41.
—— (1955*b*) What is learned in perceptual learning? A reply to Professor Postman, *Psychol. Rev.*, **62**, 447-50.
GÖDEL, K. (1931) Über formal unentscheidbare sätze der principia Mathematica und reswandter systeme. *J. Monats. für Math. u. Phys.*, **38**, 173-98.
GOTTSCHALDT, K. (1926) Über den Einfluss der Erfahrung ant die Wahrnehmung von Figuren. I. *Psychol. Forsch.* **8**, 261-317.
GUTHRIE, E. R. (1935) *The psychology of learning*. Harper Bros.
HANEY, G. W. (1931) The effect of familiarity on maze performance of albino rats. *Univ. Calif. Publ. Psychol.*, **4**, 319-33.
HAYEK, S. A. (1952) *The sensory order*. University of Chicago Press.
HEBB, D. O. (1949) *The organization of behaviour*. John Wiley.
HEBB, D. O., and FOORD, E. N. (1945) Errors of visual recognition and the nature of the trace. *J. exp. Psychol.*, **35**, 335-48.
HEIDBREDER, E. (1946) The attainment of concepts: I. Terminology and methodology. *J. gen. Psychol.*, **35**, 173-89.
—— (1947) The attainment of concepts: III. The Process. *J. gen. Psychol.*, **24**, 93-138.
HERBART J. F. (1816) *Lehrbuch zur psychologie*.
HILBERT, D. (1922) Die logischen Grundlagen der Mathematik, *Math. Ann.*, vol. 88, 151-65.
HILGARD, E. R. (1948) *Theories of learning*. Appleton-Century-Crofts.
—— (1958) *Theories of learning*. Methuen.

HILGARD, E. R., and MARQUIS, D. G. (1940) *Conditioning and learning*. Methuen.
HIRST, R. J. (1951) Perception, Science and Common Sense. *Mind. LX*, 481–505.
HULL, C. L. (1943) *Principles of behaviour*. Appleton-Century-Crofts.
—— (1950) Behaviour postulates and corollaries – 1949. *Psychol. Rev.*, **57**, 173–80.
—— (1951) *The essentials of behaviour*. Yale University Press.
—— (1952) *A behaviour system: an introduction to behaviour theory concerning the individual organism*. Yale University Press.
HULL, C. L., HOVLAND, C. I., ROSS, R. T., HALL, M., PERKINS, D. T., and FITCH, F. B. (1940) *Mathematico-deductive theory of rote learning: a study in scientific methodology*. Yale University Press.
HUMPHREYS, L. G. (1939a) The effect of random alternation of reinforcement on the acquisition and extinction of conditioned eyelid reactions. *J. exp. Psychol.*, **25**, 141–58.
HUNTER, W. S. (1913) The delayed reaction in animals and children. *Animal Behaviour*, **2**, 1.
—— (1920) The temporal maze and kinaesthetic sensory processes in the white rat. *Psychobiol.*, **2**, 1–18.
HOVLAND, C. I. (1938) Experimental studies in rote learning theory: I. Reminiscence following learning by massed and by distributed practice. *J. exp. Psychol.*, **22**, 201–24.
JACOBSON, E. (1929) *Progressive relaxation*. University of Chicago Press.
—— (1932) Electrophysiology of mental activities. *Amer. J. Psychol.*, **44**, 677–94.
JENNINGS, H. S. (1906) *The behaviour of the lower organisms*. Macmillan, New York.
KAPPERS, C. U. A., HUBER, G. C., and CROSBY, E. C. (1936) *The comparative anatomy of the nervous system of vertebrates, including man*. Vol. I., Macmillan, New York.
KENDLER, H. H. (1947) An investigation of latent learning in a T-maze. *J. comp. physiol. Psychol.*, **40**, 265–70.
KILPATRICK, F. P. (ed.) (1952) *Human behaviour from the transactional point of view*. Princeton, Institute for Associate Research.
—— (1954) Two processes in perceptual learning. *J. exp. Psychol.*, **47**, 362–70.
KOCH, S. (1954) Clark L. Hull. In W. K. Estes and others. *Modern learning theory*. Appleton-Century-Crofts, 1–176.
KOFFKA (1924) *The growth of the mind*. Harcourt Brace.
KÖHLER, W. (1925) *The mentality of apes*. Kegan Paul.

KONORSKI, J. (1948) *Conditioned reflexes and neuron organization.* Cambridge University Press.

KORNER, S. (1959) *Conceptual thinking.* Dover.

KRECHEVSKY, I. (1932a) The genesis of "hypotheses" in rats. *Univ. Calif. Publ. Psychol.* **6**, 45–64

—— (1932b) "Hypotheses" in rats. *Psychol. Rev.,* **39**, 516–32.

—— (1935). Brain mechanisms and "hypotheses". *J. comp. Psychol.,* **19**, 425–68.

LASHLEY, K. S. (1929b) *Brain mechanisms and intelligence.* University of Chicago Press.

—— (1950) *In search of the engram. Experimental biology symposium.* Cambridge University Press.

LENZEN, V. F. (1945) The concept of reality in physical theory. *Philos. Rev.,* **18**.

LEWIS, C. I. (1946) *Analysis of knowledge and valuation.* Open Court Publishing Co.

LOEB, J. (1918) *Forced Movements, Tropisms and Animal Conduct.* Lippincott, Philadelphia.

LORENZ, K. (1950) The comparative method of studying innate behaviour patterns. *Sympos. vol. 4 of Soc. Exp. Biol. on Physiological Mechanisms in Animal Behaviour,* Cambridge.

—— (1954) *Man meets dog.* Methuen.

LOUCKS, R. B. (1938) Studies of neural structures essential for learning II. The conditioning of salivary and striped muscle responses to faradization of cortical sensory elements, and the action of sleep upon such mechanisms. *J. comp. Psychol.,* **25**, 315–32.

MACCORQUODALE, K., and MEEHL, P. E. (1954) Edward C. Tolman. In Estes and others. *Modern Learning Theory.* A. T. Poffenberger (Editor). Appleton-Century-Crofts.

MAIER, N. R. F. (1929) Reasoning in white rats. *Comp. Psychol. Monogr.,* **6**, No. 29.

—— (1931) Reasoning and learning. *Psychol. Rev.,* **38**, 332–46.

MAX, L. W. (1935) An experimental study of the motor theory of consciousness: III. Action-current responses in deaf-mutes during sleep, sensory stimulation, and dreams. *J. comp. Psychol.* **19**, 469–86.

—— (1937) An experimental study of the motor theory of consciousness: IV. Action-current responses in the deaf during awakening, kinaesthetic imagery and abstract thinking. *J. comp. Psychol.,* **24**, 301–44.

MCFARLANE, D. A. (1930) The role of kinesthesis in maze learning. *Univ. Calif. Publ. Psychol.,* **4**, 277–305.

MICHOTTE, A. (1962) *The Perception of Causality.* Methuen.

MILLER, N. E., and DOLLARD, J. C. (1941) *Social learning and initiation*. Yale University Press.

MORRIS, C. W. (1946) *Signs, language and behaviour*. Prentice Hall.

MOWRER, O. H., and JONES, H. M. (1943) Extinction and behaviour variability as functions of effortlessness of task. *J. exp. Psychol.* **33,** 369–86.

MOWRER, O. H. (1950) *Learning theory and personality dynamics*. Ronald Press.

—— (1960*a*) *Learning theory and behaviour*. John Wiley.

—— (1960*b*) *Learning theory and the symbolic process*. John Wiley.

MUNN, N. L. (1955) *The evolution and growth of human behaviour*. Harrap.

MURPHY, G. (1950) *An introduction to psychology*. Harrap.

NAESS, A. (1952) Towards a theory of interpretation and preciseness. In Linsky L (Ed.). *Semantics and the philosophy of language*. University of Illinois Press.

OETTINGER, A. E. (1950) Programming a digital computer to learn. *Philos. Mag.*

OLDS, J. A. (1954) A neural model for sign-gestalt theory. *Psychol. Rev.*, **61,** 59–72.

OSGOOD, C. E. (1948) An investigation into the cause of retroactive interference. *J. exp. Psychol.*, **38,** 132–54.

—— (1953) *Method and theory in experimental psychology*. Oxford University Press.

PANTIN, C. F. A. (1950) Behaviour patterns in lower invertebrates. Symposium, vol. 4. S.E.B. *Physiol. mechanisms anim. behav.*, 175, 95.

PAP. A. (1949) *Elements of analytic philosophy*. Macmillan.

PASCH, A. (1958) *Experience and the analytic*. University of Chicago Press.

PASK, A. G. (1958) The growth process in a cybernetic machine. *Proc. Second Congress International association of Cybernetics*.

—— (1959*a*) Organic control and the cybernetic method. *Cybernetics*.

—— (1959*b*) Physical analogues to the growth of a concept. In mechanization of thought processes. NPL Symposium.

PAVLOV, I. P. (1927) *Conditioned reflexes*. Oxford University Press.

PEIRCE, C. S. (1931–35) *The collected papers of Charles Sanders Peirce*. 6 vols. Harvard University Press.

PIAGET, J. (1928) *Judgement and reasoning in the child*. Harcourt Brace.

—— (1930) *The child's conception of physical causality*. Harcourt Brace.

PIAGET, J. (1955) *The child's construction of reality*. Kegan Paul.
PLATONOV (see Pavlov, I. P. (1927)).
PRICE, H. H. (1953) *Thinking and experience*. Hutchinson.
REED, H. B. (1946a) Factors influencing the learning and retention of concepts: – I. the influence of set. *J. exp. Psychol.*, **36**, 71–87.
—— (1946b) The learning and the retention of concepts: II. The influence of length of series. III. The origin of concepts. *J. exp. Psychol.*, **36**, 166–79.
—— (1946c) The learning and retention of concepts: IV. The influence of complexity of the stimuli. *J. exp. Psychol.*, **36**, 252–61.
REICHENBACH, H. (1938) *Experience and Prediction*. University of Chicago Press.
RUBIN, E. (1921) *Visuell wahrgenommene Figuren*. Copenhagen.
RUGER, H. A. (1910) The psychology of efficiency; an experimental study of the process involved in the solution of mechanical puzzles and in the acquisition of skill in their manipulation. *Amer. Psychol.*, New York, **2**, 15.
RYLE, G. (1949) *The concept of mind*. Hutchinson.
SCHUMANN, F. (1900) Beiträge zur Analyse der Gesichtswahrnehmungen. *Z. Psychol.*, **23**, 1–32, **24**, 1–33.
SEWARD, P. J. (1942) An experimental study of Guthrie's theory of reinforcement. *J. exp. Psychol.*, **30**, 247–56.
—— (1950) Secondary reinforcement as tertiary motivation: a revision of Hull's revision. *Psychol. Rev.*, **57**, 362–74.
—— (1951) Experimental evidence for the motivating function of reward. *Psychol. Bull.*, **48**, 13–49.
—— (1952) Delayed reward learning. *Psychol. Rev.*, **59**, 200–1.
—— (1953) How are motives learned? *Psychol. Rev.*, **60**, 99–110.
SHANNON, C. E. (1950) Programming a computer for playing chess. *Phil. Mag.* **41**, 256–75.
SHANNON, C. E., and WEAVER, W. (1949). *The mathematical theory of communication*. University of Illinois Press.
SHEFFIELD, F. D. (1949) Hilgard's critique of Guthrie. *Psychol. Rev.*, **56**, 284–91.
SHEFFIELD, F. D., and ROBY, T. B. (1950) Reward value of a non-nutritive sweet taste. *J. comp. physiol. Psychol.*, **43**, 471–81.
SHEFFIELD, F. D., WULFF, J. J., and BACKER, R., (1951) Reward value of copulation without sex drive reduction. *J. comp. physiol. Psychol.*, **44**, 3–8.
SKINNER, B. F. (1933) "Resistance to extinction" in the process of conditioning. *J. gen. Psychol.*, **9**, 420–9.
—— (1938) *The behaviour of organisms: an experimental analysis*. Appleton-Century-Crofts.

SPENCE, K. W. (1950) Cognitive versus stimulus-response theories of learning. *Psychol. Rev.*, **57**, 159–72.
SPENCE, K. W. (1952) Mathematical formulations of learning phenomena. *Psychol. Rev.*, **59**, 152–60.
—— (1956) *Behavior theory and conditioning*. Yale University Press.
SPENCE, K. W., and LIPPITT, R. (1940) "Latent" learning of a simple maze problem with relevant needs satiated. *Psychol. Bull.*, **37**, 429.
THISTLETHWAITE, D. L. (1951) A critical review of latent learning and related experiments. *Psychol. Bull.*, **48**, 97–129.
—— (1952) Reply to Kendler and Maltzman. *Psychol. Bull.*, **49**, 61–71.
THORNDIKE, E. L. (1898) Animal intelligence: an experimental study of the associative processes in animals. *Psychol. Rev. Monogr. Suppl*, 2, No. 8.
—— (1911) *Animal intelligence*. Macmillan, New York.
—— (1949) *Selected writings from a connectionist's psychology*. Appleton-Century-Crofts.
THORPE, W. H. (1950) The concepts of learning and their relation to those of instinct. Symposium Vol. 4 of society for Experimental Biology on *Physiological mechanisms in animal behaviour*.
—— (1956) *Learning and instinct in animals*. Methuen.
TINBERGEN, N. (1951) *The study of instinct*. Oxford University Press.
TINKLEPAUGH, O. L. (1928) An experimental study of representative factors in monkeys. *J. comp. Psychol.*, **8**, 197–236.
TOLMAN, E. C. (1932) *Purposive behaviour in animals and men*. D. Appleton-Century.
—— (1934) Theories of learning. In F. A. Moss (Editor). *Comparative psychology*. Prentice Hall.
—— (1939) Prediction of vicarious trial and error by means of the schematic sowbug. *Psychol. Rev.*, **46**, 318–36.
—— (1941) Discrimination versus learning and the scematic sowbug. *Psychol. Rev.*, **48**, 367–82.
—— (1952) A cognition motivation model. *Psychol. Rev.*, **59**, 389–400.
TOLMAN, E. C., and HONZIK, C. H. (1930) "Insight" in rats. *Univ. Calif. Publ. Psychol.*, **4**, 215–32.
TOLMAN, E. C., RITCHIE, B. F., and KALISH, D. (1946) Studies in spatial learning, II. Place learning versus response learning. *J. exp. Psychol.*, **36**, 221–9.
TROTTER, J. R. (1956) The timing of bar-pressing behaviour. *Q. J. exp. Psychol.*, **9**, 78–87.

TURING, A. M. (1937) On computable numbers with an application to the Entscheidungsproblem. *Proc. Lond. Math. Soc.*, Ser. 2, **42**, 230–65.
UTTLEY, A. M. (1954) The classification of signals in the nervous system. *EEG CLIN. Neurophysiol.*
—— (1955) *The conditional probability of signals in he nervous system.* RRE Memorandum. No. 1109.
VERNON, M. D. (1954) *A further analysis of Perception.* Cambridge University Press.
VOEKS, V. W. (1950) Formalization and classification of a theory of learning. *J. Psychol.*, **30**, 341–62.
WALTER, W. G. (1953) *The living brain.* Duckworth.
WEAVER, G. (1927) Figure and ground in the visual perception of form. *Amer. J. Psychol.* **38**, 194.
WEISS, P. (1950) *Genetic neurology.* University of Chicago Press.
WERNER, H. (1935) Studies on contour. I. qualitative analysis. *Amer. J. Psychol.*, **47**, 40–64.
—— (1940) Studies in contour: strobostereoscopic phenomena. *Amer. J. Psychol.*, **53**, 418–22.
WERTHEIMER, M. (1945) *Productive thinking.* Harper Bros.
WHORF, B. L. (1941) Languages and logic. *The Technology Review*, XLIII, 6.
WOLFE, J. B. (1936) Effectiveness of token-reward for chimpanzees. *Comp. Psychol. Monogr.*, **12**, Np. 60.
WOODGER, J. H. (1937) *The axiomatic method in biology.* Cambridge University Press.
—— (1939) Technique of theory construction. *Encyclopaedia of unified science.* Vol II, No. 5, University of Chicago Press.
—— (1952) Science without properties. *Brit. J. Philos. Sci.*, **2**, 193–217.
—— (1954) *Language and biology.* Cambridge University Press.
YERKES, R. M. (1912) The intelligence of earthworms. *J. Amer. Behav.*, **2**, 332–52.
ZEIGARNIK, B. (1927) Das Behalten erledigte und unerledigta Handlungen. In K. Lewin (ed.) untersuchungen zur Handlungen und Affektpsychologie. *Psychol. Forsch.*, **9**, 1–85.
ZENER, K. (1932) The significance of behaviour accompanying conditioned, salivary secretion for theories of the conditioned response. *Amer. J. Psychol.*, **50**, 382–403.
ZIPF, G. K. (1935) *The psycho-biology of language.* Houghton Mifflin.
—— (1949) *Human behaviour and the principle of least effort.* Addison-Wesley.

NAMES INDEX

Ames, A., Junr., 160, 164, 204
Ashby, W. R., 211
Austin, G. A., 259
Ayer, A. J., 132, 135

Baerends, G. P., 180
Bartlett, F. C., 251, 254, 258
Beach, F. A., 177
Bentley, A., 165
Berkeley, Bishop, 130
Blodgett, H. C., 73
Bogoslavsky, G. W., 255
Boring, E. G., 141, 145
Bridgman, P. W., 209
Broad, C. D., 129
Brown, R. W., 284
Bruner, J. S., 259, 262

Cantril, H., 167
Carnap, R., 281, 283
Chapman, B. L. M., 211
Child, C. M., 173, 176, 178
Church, A., 209
Cofer, C. N., 282
Coghill, G. E., 182
Crawshay-Williams, R., 294
Culbertson, J. T., 215

Darwin, C., 20
Dewey, J., 165
Diamond, A. S., 243
Drever, J., 149, 151, 188, 287

Fitch, F. B., 87
Flourens, P., 15
Foley, J. P., 282
Foord, E. N., 254
Freud, S., 12

Galli, A., 154
Galton, F., 19
George, F. H., 76, 128, 186, 211, 217, 233, 254, 259, 291
Gibson, J. J., 141, 149, 288

Gödel, K., 209
Goodnow, J. J., 259
Gottschaldt, K., 158
Guthrie, E. R., 58, 255

Handlon, J. H., 186
Hayek, S. A., 211
Hebb, D. O., 50, 121, 225, 254
Heidbreder, E., 265
Helmholtz, H., 15
Helsen, H. E., 149
Herbart, G. F., 14
Hilgard, E. R., 31, 61
Hillel, Bar, Y., 283
Hirst, R. J., 128
Hocheimer, W., 154
Honzik, C. H., 114
Hull, C. L., 60, 77, 191
Humphreys, L. G., 117
Hunter, W. S., 251, 261

Jacobson, E., 269
Jennings, H. S., 176

Kalish, D., 114
Kappers, C. U. A., 50
Kilpatrick, F. P., 160, 165, 166, 169
Koch, S., 85
Koffka, K., 151
Kohler, W., 149, 151, 261
Korner, S., 264
Kornorski, J., 38, 49, 183
Krasnagorsky, N. I., 46
Krechevsky, J., 115, 117
Külpe, O., 139

Lashley, K. S., 142
Lewis, C. I., 277
Locke, J., 130
Loeb, J., 176, 178
Lorenz, K., 181, 184
Loucks, R. B., 117

MacCorquodale, K., 105

Names Index

McDougall, W., 19, 20
Mach, E., 130
Maier, N. R. F., 43
Max, L. W., 269
Michotte, A., 149, 157
Miller, N. E., 96, 97
Milner, P. M., 122
Morris, C. W., 58, 136, 272, 274
Mowrer, O. H., 97, 101, 289, 290

Naess, A., 284

Oettinger, A. E., 233
Olds, J. A., 121
O'Neil, W. M., 149, 151
Osgood, C. E., 149, 253, 260, 276, 283

Pantin, C. F. A., 182
Pap, A., 133
Pask, A. G., 211
Pavlov, I. P., 31, 37, 45
Peirce, C. S., 136, 137
Piaget, J., 262
Platonov, 65
Price, H. H., 127, 132, 139, 263

Reed, H. B., 265
Reichenbach, H., 136
Ritchie, B. F., 114
Roby, T. B., 99
Rubin, E., 154
Ruger, H. A., 261
Ryle, G., 128, 134, 263

Schumann, F., 154
Seward, P. J., 59, 101

Shannon, C. E., 211, 233, 283, 288
Sheffield, F. D., 99
Sherrington, C., 17
Skinner, B. F., 62, 65, 149
Smoke, K. L., 262
Spence, K. W., 99, 117

Thistlethwaite, D. L., 72
Thorndike, E. L., 62, 63, 151
Thorpe, W. H., 38, 183, 184
Tinbergen, N., 179, 181, 184
Tinklepaugh, O. L., 106
Titchener, E. B., 139
Tolman, E. C., 103 et seq.
Trotter, J. R., 71
Turing, A. M., 209

Uttley, A. M., 211, 215, 259

Vernon, M. D., 141

Walter, W. Grey, 211
Weaver, G., 283, 288
Weiss, P., 184
Werner, R., 153
Wertheimer, M., 152
Whorf, B. L., 282
Wolfe, J. B., 41
Woodger, J. H., 249
Wulff, J. J., 99
Wundt, W., 139

Yerkes, R. M., 29

Zeigarnik, B., 158, 255
Zener, K., 58
Zipf, G. K., 283

SUBJECT INDEX

Activating Stimulus, 113
After-Effect
  Figural, 142
  Inhibitory, 46
  Movement, 144
  Spiral, 143
Ambiguous figures, 147
Associations, 101, 122, 242
Associative shifting, 63
Auto coding, 238
Automaton
  Finite, 210
  Infinite, 210
Avoidance training, 60

Behaviour family, 275
Behavioural Nets, 212
Behaviourism, 13, 62, 125
Beliefs
  Acquisition of, 188, 189, 214
  Formation, 266
  Strength of, 189, 194, 214
  Value, 106, 108
Believing, 169, 171, 196, 197, 204
Binary code, 232
Body-mind, problem of, 141
Brain
  Cerebellum, 17
  Cerebral cortex, 17, 47, 145
  Diencephalon, 16
  Hypothalamus, 17
  Medulla oblongata, 16
  Mesencephalon, 16
  Metencephalon, 16
  Mylencephalon, 16
  Olivary body, 16
  Pons, 16
  Telencephalon, 16
  Thalamus, 17

Capability, 47
Cathexis, 112, 113, 121
Causality, 132
Cell assemblies, 217

Classification systems, 220, 223, 249, 259
Clues, 194
Communication systems, 208
Computers, 232
Concept formation, 264
Concepts, 98
Conditioned responses, 37, 52, 58, 92
Conditioning
  Classical (Type I), 40
  Instrumental (Type II), 40
Conditioning process, 40, 42
Consciousness, 194, 199
Constancy, 146
Cues, 79, 194
Cybernetics, 54, 208, 248

Decision procedure, 209
Delayed reaction, 180
Differentiation, 46
Discrimination, 39, 81
Drive, 60, 79, 83, 88, 191

Effect, law of, 56, 60, 81
  principle of, 60, 79
  spread of, 64
Elicitor-cathexis, 113
Emotions, 291
Epistemology, 25
Equalization, 47
Ethology, 179
Excitation, 45, 48
Exercise, law of, 57
Expectancy, 61, 96, 104, 105, 110
Experimental neurosis, 39
External inhibition, 46
External question, 172
Extinction, 111

Field theory, 117
Figure ground, 196
Formalization, 86, 87, 93
Frequency, 57, 227, 252

307

Generalization, 46, 112, 230, 237, 259, 289
Gestalt theory, 146, 151, 153, 165
Goal, changing, 243, 247
    seeking, 104
Goal gradient theory, 81, 88, 95
Gradient of generalization, 39, 81

Habit, 80, 81, 85, 231
Habit family hierarchy, 81

Ideas, 200
Illusion, 127
Imagination, 200
Imprinting, 184
Induction, 46, 246
Inductive programming, 239, 243
Inference, 112, 129
Information theory, 210
Inhibition, 45, 85
Inhibition of delay, 46
Insight, 34, 114, 233, 237, 243
Internal inhibition, 46
Internal question, 172
Intervening variables, 78
Introspection, 12, 33

Language, 186, 202, 227, 242, 272, 274
Language experiments, 282, 284
Lansigns, 54, 276
Learning
    Definitions, 31, 53, 124
    Discrimination, 261, 289
    Insight, 36, 114, 151, 152, 261
    Latent, 72, 82, 110, 115
    Machines, 212
    Perceptual, 132, 141, 170, 193, 214
    Rote, 93, 94
    Theory, 56, 77, 103, 291, 292
    Trial and Error, 35, 151
Levels of investigation, 123, 124, 184
Logical constructs, 78
Logical Nets, 210, 211, 217

Maturation, 182
Maze-running, 29, 73, 114
Meaning, 201, 277, 278
Memory, 197, 251
Methodology, 77, 86, 105
Mind-body problem, 141

Mnemonization, 111
Molar approach, 26, 103
Molecular approach, 27, 30, 217
Models, 28, 106, 210, 219
Motivation, 83, 106, 147, 191, 214, 250

Nativist-Empiricist controversy, 15, 168, 206
Need, 60, 80, 106, 109, 113
Noughts and crosses, 233

Organism, 173, 174

Paranormal cognition, 11
Perception, 32, 126, 132, 141, 168, 170, 193
Perceptual consciousness, 127
Performance, 73, 116, 117
Phenonmenalism, 129, 132, 134
Philosophy, 123, 263
Phonetics, 284
Physiological gradients, 176
Pragnanz, Law of, 156
Probability, 210, 212
Problem solving, 44
Programming, 232, 239
Psycho-analysis, 18
Purpose, 226

Realism
    Critical, 126, 127, 136
    Naïve, 125, 139
Recency, 56, 227, 252
Reflexes, 42, 50
Rehearsal, 192
Reinforcement, 35
    delay in, 84
    Heterogeneous, 60
    Homogeneous, 60
    Partial, 38, 64, 97, 117
    Primary and secondary, 80, 82, 84, 98
Response, 37, 52, 58, 79, 87, 88, 92, 195
Response substitution, 289
Retinal elements, 217, 219
Retroactive inhibition, 228
Retrospection, 12

Semantics, 133, 281
Set, 33, 75, 148, 158, 256
Sign learning, 274

Subject Index

Signs, 54, 272, 275
Stimulus, 46, 51, 80, 84, 87, 88, 103, 187, 191
Stimulus generalization, 75, 85
Stimulus substitution, 57, 289
Stochastic process, 213, 245
Storage systems, 214, 215, 221, 226, 234, 249
Synapses, 17

Thinking, 121, 234, 255, 260
   definitions of, 258
   motor aspects of, 269
Training schedules, 40, 50

Transactionalism, 146, 160
Transactional theory, 164
Transfer of training, 74, 96
Tropism, 178
Turing machine, 209, 210, 211
Two factor theory, 290

Valence, 113, 192
Value, 56, 192, 214, 227, 252
Variables, 105
Variables, intervening, 78

Words, 243, 273